© British Telecommunications plc 1992.

ou to you?

s you expand, from BT.)

Staying Closer. The more closely in touch your people stay with each other, the more you can work as a team. To help you communicate effectively across oceans and continents, BT becomes part of that team. Our approach is to stay close to you, working from the outset to understand your ethos, your culture, your way of doing business. So that we can move from merely answering your needs to helping you achieve your vision – with communications that make you more responsive to your people, your partners and your customers around the world. "Going Further, Staying Closer" is the BT difference. If you'd like a brochure that explains that difference more fully, call us on **+44 272 217777.**

TSOURCING FROM SYNCORDIA.

BT

Going Further   Staying Closer

The sign of a perfect partnership

Omega Constellation.
Ladies' and gents' watches in 18 k gold and steel.
Ladies' model with diamond-set bezel.
Scratch-resistant sapphire crystal.
Water-resistant.
Swiss made since 1848.

Ω
OMEGA
The sign of excellence

Dudley Fishburn: Member of Parliament for Kensington and on the Board of Overseers, Harvard University.

1993 will start with the world in a pessimistic frame of mind. That gloom should soon dispel itself. A clear economic recovery is under way. Though it will be hesistant at first, it will last the longer for being so. If you are sitting in one of the world's blackspots—Britain, the Japanese financial markets, southern California or the headquarters of an over-large organisation—this prediction will seem hopelessly optimistic. Next year's wealth won't return to yesteryear's winners. If you are working in a company with much more than 100 people, do not expect to be in the vanguard of recovery. If you see your job as a job for life, you may well lose it in 1993. And if your markets are not wholly international, you have reason to be gloomy: world trade will expand at double the rate of domestic business next year, foreign investment at twice the rate of domestic investment.

Europe will spend 1993 squabbling about nonsenses, grand schemes dreamt up by politicians, but laying down, in fact, a pattern of prosperity that bodes well for the rest of the century. Watch next year's two most important European elections, in France and Spain, for evidence of this. Expect the European single market to arrive in good technical shape on January 1st: proof that the European Community, when it sticks to things economic, works and works well. For this reason a handful of new countries will apply to join the club next year. Even Eastern Europe will make progress: in 1993, for the first time since the war, more East Europeans will work for private enterprise than for the state.

Across the world the baby boomers of the 1960s will be growing ever-more middle-aged: being wise, they will (unlike their governments) seek to save rather than spend, creating ample capital to finance the next stage of the economic cycle, if delaying any new consumer boom. They are already well housed, so don't expect the property market to take off.

But these middle-aged rich people need to look over their shoulders to the younger world that is closing in on them. A large number of successful newly industrialising countries, with young populations and eager ambitions, will grab a greater share of the world's wealth next year. Whether it is China or Chile, Mexico or Turkey, these countries will grow at substantially faster rates next year than the rich world. Indeed China will grow as fast in 1993 as Japan ever did in the 1950s. This is the single greatest economic change that is happening in the world.

Next year's wårs will be tribal affairs: brutal but local. They will have neither the energy nor the ambition to spill over their borders or disrupt the world at large—with one terrifying exception. Some tribal leader may get hold of one of the 30,000 nuclear warheads that are lying around in the ex-Soviet Union. With everything so out of control in Russia (which may just write itself a legitimate constitution next year) the West's nonchalance at the fate of the country's redundant nuclear armoury seems risky.

These are some of the ideas running through *The World in 1993*. Not all its predictions will be right, but right enough, I hope, to make a good read in the 70 countries and 12 different languages in which it appears.

Dudley Fishburn

Editor

WHO WOULD
KNOW BETTER HOW TO
MAKE YOU FEEL

WELCOME

IN EUROPE?

Every day, warm, attentive staff welcome guests to Holiday Inn hotels throughout Europe. To spacious and well appointed rooms. To thoughtfully prepared meals. Each Holiday Inn has meeting rooms, and provides fax machines and audio visual equipment to help you keep in touch with colleagues and clients alike. Wherever your business takes you in Europe, that's a welcoming thought.

STAY WITH SOMEONE YOU KNOW.

FOR RESERVATIONS, CALL BELGIUM (02)7710200, FRANCE (1)43553903, GERMANY (0130)5678, ITALY (02)6598432, THE NETHERLANDS (020)6279279, SPAIN (91)5555162, SWITZERLAND (01)3020837, THE UNITED KINGDOM (071)7227755.

EDITOR: Dudley Fishburn

MANAGING EDITOR: Harriet Ziegler
DEPUTY EDITOR: Jack Grimston

DESIGN AND ART DIRECTION: Bailey and Kenny
DESIGN ASSISTANCE: Andrew Franklin
CHARTS AND MAPS: Michael Robinson
ILLUSTRATIONS: Derek Cousins
PICTURE RESEARCH: Juliet Brightmore

ADVERTISING DIRECTOR: Jon Humphrey
PRODUCTION DIRECTOR: David Gill
PRODUCTION ASSISTANT: Susie Canitrot
CIRCULATION DIRECTOR: Helen Alexander
FOREIGN RIGHTS: Hutton-Williams Agency

PUBLISHER: David Hanger

All the information and forecasts in this magazine have been checked to the best of the authors' and publishers' ability but they do not accept responsibility for loss arising from decisions based on them. Where opinion is expressed, it is that of the authors and editors.

ISBN 0 85058 4256
© 1992
The Economist Publications Ltd

The Economist Publications Ltd is the specialist publishing arm of The Economist Group. It is editorially independent of *The Economist* Newspaper.

PHOTOGRAPHIC SOURCES: Associated Press; Austin J. Brown; Colorific/Wood-in Camp; International Stock Exchange Library; Katz Pictures; Katz/REA; Magnum Photos; Network Photographers; Rex Features/SIPA; Science Photo Library; Select Photos; Sygma

Printed by BPPC Magazines Ltd
(Blackpool and Carlisle, England)
Reprographics by Copeland Origination Services

The Economist Publications

25 St James's Street, London, SW1A 1HG
TELEPHONE 071-839 7000

*D*esigning your competitive edge with Singapore.

Singapore offers more than superb infrastructure, excellent IT and telecommunications networks, worldwide distribution linkages, and a total value chain to support a diversity of manufacturing and service businesses.

With our total business capabilities, we can be your strategic partner. To develop and capitalise on new business opportunities, especially in the world's fastest growing market: the Asia-Pacific.

Banking on 30 years of successful economic planning, and the testimony of over 3,000 MNCs operating here, Singapore is the business architect that can enhance your competitive edge.

You can leverage our strategic alliances with other economies, our familiarity with regional markets, and not least our expertise in distributing and configuring businesses to stay ahead.

So use our value-added solutions to your advantage now, call the Singapore Economic Development Board today.

Europe: Frankfurt (69) 233-838 • London (71) 839-6688 • Milan (02) 799-277 • Paris (01) 45001183 • Stockholm (08) 6637488 **North America:** Boston (617) 261-9981 • Chicago (312) 565-1100 • Los Angeles (310) 553-0199 • New York (212) 421-2200 • San Francisco (415) 591-9102 • Washington DC (202) 223-2571 **Asia-Pacific:** • Hongkong (852) 810-0036 • Jakarta (21) 520-1489 • Osaka (06) 261-5131 • Singapore (65) 336-2288 • Tokyo (03) 3501-6041

SINGAPORE
▶ YOUR GLOBAL BUSINESS ARCHITECT ◀

ECONOMICS '93

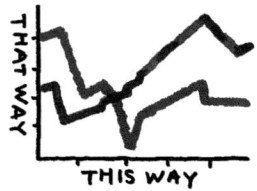

The world will pick itself out of recession next year, **Clive Crook**, economics editor of *The Economist*, page 13. And Britain will stage a rapid turnaround, **Anatole Kaletsky**, economics editor of *The Times*, page 50. Expect the American recovery to be tantalisingly slow but long-lasting, **David Hale**, *Kemper Financial Services*, page 67. **Horst Siebert**, *German Council of Economic Advisers*, sees a Germany puzzled but prosperous, page 30. Russia will end 1993 half as rich as when it began 1991, **John Parker**, *The Economist*, page 46. Environmentalists will devastate the third world, **Deepak Lal**, *University College London*, page 16. China and the Chinese everywhere will thrive, **Jim Rohwer**, *The Economist*, page 77. Foreign investment will be next year's saviour for Britain, **Iain Carson**, *BBC*, page 55.

ELECTIONS '93

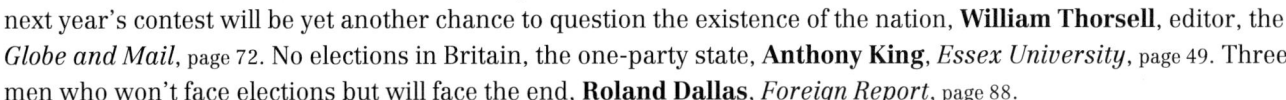

France will start two years of miserable politics, **Yann de l'Ecotais**, editor, *L'Express*, page 24. Spain goes to the polls nursing a hangover, **Juan Luis Cébrian**, publisher, *El Pais*, page 35. It will be a bitter election in Australia, **Paul Kelly**, editor, the *Australian*, page 79. In Canada, next year's contest will be yet another chance to question the existence of the nation, **William Thorsell**, editor, the *Globe and Mail*, page 72. No elections in Britain, the one-party state, **Anthony King**, *Essex University*, page 49. Three men who won't face elections but will face the end, **Roland Dallas**, *Foreign Report*, page 88.

MANAGEMENT '93

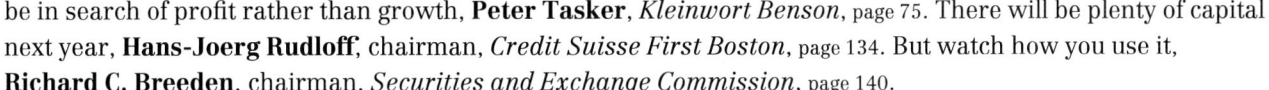

If you have more than 100 people in your company, break it up, **Tom Peters**, arch-guru of management theories, page 126. **Richard Branson**, *Virgin Group of Companies*, argues for more competition in the air, page 112. Next year's winners will be small and nifty, **David Manasian**, *The Economist*, page 107. Japan's companies will be in search of profit rather than growth, **Peter Tasker**, *Kleinwort Benson*, page 75. There will be plenty of capital next year, **Hans-Joerg Rudloff**, chairman, *Credit Suisse First Boston*, page 134. But watch how you use it, **Richard C. Breeden**, chairman, *Securities and Exchange Commission*, page 140.

HEADACHES '93

Explaining "subsidiarity" to Europe, **Leon Brittan**, *EC commissioner*, page 43. Uniting America's many races to a common purpose, **Bill Bradley**, *United States senator*, page 70. Nuclear proliferation and the next war, **Dudley Fishburn**, editor, *The World in 1993*, page 12. And how to stop it, **Frank von Hippel**, *Princeton University*, page 81.

SCIENCE '93

Next year's scientific breakthroughs, **John Maddox**, editor, *Nature*, page 142. Scientific toys you'll have to have, **Tim Jackson**, the *Independent*, page 116. Go kick a drug company, **Moira Dower**, editor, *Scrip World Pharmaceutical News*, page 117. The science of the seas, **John Woods**, chairman, *Global Ocean Observing System*, page 145. The human genome project, **Leroy Hood**, *University of Washington*, page 143. Science will change television viewing next year, **Norman Macrae**, the *Sunday Times*, page 60.

''I assess fire risks for a living,

but my life's work is preventing them.''

Stan Woodward

LONDON & EDINBURGH INSURANCE

Stan Woodward is Chief Property Surveyor at ITT's London & Edinburgh Insurance Group. And he takes his job home with him every night, devoting much of his free time to the local Fire Liaison Group, educating the community about fire safety.

ITT Insurance is one of eight diverse businesses that make up today's ITT Corporation. This, along with our investment in Alcatel Alsthom, makes us a multinational, US $20.6 billion enterprise employing 110,000 people around the world.

In fact, one out of three ITT employees lives and works in Europe. And whether it's ITT Defense and Electronics, or ITT Sheraton, these companies and all of our businesses share a common goal: To improve the quality of life. Because it's not just how you make a living that's important, it's how you live. Just ask Stan Woodward. For more information about ITT phone us on: 0903 273521. Or write to: ITT Europe, The Warren, Worthing, West Sussex BN14 9QD.

THE WORLD IN 1993

What's in a nationality?

Sovereign countries, the invention of the past 200 years, will fade as the century draws to its close. Most of the political arguments next year will be over this uncomfortable fact, argues *Jim Rohwer*.

The growing integration of the world economy is pushing human society into a borderless future. On January 1st 1993 the European single market starts: 350m people will be able to trade between themselves without so much as a wave to their border guards. The commercial divides between 12 of the world's richest countries, with 30% of its GDP, will vanish. And on the same date the European Economic Area gets under way, bringing another seven countries into the free-trade net. By December 31st 1993 the North American Free Trade Area will, somewhat less ambitiously, link together three countries with 370m people and 31% of the world's wealth—and a queue of Latin countries will be forming to join it.

Capital first, then goods and at last services will be ever more inclined to flow to places where they earn the best returns, not necessarily where governments would like them to go; the companies and people who provide all these things are increasingly following suit. Foreigners will form a greater minority in every advanced country next year than ever before.

But not so fast. The attachments of blood, race, religion and language will be lessened hardly a jot by all these developments. Indeed, they will continue to weigh more heavily in the world's emotional scales than economic cosmopolitanism does; and they will be the root cause of most of 1993's rows. The effects of these ancient calls on loyalty can sometimes be horrifying, as the murderous

events in ex-Yugoslavia show. Yet sometimes the old sorts of identity give significant and welcome clues about how much change societies are ready for; the rebellion of some of Europe's voters against the Maastricht treaty on closer European union is a good example.

How will these currents interact? The logic of economic integration is both flawless and powerful. It has always made sense for resources to be channelled into the uses that an undistorted system of price signals says will give the best returns. Modern technologies—the computer, digital telecommunications and long-haul jet aircraft—are making it increasingly easy for this to be done on a global scale and at a speed that would have been unimaginable only decades ago.

The $1 trillion a day that is now traded round-the-clock in the global foreign-exchange market is triple the figure of 1986; this is a tide that many European governments, notably Britain's, found themselves unable to hold back in the autumn of 1992 when the market concluded that the parities of the European exchange-rate mechanism were wrong. The diffusion of innovations and information shows the same pattern of increasing speed and thoroughness. To take one example, wherever the most advanced semiconductor technologies first appear, they spread throughout the rich world's chip makers within just two-and-a-half years.

Conventional capital flows—investment in stocks, bonds and currencies—and merchandise trade have in the past been the main engine of economic integration.

Jim Rohwer: Asia correspondent for *The Economist*.

They are still growing fast. The value of world trade in 1993 will be around $8 trillion. That figure is more than 20 times bigger in real terms than it was in 1950 and is equal to more than a third of gross world product. The volume of world trade grew by 3% a year on average in 1974-83; in the decade 1984-93 it will have grown nearly twice as fast, by 5.7% a year, despite rising protectionism in the rich world.

But another sort of flow can be expected to do even more in 1993 to erase national boundaries. Foreign direct investment, the stock of which already amounts to some $2 trillion worldwide, is significant enough for the push it gives to economic growth to be courted by countries across the world. This is why poor countries, most momentously China, have begun welcoming foreign investors instead of spurning them. More radically, foreign direct investment is changing the nature of the corporation and of competition.

With companies, technologies, parts, products and employees increasingly flowing between different countries, it is becoming hard to tell the "nationality" of either a product or a firm. This undermines the ability of national governments to control their economies—or even to define "national" economic aims beyond the most basic ones like price stability.

Few advanced industrial companies can call themselves national any more—a large fraction of their very ownership is often foreign. The new jet that Boeing is launching next year has major elements coming from a dozen foreign countries. Will it be an American plane? No, but it will still swell a feeling of national pride in American hearts. That is the paradox.

Societies are not responding to the fuzzing of national borders in the same way economies are. It would be easy to conclude, not just from that chilling Serbian phrase "ethnic cleansing", but also from the conflicts in the Mid-

dle East, the Indian subcontinent and the former Soviet Union, that ethnic, religious or family identification is always a force for destructive divisiveness. This is not true. One of the greatest recent exercises in the erasure of borders has been the economic co-operation of the overseas Chinese, first among themselves and in the past decade with China too. Scattered through a dozen countries in East and South-East Asia, the ethnic Chinese have used ties of kinship, language and now schooling to build private channels through which capital, goods and people flow largely unimpeded by any national or political considerations.

The common lesson is how powerful the old identifications still are. People are quite happy, indeed demand, to buy whatever products appeal to them, whatever country they come from; this applies as much to cultural products like films and music as it does to cars. Yet when it comes to matters like their safety, their security (financial and otherwise) and their identity, people show an extremely strong inclination to rely on old loyalties: family, religion, race and nation. The outcome can be as basic as the mutual mistrust of Jew and Arab; or as sophisticated as the business network of the Chinese diaspora or the attachment of Germans to their Bundesbank.

For about 200 years the political instrument for trying to harness the divergent currents of economy and society has been the nation-state. If this sounds awfully recent, that is because it is. Germany and Italy did not even exist as the world now knows them until just over a century ago. In general, for thousands of years empires like those of China and Rome and city-states like those of Venice and Lubeck were the political units that counted. With the strains being increasingly put on the nation-state by both the race to a single global economy and by the enduring strength of local attachments, might not a world of city-states become attractive again?

Nuclear nightmares

Next year's most likely war will be to stop some barmy dictator from using a nuclear bomb. Will it be too late, asks *Dudley Fishburn*?

The television news item will sound like this: "Last night American stealth bombers launched a surprise attack on a factory in North Korea thought to be housing nuclear warheads stolen from Russia." If not North Korea, supplement Libya, a Palestinian refugee camp, or an unpronounceable corner of the old Soviet empire. Someone, somewhere, will get their hands on one of the 30,000 nuclear warheads now lying around the Russian landmass. Just as disarmament between the major powers seems assured, the nuclear rearmament of some lunatic in a tiny country seems all too possible.

When everything in Russia is up for semi-illicit sale—from ex-Soviet army hats bought by visiting tourists to any bit of the Black Sea fleet that you care to sail away—the risk is frighteningly high that a fragment of Russia's vast nuclear armoury will go missing. It will then turn up

in the hands of some dictator to whom the old constraint of the cold war—the fear of mutually assured destruction—means nothing but glorious martyrdom. Hence those stealth bombers.

The dictator does not need a complete weapons system. Next year, 6,000 Russian weapons will be taken apart (leaving 24,000 under not-very-safe lock and key, mostly in some military car park near Tomsk). That means dismantling thousands of thermonuclear triggers from their surrounding "pits" of weapons uranium or plutonium. These are the bits, perhaps not weighing more than 50kg, that a dictator will want to get hold of: fancy delivery systems are scarcely going to concern him.

Over the next five years 700,000kg of weapons uranium and 140,000kg of plutonium are going to be extracted from the ex-Soviet armoury, and yet the "secure" storage space, which should be a veritable Fort Knox, has not yet been built or financed. Nor will it be without western, most probably American, finance. It will not take many millions of dollars to persuade someone, perhaps even a Russian republic, to let slip a bit of this surplus explosive. It has, after all, no other value.

The immediate blame—the incompetence, the easy bribe, the disappearing box of tricks—will be Russia's: but not Russia's alone. Western leaders are negligent too: un-willing to admit that getting out of the nuclear age will be as dangerous (and the key danger will be in the next five years) as getting into it. Rather than bossily taking in hand the problem where it exists—on the ground in the former Soviet Union—they will wait until one of the weapons crops up in the backyard of The Great Leader, Kim Il Sung, of North Korea. In will go the stealth bombers—but perhaps too late to avoid the detonation of the first atomic bomb since Hiroshima.

A mixture of frailties

With luck, growth next year will be better than in 1992.
But, warns *Clive Crook*, don't bet the farm.

A year ago it seemed likely that the world economy would grow soundly in 1992. Not spectacular growth, because 1991's slowdown in the industrial economies had itself been comparatively mild, and the boldest recoveries follow the bleakest slumps. But the past year has disappointed even modest hopes. In October 1991 the IMF predicted that the industrial countries' output would expand by 3% in 1992. In October 1992 that projection had been "trimmed" to 1½%. Growth that slow does not prevent unemployment rising or persuade those in work that their standard of living is improving. For 1993, the forecasters now predict growth of—you guessed—3%. That much growth, it seems, is always on the horizon. (Horizon: an imaginary line that recedes as quickly as you approach it.) By the spring that forecast will have been trimmed again. Think of 2% growth as the likeliest outcome for the next 12 months. But never rule out nasty surprises.

The world cannot have solid growth without a stronger expansion in America. There, much the most important brake on growth is debt. During the 1980s America's consumers and businesses borrowed eagerly. Between 1980 and 1991, the assets of the American corporate sector (measured in relation to national income) fell by nearly 20%. Liabilities (measured on the same basis) increased by nearly 30%. Assets declined because companies invested too little; liabilities grew because companies borrowed to pay for lots of mergers, takeovers, stock repurchases and leveraged buy-outs.

The result is a frail economy. As profits and incomes are squeezed, an over-borrowed America is questioning its capacity to meet the payments. Borrowers have begun to pay down debt urgently. Banks and other lenders are chosing their debtors with greater care. The Federal Reserve has cut America's short-term interest rates repeatedly; by the end of 1992 they stood at less than 3%. Even so, saving remains high, and consumer spending low. As in any economic recovery, the pace of expansion is driven mainly by demand: consumer-demand for goods and services, producer-demand for equipment and raw materials. In 1993's recovery, demand will grow more slowly than usual.

Some have begun to fear that America's recovery is fizzling out altogether. If it is, there are no obvious remedies: fiscal policy is already so loose (the budget deficit is 5% of GDP) that a further loosening might push long-term interest rates sharply up, making matters worse, and monetary policy has already been relaxed nearly to the limit (nominal interest rates cannot turn negative).

Financial fragility looks an even bigger worry in Japan. Crashing property prices and the collapse in Tokyo's stockmarket—no less startling for being so long drawn out—have exposed the weakness of many of the country's banks and other financial institutions. Business and consumer confidence has plunged. Alarmed at slowing growth, Japan's government announced a big new infrastructure programme in the summer. All being well, this should help the economy to grow by more than the benchmark 3% next year. But will all be well? If the government bungles its handling of the distressed financial sector, a much worse outcome is easy to imagine.

Germany's economic difficulties are historically unprecedented—and, as Europe found in September, not confined to itself. Public borrowing rather than private debt is the crux of the matter. The government has chosen to finance the enormous costs of unification mainly through borrowing, not taxes; the Bundesbank, steadfast as ever in its defence of low inflation, pushed interest rates high.

By the summer of 1993 German interest rates will be several percentage points lower. Before then, evidence of slowing German growth will have become clear enough to convince the Bundesbank that the threat of inflation has receded. This will be the key to restoring stable currencies in Europe—for the interest paid on D-marks sets the floor for interest rates in other countries in the European exchange-rate mechanism (ERM).

If the ERM can hold together that long—another big if—Britain will probably rejoin the system then. It would do so with the brief benefit of a devalued pound (hence, more competitive industries) but with the drawback of rising "core" inflation. Its government would have to fight for credibility all over again. If the ERM falls apart—and after September's experience that cannot be ruled out—a smaller group of countries (Germany, France, the Bene-

Clive Crook: economics editor of *The Economist*.

lux countries and Denmark) will press on to create a single currency for Europe's low-inflation elite. Britain would have cause to mourn that event—and would start to date its renewed economic decline from it. Floating exchange rates are not the answer. They spur inflation and distort trade; the greater the volatility in currencies, the steeper these costs. Britain will rediscover this soon, when the inflationary consequences of a collapsing currency arouse more concern in 1993.

There is no perfect monetary system. The expansion of international finance has made all such systems—fixed, floating and everything in-between—more imperfect than before. But whatever the monetary regime, the best way to help economies has not changed: keep budget deficits small and markets open. In most industrial countries, budget deficits have widened by much more than can be blamed on recession alone. And the stalemate in the Uruguay round of trade talks has been allowed to drag on for months. Both failures hurt the rich economies. More distressing is that they hurt the poor ones more—economies less able to cope, and struggling to push through reforms that the rich countries have demanded.

Excessive public borrowing will continue in the G7 countries next year. It will keep long-term interest rates high, punishing countries in Latin America, Africa, South Asia and Eastern Europe, whose need for affordable imports of capital is much greater than the G7's. The rich countries will also maintain barriers against many exports from the poor, robbing those countries, as for years past, of their best chance to escape poverty. Unfortunately, some of the cruellest economic forecasts are certain to come true.

Everything is relative

Next year things won't just change. The rate at which they change will change.
Most measurements of human progress are bunk, argues *Matt Ridley*.

"The trend in the increase is still downward." With those words Britain's secretary of state for employment recently tried to reassure the country about its unemployment figures. A year before, her predecessor had greeted the unemployment statistics with equal hope. It was, he pointed out, "the third successive month in which the rate of increase has fallen." The age of progress is over. Welcome to the age of rate of change of progress.

There once was a time when the best that anybody could expect was that things would stay the same. Medieval Europe, with one eye looking back at the golden age of Rome and one looking anxiously forward to the future, did not much believe in progress.

In the dreadful 14th century, when war and plague and bad weather and inflation all came at once, most Europeans would have been thrilled by 0% real growth. Then came the enlightenment and the idea that things would always improve forever.

Progress itself began to be taken for granted and rates of progress came to matter more. Going Mach 2 (speed) is old hat for fighter pilots; pulling 7G (acceleration) is not. For some decades economists and politicians have been more interested in rates of change than in the absolute sizes of things. Growth replaced wealth as a measure of national well-being. Compared with 30 years ago, the average American lives longer, eats better, has more time-saving devices to help in the house, infinitely more entertainment options, vastly more money (in real terms)—and is miserable. Even in stagnant Britain, the average unemployed person is now paid the same in benefit as his father earned in an average job in 1957—in real terms. Who still knows or cares that America is wealthier than Japan? Nobody. Who knows that over the past decade Japan's growth rate has been vastly higher than America's? Everyone. A politician facing re-election in 1993 will not equate negative growth with misery; he will equate 1% growth with misery, too.

Growth's benefits depend on how others are doing. In a world growing at 1%, the country that grows at 2% is king. It can soon afford to buy its neighbour's assets and travel cheaply along its quaint byways. Two philosophers were once out walking in the woods when they stumbled on an angry bear, which charged them. "It's no good; you cannot outrun a bear." "I know," replied the other, "I don't have to outrun the bear; I have only to outrun you."

In the past decade or so politicians have become obsessed not with rates of change, but with the rates at which rates of change change. No economic statistic is ever given straight nowadays: unemployment is X or consumer confidence is Y. Nor, even, is its rate of change the only thing commented on: unemployment has risen; confidence has fallen. Far better, in the modern world, to fill the citizen in with the true significance: the slowing rise in the rate of unemployment; the accelerating fall in consumer confidence. "Output fall shows signs of slowing," trumpeted the *Daily Telegraph* in a headline in May 1992, perceiving a break in Britain's economic clouds.

It all started in 1672, the year that Isaac Newton realised that he could express the rate of change of a planet's velocity by dividing its path into infinitely many, infinitely small steps, and so invented calculus (he spent the next 60 years vilifying Gottfried Leibniz for making the same discovery). But not even Newton realised that he had found a principle that applies outside mathematics. In the recent American general election a curious beast called the spin doctor has been much in evidence. Spin doctors' jobs are not so much to explain and justify what their candidates say as to tell reporters that what the candidate has said is what the electorate wants to hear. Thus their best ammunition is the snap poll showing how well a candidate's

Matt Ridley: freelance journalist formerly with *The Economist*. He is currently writing a book about evolution.

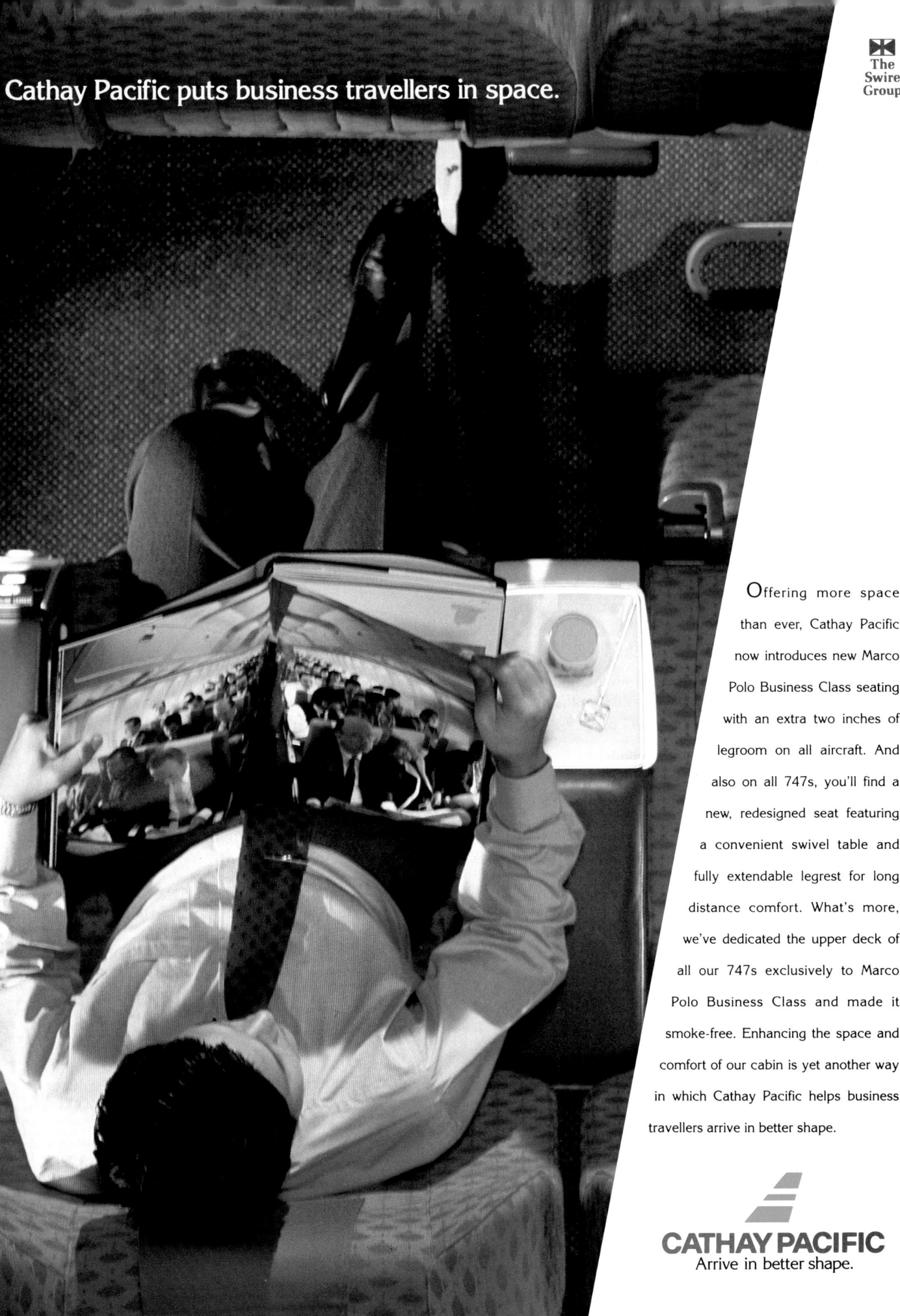

Cathay Pacific puts business travellers in space.

Offering more space than ever, Cathay Pacific now introduces new Marco Polo Business Class seating with an extra two inches of legroom on all aircraft. And also on all 747s, you'll find a new, redesigned seat featuring a convenient swivel table and fully extendable legrest for long distance comfort. What's more, we've dedicated the upper deck of all our 747s exclusively to Marco Polo Business Class and made it smoke-free. Enhancing the space and comfort of our cabin is yet another way in which Cathay Pacific helps business travellers arrive in better shape.

CATHAY PACIFIC
Arrive in better shape.

performance has gone down in, say, a debate with his opponent. This can be used to persuade the reporter to write an article claiming that the candidate "won" the debate in that he proved more popular. The article in turn will convince the electorate that the candidate is a better candidate because he won the debate. In other words, what sways the voters is not what the candidate says, nor even whether what he says is popular, but whether what he says is reported by spin doctors and reporters to be likely to be popular with voters. I'm going to vote for X because I think he's the kind of guy who will appeal to people like me. This is meta-meta-politics.

In reading this page, you are using second derivatives. Neuroscientists have recently realised that the brain of a monkey can do calculus, though not consciously. Cells that respond to a rate of change of light on the eye are used to measure the speed of a moving object. Cells that respond only when the rate of change of rate of change of light reaches zero are used to find the edges of objects, or letters on a page. And it is conceivable, though not describable, that there are cells that respond to rates of change of rates of change of rates of change: third derivatives.

A bold prediction for 1993. Some economist or politician will for the first time in history spin a statistic by drawing attention to how favourable its third derivative is. Somebody, somewhere, will say: "Yes the annualised inflation rate is high, and yes it is going up, but at least the rate at which it is going up has at last begun to slow down." In other words, the rate at which the rate of change of the rate of change of prices has changed is encouraging.

Green imperialists

Being bossy about the world's environment is the new form of imperialism towards the third world, asserts *Deepak Lal*.

Just as the dead hand of socialism blighted the prospects of the world's poor during much of this century, there is a danger that international greenery, an emotional concern for the environment, will do the same for the next few decades. Both are well-intentioned, and their proponents look upon themselves as progressive. In fact with the death of socialism, greenery is now the faith of idealists, providing a new focus for their inherent dirigisme, likely to harm rather than benefit humanity, not least those living in the third world.

The centrepiece of the international green agitation concerns the control of the so-called greenhouse gases— CO_2, CH_4, N_2O and CFCs. Much of the other aspects of their programme—preserving the tropical rain forests and their diversity of species, controlling population—follows on from this. It is indubitable that these gases have increased over the past 100 years and their emissions will accelerate with growing global economic activity. What is highly controversial is the purported link between this fact and the prospects of catastrophic climatic change, and the destruction of the ozone layer. Many scientists say that the recent rise in global temperatures is associated with a high point in the sun-spot cycle. Some cast doubt on the link between CFCs and the ozone hole, and argue it too may be linked to variations in the solar cycle.

Remember past scientific predictions of doom—the global food shortage, the limits to growth imposed by non-renewable fossil fuels and minerals, the danger of a new ice age. All have been speedily falsified. Thus even with low technology the world could support one-and-a-half times the expected population in 2000, and over nine times that level using the best currently-available technology at the United Nations' recommended calorie intake a head. The commercial reserves of non-renewable resources have risen markedly since 1970 (with those for oil rising by 63% and natural gas by 163%), and declines in their price trends, as well as in their current consumption as a proportion of reserves, all point to a growing abundance rather than scarcity of many non-renewable natural resources.

If global warming does occur, it is likely to affect only those economic activities which are subject to climatic influence— mainly agriculture. Developed countries are less dependent on agriculture, in terms of both GDP and employment, than developing countries. Industrialisation and urbanisation—the two great forces of economic progress in this century—have made making a living in developed countries virtually climate-proof. The same process of economic growth will do the same in developing countries. For the world as a whole there is no evidence that agricultural output will fall with global warming.

To delay the doubling of CO_2 emissions by four decades will cost roughly 2% of gross world product in perpetuity. Whilst the cost of this reduction is trivial for developed countries, it will not be for many poor countries. They are therefore right to ask the developed countries to pay for the costs of their dubious eco-morality. But whether the developed countries will be willing to commit themselves to official transfers about four times current aid flows to developing countries, in perpetuity, must be in serious doubt. This would then open up the real danger of an era of direct or indirect imperialism, to discharge a green variant of the 19th century's white man's burden. For one little-noticed aspect of the attitudes which underlie greenery is its implicit misanthropy, whose close cousin is racism. Burgeoning third-world populations, polluting the atmosphere and degrading its natural resources and habitats for plants and insects, can easily be turned into the enemy on Spaceship Earth.

Deepak Lal: Professor at University College London and at the University of California, Los Angeles. His publications include "The Limits of International Co-Operation".

Dancers With Unlimited Vitality Need A Wider Stage To Perform.

The people of the Republic of China on Taiwan have been working hard to achieve economic prosperity and a democratic society for themselves. Having won highly favorable reviews for their domestic economic performance, they are now ready to play a larger role on the international stage, and help less developed nations achieve their economic potential.

The Republic of China on Taiwan is already a major player in regional organizations such as the Asian Development Bank. It has formally applied for membership of GATT, and is seeking to enter other international economic, cultural, and humanitarian organizations.

Like dancers who have proved themselves on their national stage, they are looking to play to wider audiences, and to contribute their vitality, their skills, their experience, and their resources to development of a new world order based on peace, progress, and prosperity.

TODAY'S TAIWAN

REPUBLIC OF CHINA

FOR FURTHER INFORMATION:
Amstelveen: Tel: (020)6412536, 6451470 • Fax: (020)6458651
Bruxelles: Tel: 5115284 • Fax: 5141015
Copenhagen: Tel: (31)197511, 197696, 197311• Fax: (38)332888
London: Tel: 9309553 • Fax: 3210043
Madrid: Tel: 4112807, 4113761 • Fax: 5636659
Paris: Tel: (1)44709150 • Fax: (1)44709157

Roma: Tel: 8083278, 8083166 • Fax: (06)3224632
Vienna: Tel: (1)512468183 • Fax: (1)5138775
Germany
Bonn: Tel: (0228)364014-18, 356770 • Fax: (0228)357520
Hamburg: Tel: (040)462322, 472724 • Fax: (040)464533
München: Tel: (089)2711958 • Fax: (089)2731121

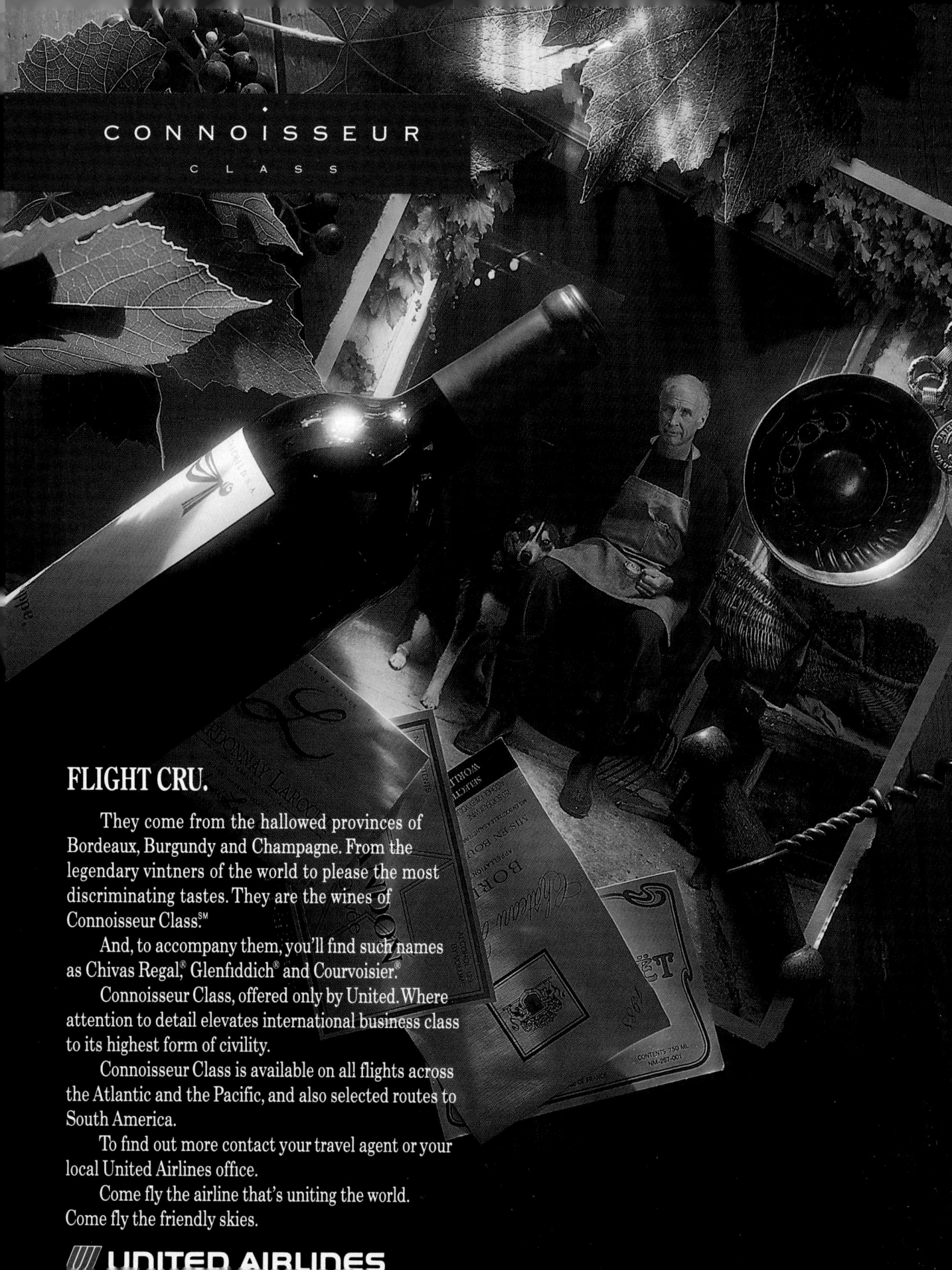

CONNOISSEUR
C L A S S

FLIGHT CRU.

They come from the hallowed provinces of Bordeaux, Burgundy and Champagne. From the legendary vintners of the world to please the most discriminating tastes. They are the wines of Connoisseur Class.℠

And, to accompany them, you'll find such names as Chivas Regal,® Glenfiddich® and Courvoisier.®

Connoisseur Class, offered only by United. Where attention to detail elevates international business class to its highest form of civility.

Connoisseur Class is available on all flights across the Atlantic and the Pacific, and also selected routes to South America.

To find out more contact your travel agent or your local United Airlines office.

Come fly the airline that's uniting the world. Come fly the friendly skies.

UNITED AIRLINES

DIARY FOR 1993

January

Single European market starts. So does the European Economic Area: 18 countries, 380m people, 10,000 pages and the freest trading system in Western Europe since the Roman Empire. It will be the world's largest market.

Denmark takes over EC presidency.

Czechoslovakia (1918-93) splits into the Czech republic and Slovakia.

Elections in Aruba, Niger and Monaco.

American pullout from bases in the Philippines is complete.

Trial of former American secretary of defence Caspar Weinberger.

Military government in Nigeria hands over to civilians.

Inauguration of United States president and vice-president.

Chinese year of the rooster begins.

February

Elections in the Greek half of Cyprus, Senegal, Tonga and the Solomon Islands.

Birth of the British Labour Party, 1893.

Execution of Louis XVI, 1793.

World Economic Forum, Davos, Switzerland.

Ramadan begins.

German budget goes to the Bundestag.

Source: FENS, 46 Collamore Avenue, London, SW18 3JT
Contact Tom Arms, tel. 081 877 1871

March

Hollywood Oscars awarded.

Parliamentary elections in France.

Presidential elections in Indonesia.

Reform-minded new apparatchiks take office in China.

April

Elections in Iraq. Send in UN opinion pollsters.

Italy votes on electoral reform; Brazil votes on its form of government; Eritrea votes on independence from Ethiopia.

First Asian Grand Prix to be held in Japan to add to the Japanese Grand Prix. A reward for Japan's growing power in the sport.

UN-supervised elections in Cambodia; first ever multi-party elections due in Kenya; election in Cameroon.

May

Eurovision Song Contest.

Austria takes over presidency of the Council of Europe.

Danes pillage the Thames valley, 893.

Elections in Bolivia.

East Asian Games in Shanghai.

Cannes Film Festival.

The first $100,000 award in memory of Russian dissident Andrei Sakharov is made.

June

Royal Ascot and Wimbledon fortnight.

Robin Leigh-Pemberton steps down as Bank of England governor and Arthur Dunkel as head of GATT.

Latest date for Australian general election.

40th Paris Air Show.

EC heads-of-government summit, Copenhagen.

United Nations World Conference on Human Rights, Vienna.

Hillary and Tensing conquer Everest, 1953.

July

ASEAN foreign ministers meet in Singapore.

Belgium takes over the EC presidency.

Elections for lower house of the Japanese Diet.

Caribbean Economic Community summit.

Economic Community of West African States summit.

British Grand Prix.

G7 meeting in Japan.

August

Withdrawal of Russian troops from Lithuania.

General election in Paraguay.

September

The Economist first published, 1843.

Helmut Schlesinger steps down as Bundesbank chief. Hans Tietmeyer becomes Europe's chief cashier.

General election in Holland.

OPEC oil ministers meet.

Latest date for Norwegian general election.

Francophone heads-of-government summit.

Frankfurt Motor Show.

International conference of environmental non-government organisations meets in London.

IMF and World Bank meet in Washington.

International Olympic Committee decides venue for Olympic Games in 2000.

UN General Assembly.

Jewish New Year 5754.

October

Nobel Prize winners announced.

Current term of Egypt's Hosni Mubarak ends. New one guaranteed.

Frankfurt Book Fair.

Latest date for general elections in Spain and New Zealand.

Tokyo Motor Show.

November

Latest date for elections in Canada.

EC-USA summit expected.

Prime antipodean horseflesh contests the Melbourne Cup.

G-15, the 15 developing countries, have a summit.

International Trade Fair in Santiago, Chile.

Cairo Defence Trade Fair. The major tank market in the Arab World.

New York Marathon.

Election in Honduras.

OPEC oil ministers meet in Vienna.

December

Presidential and congressional elections in Chile.

Presidential and congressional elections in Venezuela.

EC heads-of-government summit, Brussels.

CSCE foreign ministers meet.

Summit of the South Asian Association for Regional Co-operation.

Channel Tunnel opens.

North American Free Trade Area takes effect tomorrow.

Global Excellence

Singapore Airlines and Swissair have both chosen Delta Air Lines as their partner in a global alliance. If you're familiar with their standards, then you're familiar with ours.

Come Experience Travel That's Anything But Ordinary.

DELTA AIR LINES
We Love To Fly And It Shows.

Not Only do We Have Great Golf Courses.
We Also Have Great Bunkers.

IMAGINE STARTING a round of golf in St. Andrews and ending up on the 18th green in St. Thomas. That's the kind of startling contrast playing golf in Spain brings to mind. The sea and the mountains are never very far away on a Spanish course. Naturally, whether the backdrop is Caledonian or Caribbean, it helps to play the game with some sun on your back. And in Spain, there's no shortage of that. In fact, a round or two at Christmas time is always on the cards. Which is probably why so many of the locals are up to scratch. Even with the natural talents of a *Ballesteros* or an *Olazabal*, it helps it you can practise your putting all year round, a short drive from some of the most beautiful scenery on earth. Once you've played a round in Spain, nine holes can easily turn into nine hundred. And who cares whether you spend most of your time in a bunker. In Spain there's never any rush to finish a round. Whether it's on the golf course or in the beach-bar.

ESPAÑA

Passion for life.

Life in a one-party state

Anthony King

The British in 1993 will grow accustomed to living in a one-party state. Elections are still held every four or five years, but the Conservatives always win. By the time of the next election, in 1996 or 1997, students entering Britain's colleges and universities will not have been born when a party other than the Conservatives last held office.

Since the Social Democrats lost their permanent majority in Sweden in the 1970s, the British Tories have become Europe's most successful political party. They win more votes than most other European parties. They win them more often. And, unlike the Italian Christian Democrats or the German CDU-CSU, they do not have to share their power with anyone else. There has not been a coalition government in Britain since 1945.

Moreover, the state the Tories dominate is a powerful state. Britain lacks a regional or provincial tier of government. Local government is weak. The courts

Anthony King: professor of government at Essex University, election commentator for the BBC and regular contributor to the *Daily Telegraph*.

have no power to declare acts of parliament unconstitutional. There is no bill of rights. Britain's political culture is likewise one of winner-take-all. The opposition parties are seldom consulted. Consensus-building is seen as a strange activity engaged in by Japanese businessmen.

Pressure groups used to exercise a (frequently excessive) countervailing influence, but Margaret Thatcher put a stop to that. Privatisation largely destroyed the power of the public-sector unions. Unemployment weakened the private-sector unions. Other interest groups found their legitimacy questioned. Mrs Thatcher shared Charles de Gaulle's horror of "intermediaries", self-appointed bodies with the temerity to interpose themselves between government and people. In a symbolic gesture, John Major's government last summer abolished the National Economic Development Council, the last relic of an age when government ministers, trade-union leaders and businessmen used to sit down together.

Centralised power moulds the politics

around it. The Conservatives dominate British government. Therefore British politics is increasingly Conservative party politics. Conservative MPs, not British voters, ousted Mrs Thatcher. In 1993 the two great issues of British politics, Europe and the economy, will be fought out inside the Tory party. Government ministers used to confront opposition spokesmen across the dispatch box. In 1993 they will be looking over their shoulders at their own supporters.

Mr Major, unlike Mrs Thatcher, has tried to come to terms with the new realities. Her closest confidants were civil servants, businessmen and right-wing intellectuals. His are the Tory chief whip, the party chairman and the Tories' leader in the House of Lords. Affairs of state are now affairs of party. Mr Major used to be a whip. He still thinks like one.

The effects are already apparent. Britain's European policy is largely a function of the prevailing balance of forces within the Conservative Party. So is its economic policy. Tory backbenchers were once obscure figures. Now they have clout and are even interviewed on television. Pressure groups, with less direct access to ministers, now focus much of their lobbying on backbench Tory MPs, whose newfound self-importance is palpable.

As the Conservative nexus between government and party strengthens, the opposition parties become increasingly invisible. The election of John Smith to succeed Neil Kinnock as leader of the Labour Party in 1992 went largely unremarked. Labour's internal divisions on Europe attract attention only in so far as they mirror Tory splits. Britain's newspapers today assign only relatively junior reporters to cover the affairs of the Labour Party. The Liberal Democrats, following their failure to secure as much as 18% of the vote last April, are no longer taken seriously by anyone but themselves.

Apart from Europe, the Conservatives' greatest anxiety in 1993 will be to control public spending. Pressure from government departments for increased spending, mainly on the welfare state, is

Me and my enemy

intense. So is public pressure for increased infrastructure investment to aid the ailing construction industry. But Mr Major's abhorrence of inflation is genuine and Britain's public thrashing over the exchange-rate mechanism hit him hard.

The prime minister and his chancellor have another motive for wanting to contain expenditure. The Conservatives lost seats at the last election because they had allowed the economic cycle and the electoral cycle to get out of phase. The boom came in 1988-89 instead of 1991-92. Ministers are determined not to repeat that mistake. Restraint now should facilitate munificence in 1996-97, when the British people are again given a chance to vote Tory.

Losing touch

But a danger for the Conservatives arises directly out of their dominant-party status. Power can induce carelessness. Tory ministers and MPs tend to be well-heeled and to have well-heeled friends. Cars are lent, consultancies offered, free holidays abroad provided. Actual corruption is rare, but Conservative politicians are usually shielded from worries about the mortgage, fears of joblessness or rides in crowded commuter trains. They live life at one remove. Losing touch in the short run could mean losing votes in the long.

A greater danger for both party and country is authoritarianism. Mrs Thatcher had authoritarian tendencies. Under an earlier Queen Elizabeth, she would probably have caused heads to roll. Her successor tolerates dissent more readily, but all prime ministers and governments are liable to confuse the national interest with their own. The longer they have been in power, the greater the confusion is liable to be. After 22 years in office, Canada's Liberals lost power in 1957 partly because they had started to treat the Canadian House of Commons, and by extension the Canadian people, as a bit of a nuisance.

The British government's course for 1993 was meant to have been set by now. Mr Major is not an imaginative man. He reads little apart from official papers and is uncomfortable with general ideas. His mind-set is that of a central banker. He can usually be counted upon to go on doing whatever he happens to be doing at the moment. If anything, Mr Major is even more stubborn than Mrs Thatcher was.

And that, till now, has been his problem. Like many stubborn men, Mr Major clings to policies and people till well past their ditch-by date—and then advances new policies and people with equal fervour. In 1992 he was forced to abandon Britain's membership of the exchange-rate mechanism (ERM), to accept the resignation of his scandal-prone heritage secretary, David Mellor, and to postpone the government's proposals for swingeing cuts in coal production.

In 1992 the government doggedly pursued the single object of zero inflation by means of tight money and the ERM. In 1993 it will equally doggedly pursue the twin objects of jobs and growth by means of somewhat looser money and public spending on a range of expensive capital projects. It will be a difficult year, especially as Conservative backbenchers continue to behave as though they had recently undergone assertiveness training. Parliament will probably in the end ratify Britain's version of the Maastricht treaty, but the debates inside the Tory Party will tax the government whips and further expose the scale and depth of the Tories' divisions on the issue.

The economy may begin to come out of recession in 1993, but any upturn will be too late to save the Conservatives from a drubbing in the May local elections. The Tories' anguish will be further compounded by the government's need, early in 1993, to take the deferred decisions on pit closures and also by the introduction of the new council tax, which will hit thousands of householders in the Tory heartlands in the east and south-east.

Under constant threat will be the prime minister's personal standing and authority. Last April Mr Major was the man who won the election. In 1993 he will be the man on trial. He will need to show far greater political acumen than he did in the aftermath of his election victory. He will also need to show less stubbornness and more imagination. The odds are he will survive. He is every bit as nice as he looks. He is also a lot tougher.

Britain's coming boom

Anatole Kaletsky

The outlines of economic recovery are always hard to discern from the bottom of a recession, but Britain in 1993 is likely to be the fastest-growing economy in Europe, and possibly in the industrialised world. The economic recovery was already coming into view before September 16th 1992, when John Major's two-year love affair with fixed exchange rates suddenly and dramatically ended. Omens of economic growth are now unmistakable to all but the professional pundits, who are usually the last to wake up to unexpected changes in the business world.

Even with bank base rates at 10%, British consumers and home owners were cautiously creeping out of their bunkers before the devaluation. With interest rates falling sharply after leaving the exchange-rate mechanism (ERM) (instead of rising, as most establishment economists had predicted), consumer spending and residential investment have begun a steady advance. But, for the first time in a generation, the economic recovery will not depend entirely on personal consumption and housing. Britain may therefore avoid the traditional inflationary boom and balance-of-payments crisis that has marked the end of every past expansion. Provided the government can keep its nerve and take advantage of the sharply falling exchange rate, Britain stands a good chance of climbing on to a virtuous circle of low inflation and export-

led growth.

But to turn the devaluation into a blessing, the government will have to stick to two tough decisions throughout the year ahead. First, it must not allow itself to be panicked by the markets, the media or the business community into returning to the failed policy of ERM membership. Second, and more important, it must ensure that no such panics actually occur, by pursuing the toughest anti-inflationary policy attempted by any British government in a generation.

To offset the monetary easing and currency devaluation clearly needed by British industry and consumers, the government must aggressively tighten fiscal policy and curb public-sector wages. A total pay freeze in the public sector, accompanied by a firm plan to cut the cyclically-adjusted fiscal deficit to zero, would give John Major the leeway to cut interest rates rapidly to 6% or 7%.

Low interest rates, accompanied by a free-floating exchange rate, should have far more effect than in the United States. Britain is a variable-rate economy, while the great majority of American mortgages and business loans are made at fixed rates tied to long-term bond yields. Secondly, Britain's capacity to benefit from a competitive exchange rate is even greater than America's because of the huge scope for technological catching-up and productivity growth in manufacturing industry, an "advantage" of relative backwardness that American manufacturers have

---

Anatole Kaletsky: economics editor of *The Times*.

not enjoyed since the war.

Even with the pound valued at DM2.95 most of Britain's manufacturing and trading companies believed they were competitive with their German and French rivals. But unfortunately, after decades of de-industrialisation, there were simply not enough of those highly-competitive manufacturing companies left in Britain. This was the fundamental reason why the markets would not let the pound remain at its elevated ERM level.

Britain's tradable goods sector, while reasonably competitive, is simply too small. The share of Britain's GDP derived from manufacturing is less than 20%, compared with 31% in Germany and 29% in Japan. This is just not sufficient to keep up with the country's consumption of manufactured and other tradable goods, and explains the current-account deficit of 3% of GDP in the depths of recession.

and the country's position as the main magnet for Japanese and American investment in Europe should remain secure in the coming years. The special clauses in the Maastricht treaty, allowing Britain to keep a competitive exchange rate and exempting it from many of Europe's social and regulatory overheads, should more than make up for the foreign businessmen's visceral concerns about investing in a country that is outside the "mainstream" of Europe.

Three threats

There are, however, three potentially large qualifications to all this good news. Firstly, the government could panic and go back to targeting an exchange rate that was still overvalued and needed the crutch of high-interest rates as an artificial support. With the credibility of the ERM shattered, Britain would have to fol-

may well lack the guts to tighten fiscal policy and take on the public-sector vested interests.

Finally, the continental Europeans may notice that their economies, supposedly in the "fast lane" to monetary union, are actually being overtaken by Britain, in the slow lane.

Instead of responding rationally to this perception by making a bonfire of their excessive regulations and moving to the mix of looser money and tighter fiscal policy, they could try to change the rules of the game. Protectionist pressures in Europe were always bound to intensify as "national champions" in cosseted industries from motors and telecommunications to insurance and legal services were exposed to the 1992 programme. If, on top of the single market, continental Europe launches into a highly deflationary strategy for monetary union, while the

This recession is not the worst . . . . but there could be a shock to come

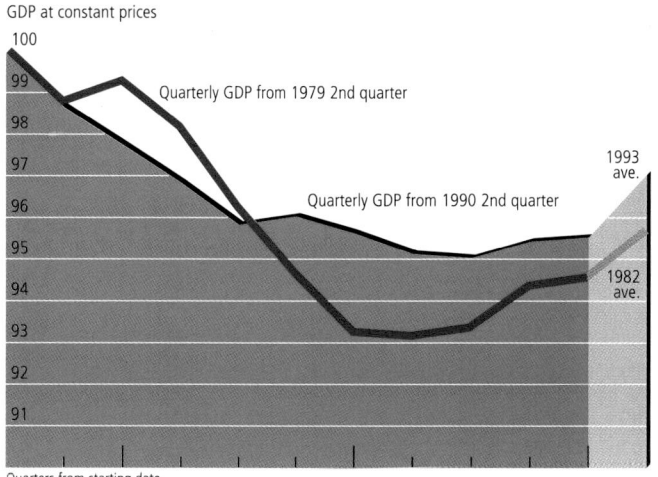

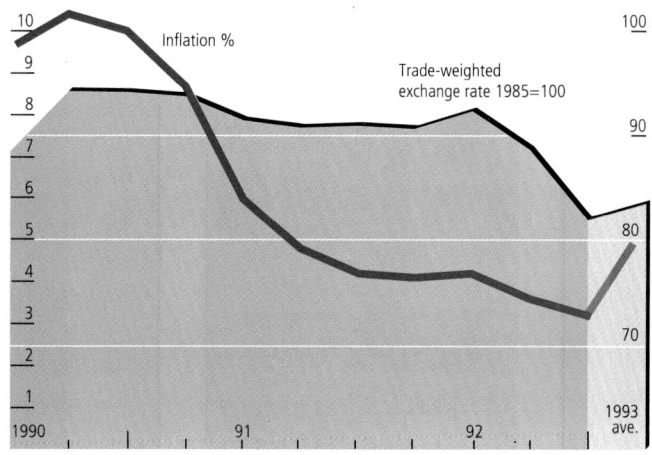

Quarters from starting date

Britain's involvement in manufacturing fell steadily throughout the 1960s and 1970s, as it did throughout the industrialised world. But manufacturing activity dropped much more abruptly from 1978 onwards, as a result of the North Sea oil shock and the high sterling policy pursued by Margaret Thatcher until 1981. It was the plunge in manufacturing output from 26% of GDP in 1978 to 19.7% in 1987 that had to be made good before Britain could hope for a stable exchange rate with Europe—and which is now likely to be reversed as a result of the highly competitive pound.

In 1993 sterling should remain well below its old ERM floor of DM2.7780, even though it will probably rise against the D-mark from its immediate post-devaluation low point of DM2.37. As a result, a big surge in domestic manufacturing investment can be expected in Britain. Foreign capital should also continue to flow in,

low even more deflationary policies than before to stabilise sterling at an artificially high level. The result would be several more years of bumping along the bottom of recession, until the deflationary policies were sabotaged again by the financial markets or Mr Major was thrown out by his own party. But Mr Major is unlikely to make the same mistake twice.

The second, and more likely, threat to Britain's future will be inflation. If the government were were to follow through on the policy of sharply lower interest rates, combined with tighter fiscal policy and wage controls in the public sector, inflation in Britain would continue to fall in 1993.

In the longer term, inflation could be stabilised at the sub-2% levels which Germany, with its exploding fiscal deficits and its deteriorating industrial relations and social consensus, will only be able to dream of. However, British politicians

United States and Britain are rebuilding their manufacturing economies with competitive exchange rates, the prospects for free trade could turn very bleak, even within the EC.

But before getting carried away with nightmares about international or even intra-European trade wars, one reassuring fact must be recalled. Germany exports 34% of its GDP and 46% of that—equivalent to almost 15% of German GDP—goes outside Europe. However tough the competition in the years ahead from Britain, the United States and other newly reindustrialising countries, Germany, France and the rest of the West European core would suffer far more than they gained from a collapse of free trade. The risks cannot be ignored, but the chances of Britain enjoying a virtuous circle of prosperity, low inflation and export-led expansion are as good as they have been for 50 years.

THE PERFORMANCE.

This Calibra has just moved up a gear.

It's the new Turbo 4x4 version with a six speed gearbox unique in its class.

The extra cog is no gimmick. Without it you simply wouldn't appreciate the car's finely-tuned muscle-power.

Balancing the increased performance is a safer, more refined turbo system.

It cuts in swiftly at unusually low engine speeds, giving an immediate response when you want to overtake a slow-moving vehicle.

For the interior, a spot of power-dressing seemed appropriate.

All-black, all-leather heated seats. All matching the door panels, gear knob and steering wheel.

What isn't new about the seats is the now legendary amount of rear legroom.

As any car magazine will tell you, no other car of its type can match the Calibra for accommodation.

(One summed it up rather nicely, claiming it actually defies coupé law.*)

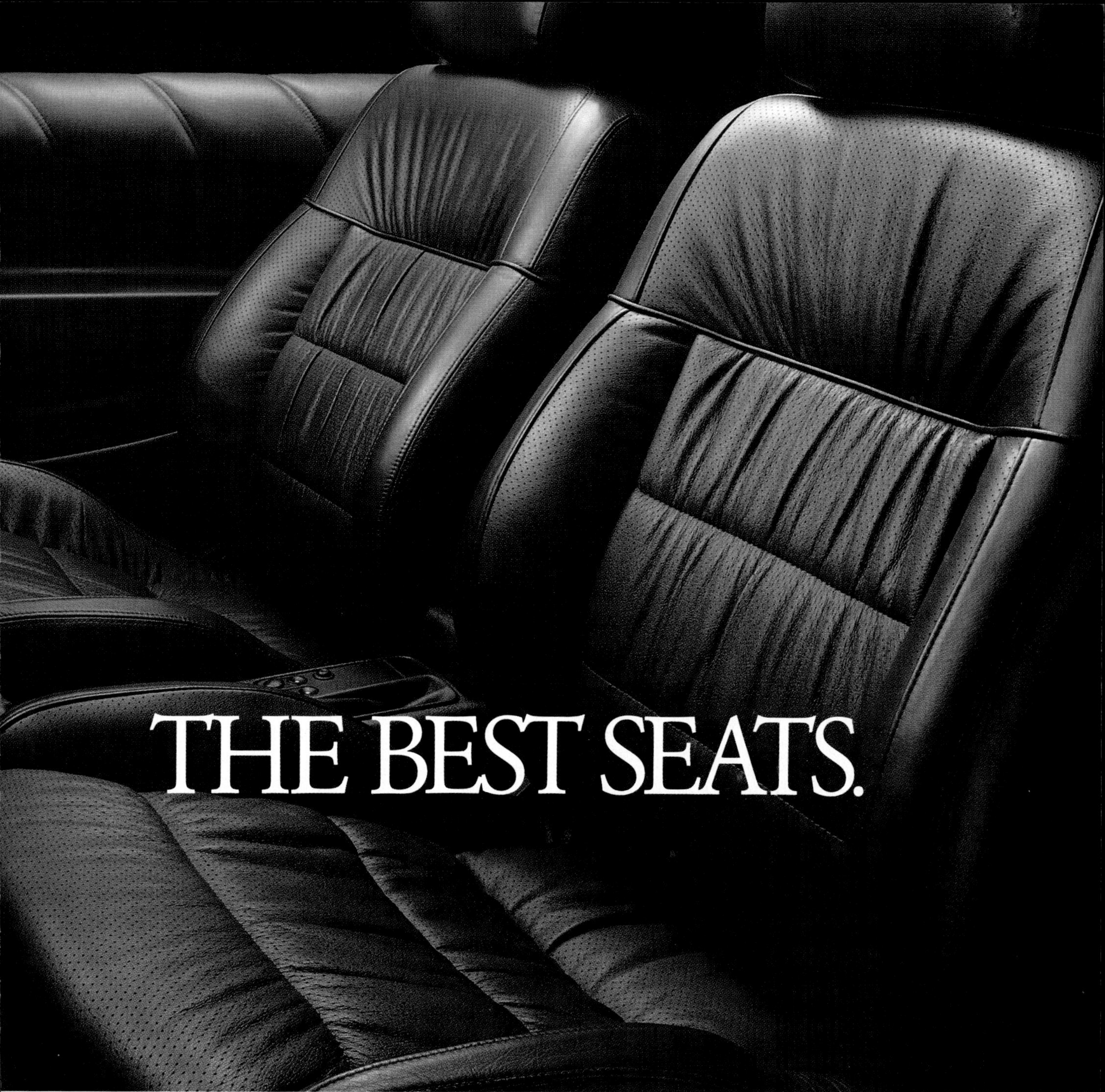

THE BEST SEATS.

Standard features include power steering, trip computer, CAT, deadlocking and alarm.

And a slinky, sophisticated SC804 radio cassette with six speakers. The system has an anti-theft removable display and the latest RDS EON cut-in travel information.

Finally, before launching our flagship, we took another long hard look at the Calibra's unmistakable, sleek styling.

Not that we wanted to change anything, of course. We just like looking at it.

For more details of either the Turbo, or the 8 or 16-valve version, telephone 0800 444200.

THE CALIBRA TURBO 4x4.

 **VAUXHALL**

Once driven, forever smitten.

It's a tall order, even for Reuters.

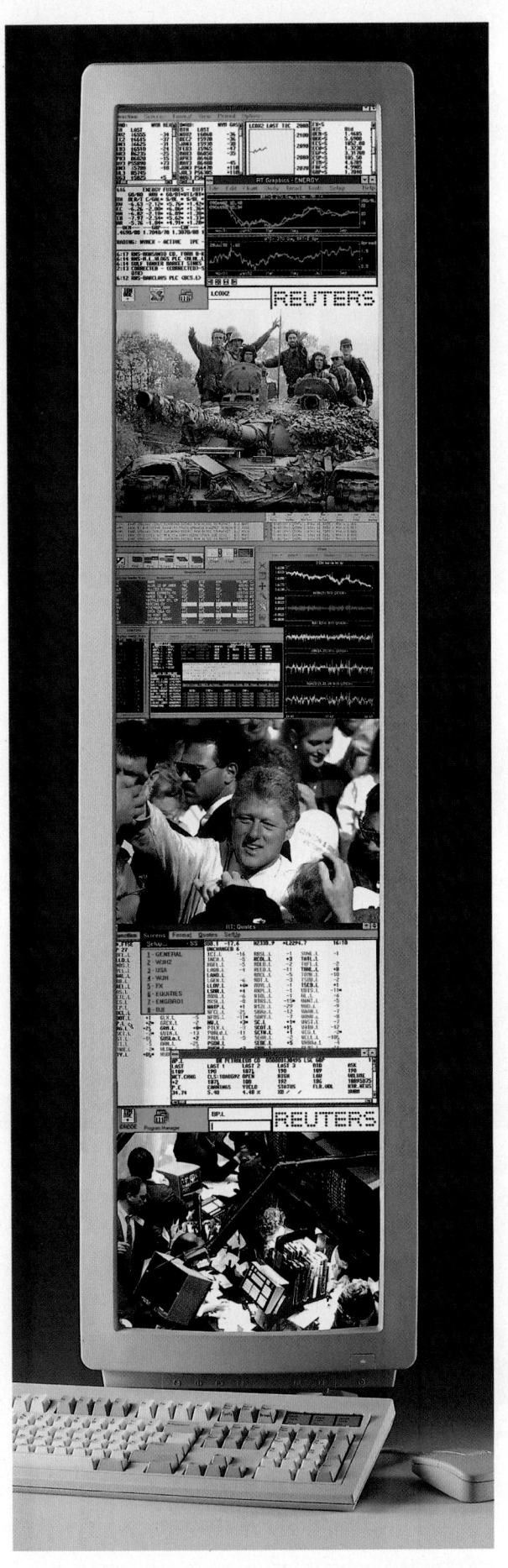

Whether it happens on your doorstep, or the other side of the world, news has a habit of moving the markets.

From a coup to a crop failure, from a war to a water shortage, financial markets can react with alarming rapidity, leaving you either nicely in the swim or high and dry.

Giving you access to market moving news, fast, knowing that you can trust its accuracy and impartiality; providing rates and data, second by second, day by day, to judge when to buy or sell, invest or divest – it's a tall order even for Reuters.

But that is our promise. And the existing population alone of Reuter screens worldwide, delivering news, rates and data direct to financial and business customers is testament to our commitment to the best products and service, wherever you are.

If you would like to know more about how our news and information products could be working to keep you in the picture, your local Reuter office will be standing by – however tall your order.

REUTERS

Making the best information work harder

For further information contact your local Reuter office.

Oh, those lovely foreigners

Iain Carson

1993 will be the year when the Japanese help to drive Britain out of its longest recession. The most striking feature of British industry since the early 1980s has been inward investment, notably by Japan. Although America and Germany still invest most in Britain, Japanese direct investment is now a fifth of the total, and three Japanese companies are about to mass-produce cars in Britain, doubling the size of the industry.

The Japanese have been filling the holes that recession has torn in Britain's industrial fabric. When industry secretary in the early 1980s, Lord Young set out to lure them: if British industry was not up to the mark, let it be replaced by the Japanese who could then raise the local game.

Since the 1980 recession wiped out a fifth of Britain's manufacturing capacity, Japanese companies have invested no less than $26 billion (£16 billion) in Britain; they employ about 50,000 Britons; they are transforming trade deficits into surpluses in products like televisions, video recorders, microwaves and now motor cars. Japanese transplant factories are taking over from the less competitive local ones; criticised once as mere screwdriver assembly plants, they are now beginning local R&D. 1993 will see the fruits of that past investment, just as the amount of new investment falls away.

In 1973 only 16% of manufacturing was owned by foreigners; now the figure is about 25%. Foreigners in 1973 accounted for 17% of investment; now the figure is 28%. One worker in six in British industry works for a foreign company. Britain has attracted more inward investment than any other EC country, and more than any other country except America.

Nomura Research Institute estimates that Japanese investment in Britain will benefit Britain's trade balance by £4 billion a year by 1995. The motor industry is the most striking example. About the only reliable sign of rising output from British industry for 1993 will come from the three Japanese car companies. Nissan is more than doubling output to about 300,000 at its Sunderland factory. In January 1993 production starts in earnest at the new Toyota factory in Derby and the Honda plant in Swindon.

Within five years, output of the three firms will be 700,000 cars a year, rising to 1m by 2000. They employ about 10,000

directly and create as many jobs outside. The Japanese have brought to Britain a new car industry as big as the traditional one (those old inward investors Ford and General Motors, plus Rover, which could soon be sold to Volkswagen or maybe Honda), taking total output back to the heights enjoyed in the 1960s.

This has sucked in continental and Japanese car-parts manufacturers, like Robert Bosch which has built a £100m-alternator factory in South Wales. Nissan has 177 suppliers in Britain, including

some Japanese firms which followed it to Sunderland.

While the old car industry languishes in the home market slump, Nissan's expansion is driven by the success of its Primera model in continental European markets. Honda and Toyota are expanding to sell across the whole EC market. The Japanese plants in Britain, with an output of around 60 cars a man a year, match productivity levels back home; other British car factories lag one-third behind this, though their efficiency doubled as they adopted Japanese methods.

The first Japanese manufacturing investment in Britain was the YKK zip factory in Lancashire; soon Japanese companies were making plastic roofing in South Wales, televisions in Devon. The

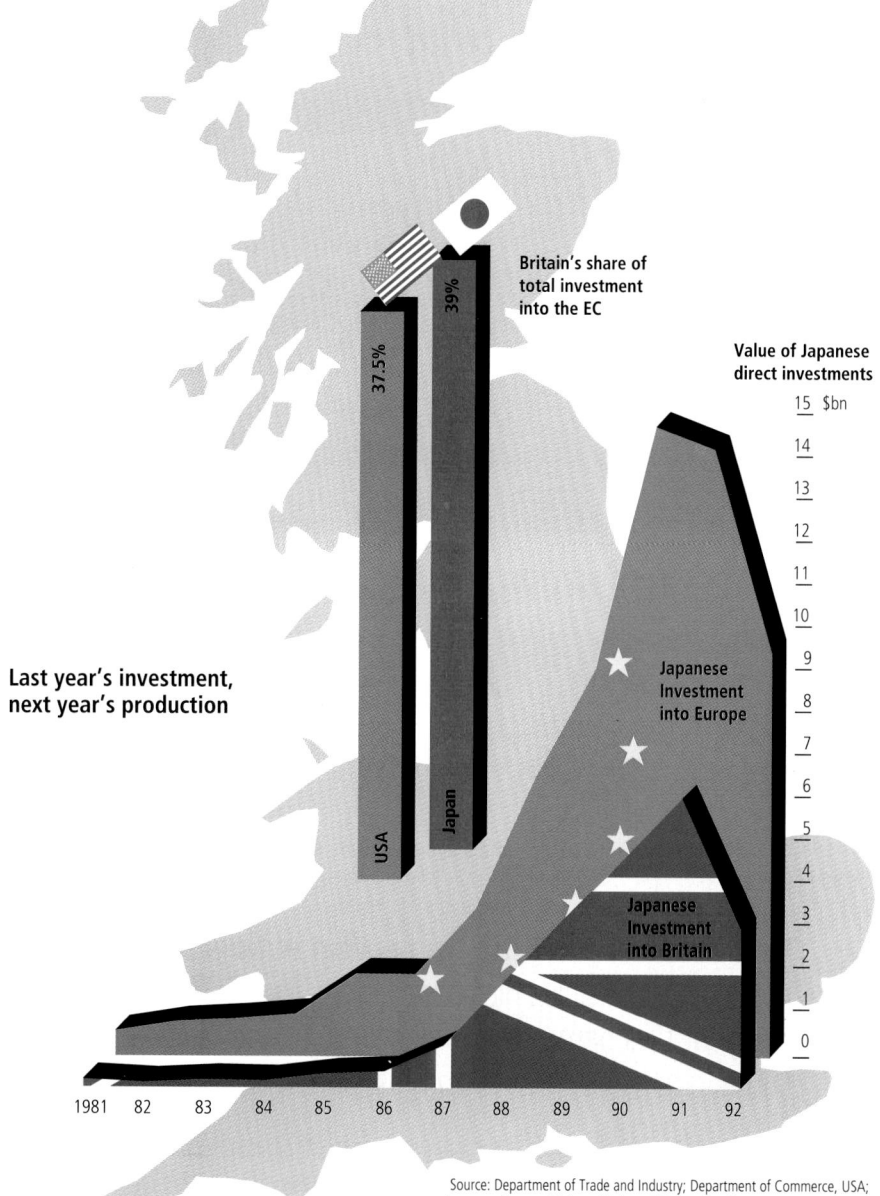

Britain's share of total investment into the EC

Value of Japanese direct investments

Last year's investment, next year's production

Japanese Investment into Europe

Japanese Investment into Britain

Source: Department of Trade and Industry; Department of Commerce, USA; Japanese Finance Ministry; Ministry of Economics, Bonn.

Iain Carson: business correspondent for the BBC.

To delete a document on his computer, Mr. Brown has to think like a computer.

#1 I inserted the floppy disk in the P.C. Nothing happened. I selected the document <u>I wanted to delete</u>. In this case I chose a letter to Susan Kilby coded <u>LETSKSEP.DOC</u>, which I'd saved on a floppy disk.

#2 From the Program Manager I double-clicked on the "Main" icon.

#3 I double-clicked on the "File Manager" icon.

#4 I selected the proper drive. Had the file been on the hard disk I would have known that the <u>C: drive</u> was where I should look, since that always represents the hard drive (but of course, you knew that.) But since <u>LETSKSEP.DOC</u> was on the floppy disk, I knew that I should select the <u>A: drive.</u>

#5 I clicked once on the document to select it.

#6 I selected "delete" from the <u>File Menu.</u>

#7 I clicked "O.K."

#8 I clicked " Yes "

It couldn't have been easier. :) - J Brown

One more of the little things that makes a Macintosh a lot easier. A Macintosh doesn't ask you to learn complex file abbreviations like AUTOEXEC.BAT and CONFIG.SYS and WIN.INI. It lets you call your files names you understand. A Macintosh doesn't ask you to reconfigure your system when you add an Apple printer. You just plug it in. A Macintosh doesn't ask you to buy and install compli-

To delete a document on his Macintosh, Mr. Mitchell has to think like Mr. Mitchell.

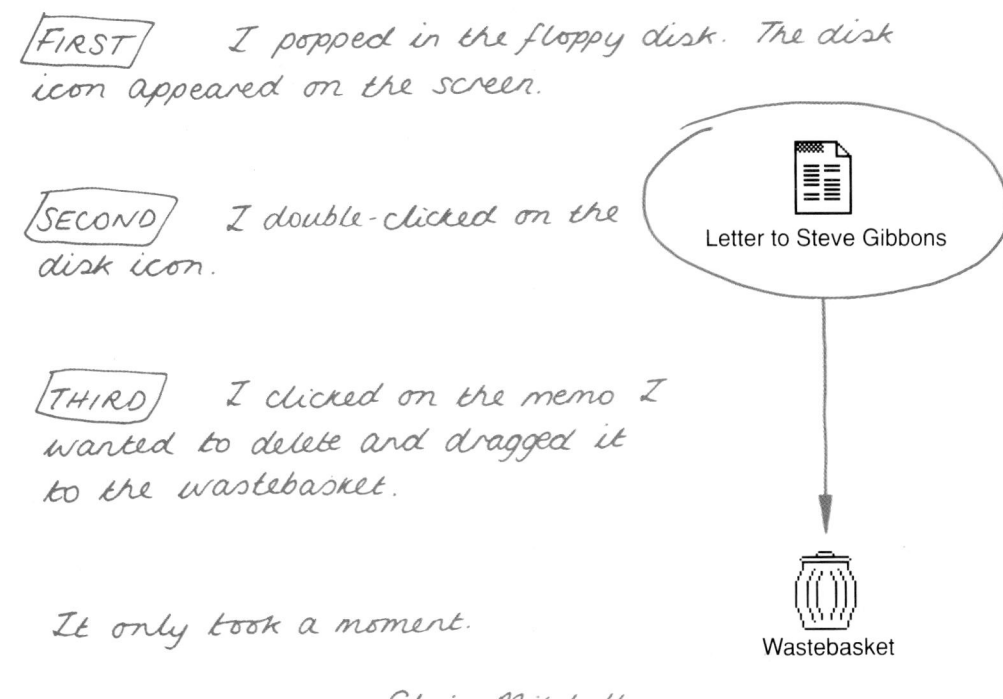

FIRST   I popped in the floppy disk. The disk icon appeared on the screen.

SECOND   I double-clicked on the disk icon.

THIRD   I clicked on the memo I wanted to delete and dragged it to the wastebasket.

It only took a moment.

Chris Mitchell

Letter to Steve Gibbons

Wastebasket

...cated networking cards or expensive file sharing software to make your computers work ...ogether. It comes with them already installed. A Macintosh understands how you work, ...o you don't have to work like a computer. For more information, dial 100 and ask for ...reefone Apple. **A Macintosh never asks you to do what a computer should do.**

Apple

Japanese Ministry of International Trade and Industry (MITI) calculates that in the 40 years to 1991, Britain enjoyed 7.4% of total Japanese direct investment; only the United States, with 42% ($148 billion), received more. The British influx was about 20% of the West European figure and 40% of the EC total.

The Japanese were attracted initially by the same factors that have also brought Britain about 40% of American investment in the EC. Britain offers a politically stable, English-language base inside the EC tariff walls. Then some of the effects of Thatcherism increased the attractions: corporate and personal income taxes are now very low; the labour market is deregulated; unions are cowed.

The number of Japanese living in Britain has quadrupled to 40,000 since 1980. There are now eight private Japanese schools around the country and a further eight Saturday schools attached to Japanese factories in Wales and the north-east. Eight Japanese estate agents help new arrivals find homes and seven Japanese removal firms help them move in. In London, where the Japanese population works in banking and financial services, the bosses have settled in the cherry-blossomed streets of St John's Wood and Hampstead, the middle managers further north in Finchley and Golders Green. Japanese families think the British suburban house with its private garden is pure heaven. If they hunger for home, there are 60 Japanese restaurants in London; in 1980 there were about ten.

But now the flow of new foreign money, from Japan and elsewhere, is diminishing and will diminish throughout 1993. The Bank for International Settlements calculates that Britain's share of inward investment into the EC fell from 39% in 1990 to 33% in 1991. Although it still had the biggest share in the Community, the British catch fell by $12 billion between 1990 and 1991. The figures for Japan's foreign investment show a similar trend: in 1991 the British figure fell to $3.6 billion, from $6.9 billion in 1990. The fall is ascribed partly to recession in Britain and abroad. But Britain has acquired such a large stock of American, German and Japanese foreign direct investment that inevitably the flow is bound to decrease.

Meanwhile, Japanese investment has quadrupled in Germany since 1990, with more high-technology projects. Recognising that the Japanese wave is subsiding, the Department of Trade and Industry is looking to lesser Asian dragon economies—Singapore, Hong Kong, Taiwan and Korea—to take up the slack in 1993.

The end of the countryside

Matt Ridley

In 1993 every British farmer will take 15% of his arable land—in all some 1.5m acres—out of crop production. This will not be compulsory, but unless he does so he will not get £84 ($145) on every productive arable acre he farms. In exchange for this largesse he will be paid the world price for his produce instead of the inflated European price: about £30 less for each tonne of wheat. The effect on the appearance of the countryside will be profound and longlasting.

"Setaside", as the scheme is known, will change the look not just of England but of much of northern Europe. Although many farmers will plough their setaside fields and spray them to keep the weeds down, some will not. The countryside will start to look a mess, ragwort and thistles abounding in what were once perhaps all-too-manicured fields. A few farmers will grow "industrial" rather than agricultural crops on them—such as rape or other forms of "biomass" for fuel.

And expect ponies and horses, which are notoriously bad grazers, to pop up everywhere: if a farmer rents a setaside field out to the Master of Fox Hounds or for little darling's pony, he will not require permission from the man from Brussels. There are already more horses in Britain than there were in the 18th century. Expect still more. Polo may yet become a plebeian sport.

Only a few farmers will plant their fields with woodland (to do so would be "permanent setaside", which must be 20% of acreage to qualify for compensation). Many more may try to grow golf courses.

More significant than the new rules from the EC will be the eventual impact of Poland and Ukraine as they begin exporting cheap wheat, thus keeping the downward pressure on prices. British farmers are already paid about half of what they were paid in the 1970s in real terms for a tonne of wheat. If that were to halve again, there would come a point where many would lose money year after year, however efficient they were.

Instead of trying to earn a return from every acre, the landowner would simply stop farming. Except in terms of interest on loans or capital taxes on death, land is not costly to own: it usually rises in value faster than inflation. 1993 may see the first farmer who decides to hold his land passively, like a share on the stockmarket, and not to work it: out with all those costly combine harvesters and animals and farmhands.

In Scotland many landowners have lost the £10 an acre they once earned in rents from sheep farmers. They earn a little from deer stalking or grouse shooting, but not much. The old Caledonian forest of pines and birches is gradually coming back on some open moors. (In New England, the primeval forest of maple and oak and hickory has long since reclaimed the land that was painstakingly cleared of stones and trees by the settlers, then abandoned after the prairies were opened to the plough.)

1066 and all that

Don't get too sentimental as the English landscape fades over the next decade. It was never unchanging. Ten thousand years ago Britain was an arctic tundra. Then it filled up with pine and birch trees, which gradually gave way 5,000 years ago to mixed forest of alder, oak, lime, elm, pine and birch.

Stone-age man arrived and began to clear the forest. By medieval times, most of Britain was an open, windswept land of vast pastures and common fields hundreds of acres in extent. The woods were few. It was only in the 15th and 16th centuries, with the enclosure movement, that the "countryside" was born: the hedges of elm and thorn and oak surrounding little fields of corn and flower-strewn pasture.

After that there were gentle trends, from horn (pasture) to corn (arable) and back again as prices moved. Before the second world war much of England's farmland was run-down and scruffy. Land prices had changed little in 100 years. It was not until the 1950s that the next great shift began. Out came hedges; out went oats and turnips and non-Friesian cows; out came old coppices to be replaced by ranks of straight conifers; in came rape and linseed; out went weeds and butterflies; in came chemicals and fertilisers; out went winter stubbles and spring-sown corn.

So will the new, untilled field offend the eye? It will certainly offend the traditional landowner, and not only because he can still earn £50 an acre a year in rent from good land. Farmers believe land must be managed, like a building, or it will become "derelict". True, unmanaged land is not a neat sight: all thistles and docks and goldfinches and coltsfoot and butterflies. But it does not stay that way forever. Tussock grass soon replaces the thistles. Within 20 years derelict land is a birch wood and within 50 it is full of oak and ash and sycamore. Horrible, says the professional forester: valueless crooked trunks of uneven, useless timber. Wonderful, says the naturalist, plucking a ripe chanterelle from the mossy floor.

The British countryside will either go this way, meandering back through the ecological succession into the forest cover whence it came and losing all reputation as a money-earner—or farmers will have to be paid to farm it as it used to be farmed, without chemicals and fertilisers, with hedges and copses and winter stubbles. The choice is the townie taxpayer's.

Hold that nation

Magnus Linklater

Major constitutional change in Scotland has effectively been ruled out for the remainder of the century as a result of the 1992 general election. The vote was hardly a massive swing of opinion, very far from a ringing endorsement of the status quo; it was indeed just a notch or two on the democratic scale. But it was enough to take the country back from the brink of potentially momentous change and to make the notion of a separate parliament and Scottish autonomy once more a distant dream. In the immediate aftermath, various pressure groups urged mass protest, and took to the streets. But after a brief flurry the banners were packed away, to be replaced by the occasional angry press conference.

It would be easy to conclude that the Scottish question had disappeared from the political agenda, and to conclude as well that this is entirely for the good. No one, surely, contemplating the horrors of ethnic rivalry in Yugoslavia and the former Soviet Union, could reasonably claim that independence was a trend to be encouraged closer to home. But it would be a mistake to say that the idea of nationhood in Scotland has simply withered. It is always there; it will return as an issue, as, historically, it always has; and there is

Magnus Linklater: editor of the *Scotsman.*

no certain guarantee that the Act of Union can be preserved intact forever.

For 1993, however, what is happening in Scotland is potentially more interesting than the constant stirring of the devolution pot. The political centre of gravity has shifted. The unquestioned hold which Labour policies and attitudes have exercised over a whole range of institutions, from local government to schools, health services, unions and housing, has slackened.

One noticeable result is that there is now a far less predictable response to major reforms such as the introduction of single-tier local authorities or the private management of hospitals. Instead they are being discussed on a pragmatic basis. Government ministers are growing used to issuing policy statements without having automatically to duck.

The potential break-up of some of the vast regional authorities which have been Labour power-bases for as long as most people can remember is being discussed with relative equanimity (though that could change as reality looms). Housing has been quietly moved away from council control without arousing protest. The "council tax", successor to the poll tax, will be made to work, not because it is popular but because it seems sensible to get the revenue in rather than attack the

What worries Scotland

The sting will be out of the local tax issue in 1993. But Ian Lang, the Scottish secretary, has obligingly given the Scots a new cause to unite them against the government: water. Mr Lang wants private sector involvement to finance the £703m of investment by 1995 (and more afterwards) needed to bring Scottish water and sewage up to EC standards.

Scottish Nationalists and socialists, as well as the regional authorities, will stir up public passions against privatisation. Local Tories will be wobbly in their support for the Scottish secretary.

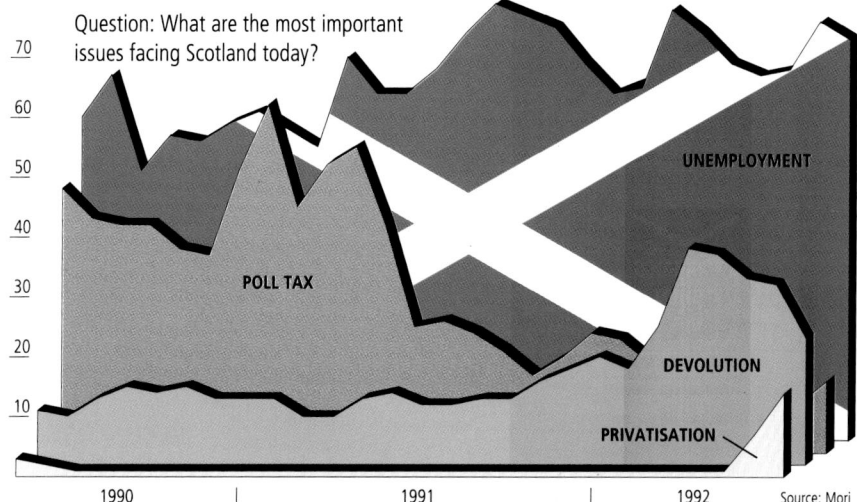

Question: What are the most important issues facing Scotland today?

POLL TAX

UNEMPLOYMENT

DEVOLUTION

PRIVATISATION

1990　　1991　　1992　　Source: Mori

Our centuries-old pursuit
of realism is starting to bear fruit.

With the advent of the YI Dynasty in 1392, came
Confucian scholarship and its emphasis on the practice
of poetry, calligraphy and painting. In the following
centuries, Korean painters achieved a remarkable
degree of perspective and realism in their monochrome
works. By studying and developing the skills and
wisdom of the past, Goldstar, the electronics arm of the
Lucky-Goldstar Group, is in the final stages of producing
another work with a remarkable degree of realism:
the Goldstar High Definition TV (HDTV). But the
HDTV is only one of the many masterpieces that the
Lucky-Goldstar Group has produced. Through dedication
to the needs of our people, and the requirements of
our customers, we've grown into a US$25 billion
corporation. Currently, we have a portfolio of over 35
diverse and well-established companies operating in
over 120 countries. Companies involved in every
aspect of electronics, chemistry, finance, trade,
construction and public service. We know where
we came from and we know where we're going.
With astute planning, development, and investment,
we aim to become one of the world's top ten
companies by the turn of the century.

Investing Our Past In The Future

change on principle. For its part, the Labour Party has been revising its position on a whole range of issues as it contemplates another five years in opposition.

There has not, however, been much evidence of triumphalism amongst Scottish ministers. Aware, perhaps, that old wounds can be easily re-opened, they appear to have become more sensitive to nationalist opinion, watering down some reforms, speaking the language of moderation rather than Thatcherite radicalism, talking to once-hostile institutions rather than ignoring them. The phrase currently in vogue is the "new unionism", described by the Scottish secretary of state, Ian Lang, as "an attractive phrase" and one which is intended to make Britain "more relevant" to its constituent parts. Whether that amounts to anything more than a marketing concept remains to be seen, and if it is not given flesh by the reforms that John Major has promised there is likely to be a re-emergence of the old discontent.

That discontent would be blunted, of course, by economic recovery, however distant that possibility seems. Scotland was not hit as badly as the south of England, perhaps because the boom had never been as great north of the border. Disposable income per head remains higher than in most regions in Britain, perhaps because the Scots have never been great borrowers; there is, therefore, some prospect of a modest recovery in the retail trade. Small businesses tend to have kept their heads down and survived better than they have in England, although recent figures on company failures show an increase. And there are some areas, such as Aberdeenshire, which have escaped the recession altogether. Here property prices remain high, and the on-shore oil industry has continued to flourish. Despite predictions that off-shore manning will continue to decline, one recent report declared that the area would continue to enjoy healthy growth for the next 25 years.

For the time being, therefore, the issues that will dominate the Scottish political scene in 1993 will tend to be ones familiar in the rest of Britain. But that does not mean that their separate quality has disappeared. As the Scottish political editor of the *Scotsman* wrote recently: "Scottish politics has not died or been banished. It has simply moved house. It has moved from Nationalist Street to Unionist Avenue, a less bohemian neighbourhood where the inhabitants hold fewer late-night parties and more coffee mornings... But if it gets too boring, the Scots might go back to the old address and start annoying the neighbours again."

You pay, he sings

The future of broadcasting

Norman Macrae

Close your eyes and ears to the tedious debate that will chatter on in Britain next year about the future of the BBC and broadcasting. Politicians will pretend that the matter rests with them. It won't, but rather with three wonderfully inescapable economic facts.

First, it is going to become very cheap to throw any number of television programmes into the boundless air. Your television set will be capable of receiving well over a hundred terrestrial and satellite programmes. You will probably have 15 buttons geared to the channels you personally decide you usually like, and a tuner to get (and record) any one of the myriad others when it has a special programme you particularly want.

Second, despite this much wider choice, watching time will go down. So lots of those sprouting channels will, like today's airlines, constantly be going bust. Those most likely to fail will not be the newer and lower-cost stations—but the familiar old ones that have been built up on the basis of absurdly top-heavy and trade-union-imposed bureaucratic costs.

Third, there will therefore be a dash towards different ways of paying. Some channels will be paid for by subscription, some by sponsorship, many by pay-as-you-view, more by advertisement, most by some mixture of these.

It is doubtful that any new channels anywhere will be financed by equivalents of Britain's upper-middle-class scam called the BBC. Its mandatory licence is a poll tax, imposed even on poor old-age pensioners in Hackney to finance programmes that they don't like, and instead to churn out upper-market stuff preferred by richer folk like most readers of this article and me.

Contrary to what most people say, these new non-public service systems will lead to a renaissance of noble art, of popular culture (including sport) and of democratic politics around the world. At present, art such as opera can be financed only by requiring huge subsidies to be paid by the 95% of taxpayers who think a fat man singing in Italian is incomprehensible rubbish, so as to service the 5% (usually richer of us) who find it divine.

Such programmes will go out via pay-as-you-view (cheaper than opera seats) along with advertisements. An audience consisting of the top 5% of worldwide admirers of Pavarotti will be a very attractive captive constituency for certain upmarket advertisements, especially as both ads and performances will be filmed ever more cheaply.

The greater revolution in innovative art will come because the video camera can cheaply open up competition. Today

Norman Macrae: columnist for the *Sunday Times*.

it is difficult for (say) work by a village dramatic society, even if written or choreographed or imaginatively directed by a new genius, to reach any audience outside the village.

Tomorrow all such societies will put their video-cameraed performances into a pool from which channels round the world will eagerly snap up original stuff, especially when written in a viewer's favourite language, like English.

The channel system of television or radio—whereby half-a-dozen controllers decide, "Can I risk showing this?"—has proved awful at stimulating new art forms. The first 70 years of the BBC produced only one original work that will live: a radio play called "Under Milk Wood" by a drunken Welsh poet. Neither prissy Puritanism nor prurient smut, constantly tinged with middle-class guilt feelings, can breed great art.

Popular sports like association football can now be watched only by the few thousand who accompany hooligans to a stadium. With pay-as-you-view, they will become richer and varied. At the top there will be transcontinental leagues. Nottingham v Roma, unlike Nottingham v Derby, will attract patriotic support, thus higher pay-as-you-view and more ads. Cheapness of transmission will mean that many new participatory sports will attract TV coverage.

The effect on politics will be the biggest. Anybody will be allowed to put any political view on his channel, as he is allowed to in his newspaper. If a channel turns absurdly Tory or Labour in its new slant, flick the switch. Most, of course, will choose the channel that reflects their own prejudices. During the period when channels were few, and supposed to be politically "fair", dreadful misinformation was poured to the public. Diverse views, even if crazy, will make better television than monopoly views that are wrong.

The most dramatic future change is that vested interests (including politicians) will now lose their battle against lie detectors. These instruments were invented just about when radio broadcasting was. Incredibly, no speaker on television ever seems to have been trussed up in one. The Japanese are now inventing non-wired or electronic lie detectors. You will point one at the screen where a speaker is uttering propaganda. If he exhibits some tell-tale sign of lying—moving his hands faster than Goebbels did, twitching his chin or eyelids, emphasising certain syllables—the instrument will start to bleep. This will have a huge effect on politicians, bishops, doomsayers, bankers and crooks. It will also affect advertisements.

The royals reform

Anthony King

The British monarchy in 1993 will continue its reversion to normal. It will be seen less as a quasi-religious institution and more as a service industry. There will be less talk of "the royal family" and more of "the royals". Veneration will gradually cease. Pay will be performance-related.

The monarchy, and individual monarchs, have not always been popular. The first four Georges, beginning in 1714, were variously stupid, lazy, stubborn and profligate. Fathers and sons typically loathed each other. All but George III kept mistresses. Before he became king in 1830 William IV sired ten illegitimate children by an actress who sometimes went on tour to help him pay his debts.

Victoria, his niece, was famously monogamous, but after her husband's death in 1861 she went on strike for a decade, refusing to perform her royal duties. She continued, however, to be paid out of state funds and one contemporary pamphlet asked, "What does she do with it?" Republicanism in Victoria's time was rife. Sober observers wondered whether her son, fat Bertie, a notorious gambler and lecher, would ever ascend the throne.

Then the age of respectability set in, quite unexpectedly. Disraeli coaxed Victoria out of her seclusion. The monarchy became caught up in the glories of empire. Victoria's successors (save only Edward VIII) became conscientious servants of the state, doting parents and models of rectitude. Ordinary British citizens looked up to the royal family—and thought of it as a family—for the first time.

In the 1990s that familiar edifice is cracking up. The monarchy is reverting to type. Elizabeth II and her consort remain respectable, but their children are re-enacting the George and Bertie show. Anne is divorced, Andrew is separated, Charles and his wife are said not to get on, and Edward, a bachelor at 28, is inevitably the subject of rumour. The British public is disoriented. The royal family clearly is too.

What happens next? Constitutionally and in the short term, nothing. In the 19th century monarchy seemed inconsistent with democracy but now almost no one holds that view. Despite the affairs of Di's phone calls and Fergie's toes, positive animus against the royals is almost wholly absent. Laughter or pity are the normal reactions. Few have any notion of what might be put in the monarchy's place. As a political institution, the monarchy in Britain itself is safe as long as the crown remains neutral between the main political parties.

Whether the same applies in the Commonwealth countries that still retain the British monarch as their head of state is more doubtful. There are republican stirrings in Canada and Australia. Large numbers in both countries no longer see Britain as the mother country. Rejection of the monarchy on nationalist grounds is likely to be fuelled by the sense that the royals are becoming risible. Elizabeth II still has her dominions beyond the seas. Charles may not inherit them.

Even in Britain, the royals' reversion to 18th-century type could have political consequences in the long term. The age-of-respectability monarchs became national symbols, embracing Scots and Welshmen as well as the dominant English. Even militant Scottish and Welsh nationalists usually fought shy of advocating republican solutions. As the royals lose esteem, so the United Kingdom may be losing legitimacy.

As a social institution, the monarchy is under more immediate threat. The junior royals, with the partial exception of Anne, are miscast as purveyors of rectitude to the multitude. Role models they are not. The queen herself, while still admired, seems increasingly out of touch—like so many bemused parents whose children have gone wrong. No longer mirror to the nation as it would like to see itself, the royal family increasingly mirrors the nation as it is. The British could become bored with their own reflection.

Attention in 1993 will focus on the civil list, the taxpayers' money that helps fund the royals. People in Britain enjoy royal cavorting; but they are less keen on paying for it. The emphasis next year will be on relatively modest payments for services actually rendered. Recipients of civil-list payments are likely to be limited to the queen and a few others close to the throne. The royal yacht Britannia is unlikely to remain afloat for long.

The more difficult question concerns the royals' public persona. Since George V's time their style has been friendly but aloof. Women curtsey. The queen is never heard asking the way to the ladies'. Social equality stops at the palace gate.

The royals and their advisers may decide that has to change. Aloofness combined with high-flying hedonism looks dangerously like arrogance. Prudence will probably begin in 1993 to point the royals towards a somewhat more egalitarian style.

WE, THE UNDERSIGNED, ARE PLEASED TO ANNOUNCE THE ACHIEVEMENT OF A EUROPEAN MONETARY UNION.

AUSTRIA / Postsparkasse

P.S.K.

BELGIUM / Postcheque

POSTCHEQUE DE POST

DENMARK / GiroBank A/S

GiroBank

FINLAND / Postipankki Ltd

POSTIPANKKI

FRANCE / La Poste

LA POSTE

GERMANY / Deutsche Bundespost Postbank

Postbank

IRELAND / An Post

POST

LUXEMBOURG / P et T

P&T LUXEMBOURG

NETHERLANDS / Postbank NV

POSTBANK

NORWAY / Postgiro

POST GIRO

SPAIN / Caja Postal

Caja Postal ARGENTARIA

SWEDEN / Postgirot

POSTGIROT

SWITZERLAND / PTT

PTT

UNITED KINGDOM / Girobank plc

Girobank

MEMBERS OF THE EUROGIRO NETWORK

A new cross-border payment system is being launched in Europe. A partnership between the above financial organisations has led to the creation of EUROGIRO — an integrated electronic network which will set new standards in transferring payments across national frontiers.

The EUROGIRO network will provide secure and paperless cross-border payments between any of the 40 million private and business customers of these organisations.

EUROGIRO will do so at low cost, at high speed and with great reliability. And it will provide the basis for a range of products designed to handle all types of transactions — from small, single and infrequent payments, to large, multiple and regular ones.

That's why EUROGIRO represents an important development in cross-border payments — and a form of monetary union which can win everyone's vote.

EUROGIRO

THE FAST, COST-EFFECTIVE PAYMENT SYSTEM

TO REQUEST FURTHER INFORMATION ON EUROGIRO, PLEASE FAX COPENHAGEN (45)42 52 62 66,
OR WRITE TO EUROGIRO NETWORK A/S, PO BOX 188, DK-2670, TAASTRUP, DENMARK, OR REFER TO THE ORGANISATION IN YOUR COUNTRY AS SHOWN ABOVE.

So many leaders, so little direction

One market, many problems

Bob Taylor

The European Community will spend a large part of 1993 digging itself out of the hole it fell into in 1992. The crisis of confidence over the ratification of the Maastricht treaty on European union, the near collapse of the Community's exchange-rate mechanism (ERM) and its poor performance as Europe's self-appointed policeman in the Balkans is far from over.

The Maastricht treaty will not therefore come into effect on the scheduled date of January 1st 1993. Look for at least a six-month delay. Finance ministers and monetary experts will examine ways of revamping the rules of the ERM to prevent a recurrence of Britain's humiliating withdrawal in September 1992. But whatever happens, the pound is likely to go on floating on its own outside the system for most, if not all, of 1993.

The Community's inability to end the fighting between the ethnic groups in former Yugoslavia means it will be more cautious before taking fresh foreign-policy initiatives of its own. It is much more likely to link up with America and the United Nations, as it ultimately did over Yugoslavia.

But 1993 will not be all damage-limitation. The Community will mark a singular achievement on January 1st, with the

Bob Taylor: writes for *The Economist* from Brussels.

formal creation of its frontier-free single market. Its launch with due fanfare at the Edinburgh summit in December 1992 is the culmination of seven years of preparation, during which more than 250 separate items of frontier-flattening legislation have been put in place. The new rules enable goods, services, people and capital to move as freely across internal borders as within one single state.

Life for businesses and citizens will not change overnight on January 1st, for several reasons. The main one is that the single market has been put in place piece-by-piece over the past few years as individual items of legislation have been adopted. It is like a motorway which has been gradually opened to traffic as successive sections are completed. Another reason is that some parts of the single market, although agreed, will take several years before they come into effect. Financial services, for instance, will not be fully freed up until 1995 and a proper single market for automobiles has been delayed until 2000.

Nor will internal border controls be entirely eliminated. These have eased everywhere with progress towards the single market. But countries like Britain and Denmark intend to keep limited controls. They believe the right to move unhindered around the Community should be

limited to EC nationals only and not granted to citizens of other countries who should be checked as they travel from one member state to the next. There will be a technical hitch too: many airports have not got round to having unhindered walk-throughs for EC passport holders.

The opening of internal frontiers within the Community will be matched by a reinforcement of controls for visitors arriving at the external borders of the Community or arriving at an EC airport on a flight from outside. The issue of immigration is high on the 1993 agenda.

One of the priorities of the Twelve will be to tighten requirements for granting asylum to political refugees and others fleeing oppression. Only a fraction of those allowed in under previous arrangements are likely to qualify in future.

For business, the focus of the single market will shift in 1993 from law-making to law enforcement. There are already signs that some governments are applying neither the letter nor the spirit of some single-market directives. Firms cite banking rules, labelling requirements, monopoly-busting telecoms directives among many instances of laws not applied properly. The European Commission has only limited resources of its own to police the single-market rules. Given the current drive by some governments to reduce the

Homeless in Brussels

Bob Taylor

Since January 1992 the Berlaymont building, seat of the European Commission for the past 24 years, has stood empty and abandoned—its staff of Eurocrats scattered to the four corners of Brussels. A year later, reflected in its grimy windows, half a dozen tower cranes fuss and wheel above the massive concrete shape of the new headquarters of the EC Council of Ministers going up just across the street. A few hundred yards away the steel and glass arched roof of the European Parliament's trendy new building glistens in the winter sunshine.

The scene is heavy with post-Maastricht symbolism. For those who wish to see it, the picture confirms that the commission has been sidelined—at least for the time being—and that the dynamic centre of EC activity is the Council of Ministers, where government ministers from the Twelve meet to take the main decisions. As for the European Parliament, it has won the post-1992 race to get its new Brussels

Europe's new talk-shop

headquarters in operation. But the building, like the parliament itself, remains more show than substance. This impression is confirmed by the fact that work is to begin in early 1993 on a second talking shop for the parliament—this time in Strasbourg, where its main sittings take place.

Even if the planned refurbishing of the Berlaymont gets under way next year, it will take four years before this asbestos-riddled fire hazard will again be fit for occupation. The council building, by contrast, will be doling out directives and, on grander occasions, hosting EC summits from 1995.

But remember the hare and the tortoise. The commission has no option but to take a back seat until the Maastricht ratification drama plays itself out. By the time the Berlaymont is back in business, the next round in the power play between EC governments and Brussels will be under way. The history of the EC since 1958 shows that time is on the commission's side.

commission's power, this is unlikely to change.

Many of the border-opening rules of the single market will be extended to the Community's neighbours of the European Free Trade Association (EFTA) under a special treaty signed with them. But for most EFTA countries, this is not enough. They have applied for full EC membership. Negotiations are due to begin in 1993, but probably not before June.

The Community must first fulfil its own internal preconditions. One is to implement a deal to set new spending limits for the EC budget. The other is to complete Maastricht ratification. The deadline for ratification is effectively the Copenhagen summit on June 21st and 22nd. By then, barring major accidents, British ratification will be completed. A second Danish referendum enabling people to vote again on Maastricht, with a few special sweeteners added, will have been held. Provided the Danes say yes this time, the first round of enlargement negotiations could take place in Copenhagen the day after the summit.

But some issues cannot be put off. Europe's farmers are due to endure their first major price cuts in the spring stemming from last year's reform of the common agricultural policy. No amount of coaxing will persuade them to remain calm until the Community has sorted out its other institutional difficulties.

France prepares for battle

Yann de l'Ecotais

The parliamentary elections to be held in France in March 1993 seem certain to produce a massive victory for the right-wing opposition. This will force the president, François Mitterrand, into a new "cohabitation" with his opponents. It will open the way for two years of continuous fighting before the next presidential election in 1995, when Mr Mitterrand goes after 14 years.

This cohabitation will be all the more difficult because Mr Mitterrand will be looking very much like a lame duck. If the referendum on the Maastricht treaty on September 20th confirmed anything, it was the widespread and deep unpopularity of the president and his Socialist Party.

So there is a real chance that Mr Mitterrand—aged 76, frail and unpopular—will throw in his hand. Although largely master of the political game under the rules of the constitution, he must hesitate when confronted by the grim prospect of the next two years. There is no doubt that his desire to work out his second term in full remains strong. Retirement would represent a physical, moral

Yann de l'Ecotais: editor-in-chief of l'*Express*.

and intellectual trial perhaps more difficult to overcome than remaining in office. Furthermore, Mr Mitterrand, skilled tactician that he is, can always hope that the obvious personal conflicts among the leaders of the opposition may make his lot happier than it seems now.

On the final lap of a political career that began half a century ago, Mr Mitterrand enters 1993 with his hand scarcely on the tiller. Politics is an ever greater struggle for him. The killer instinct has become blunted. And the great objective of his latter-day life has been reached: France, by a whisker, sits all-powerful at the heart of the EC.

Mr Mitterrand chose Europe as the grand arena for his second seven-year term. The success of the referendum assures him both of his place in French history and of a more-than-honourable exit from the Elysée. So should he risk the possible humiliations and constraints that remaining in office would entail?

On top of these personal considerations, the president of the republic will also be weighing political ones as he enters 1993. The only possible way of leaving French socialism with a chance in the

WALLONIA, EUROPE'S MEETING POINT.

Where the roads from Brussels (38 miles), Berlin (375 miles), Paris (190 miles) and London (250 miles) meet, qualification and productivity have also joined forces (according to the U.S. Labor Force Report) to attract the world's largest companies. The technology is there. We are ready to meet your industrial challenges.

PROBABLY THE EASIEST WAY TO INVEST IN EUROPE:
WALLONIA, BELGIUM'S
FRENCH-SPEAKING REGION

OFFICE FOR FOREIGN INVESTORS

MINISTRY OF WALLONIA REGION (Belgium)
Investing: O.F.I. Tel.: 32-81-32 14 53 Fax.: 32-81-30 64 00
Trading: D.A.R.E. Tel.: 32-2-211 55 11 Fax.: 32-2-211 55 70

C.T.O.

Chirac's year

short term lies in calling a presidential election before the parliamentary elections. For the left wing, some chance of winning could be retained by Michel Rocard. Once elected president, the latter could then ask the country to give him a majority in parliament to enable him to govern. In theory this is viable. It would lead to a presidential election early next year. But it has a serious problem: Mr Mitterrand does not like Mr Rocard.

Barring some dramatic unforeseen change, the government of Pierre Bérégovoy—and the president with him—will, therefore, face a real hammering next year. Three million unemployed, the weight of taxes and social insurance, insecurity, immigration: the rising anxiety, even alarm, at these—as clearly revealed by the results of the referendum—will provide the opposition with the perfect platform. Mr Mitterrand is well aware that a good part of his "left-wingers", as he used to call them in 1981, voted against him in the referendum: blue-collar workers, employees, generally low-income groups, farmers, shop-keepers made up the bulk of the "*non*" vote. Mr Mitterrand, who was expecting fragmentation among the opposition over the poll on the Maastricht treaty, lost his gamble. He will not recover from it.

Mr Mitterrand once pondered restructuring French politics by seeking an alliance between the centre-right and a large part of the Socialist Party. But even before the referendum that no longer seemed an ambition. From now on, French politics will once again be a straight battle of right against left.

Jacques Chirac will be the undoubted leader of the right-wing alliance in 1993 and its obvious candidate in an early presidential campaign. He has made few mistakes over the past two years. Above all, he has carried off two risky gambles against vociferous opposition from within his own party: he refused an alliance with Jean Marie le Pen's National Front Party, and he put himself in favour of the Maastricht treaty after calling for a referendum. He has thus acquired for himself an imposing stature that had previously escaped him. Courage and perhaps luck made him a statesman. Facing him, Valéry Giscard d'Estaing somehow cannot manage, despite his intelligence and talents, to re-awaken from the heart of his country that echo which opened up the road to the Elysée for him in 1974.

But Mr Chirac does not wish to serve again as prime minister under a Mitterrand presidency—and he probably means it. Mr Giscard d'Estaing, however, has no such qualms. It is thus that the split in the right of French politics remains a wound that might yet prove fatal.

That French politics should have become so personified by a few old enemies, who have been around for upwards of 20 years, is the very reason that the French public is in such a grumpy mood. Other European countries have their changes; in France the same old faces go on and on. The French people are worried about jobs, retirement, health and education, not about whether Mr Giscard d'Estaing is going to mess up Mr Chirac's chances. The French want—and care little where they come from—more jobs and income, and more security for the future. What's surprising about that?

The country will not then be able to postpone for much longer the one great outstanding reform: to get the state out of private and business life. The omnipresent state and its regulations, the overgrown public sector which swallows money and stifles the spirit of enterprise is long overdue for reform.

Each year, obligatory levies (taxes and contributions) cost the German economy FFr350 billion ($70 billion) less than they do the French economy. Even so, German roads, hospitals and schools can hardly be considered wanting by French standards.

On this disentanglement depends the renewal of a French society that is bogged down and bored. On it depends even the fulfilment of the monetary commitment under the Maastricht treaty. The harsh measures entailed by the move towards a single currency will not be bearable unless, in other respects, the economy is liberated from the bureaucratic yoke.

1993 ECONOMIC FORECAST

FRANCE

The French consumer will not be taking any risks in 1993. Continuing high real-interest rates and an absence of tax cuts mean another dull year on the high street. Business investment will not rise quickly as companies will not want to run too far ahead of consumers while borrowing costs are high. Still, any rise in investment will be welcome after 1992's fall of 1.3%. The increase could be 2% in 1993.

The strongest sector of the French economy is the export business, which benefits from the considerable competitiveness which French products display in world markets. Thanks to that, economic growth should reach 1.9% in 1993. That just tops the 1992 figure of 1.8%.

The government will be pleased not to have to abandon all control of its spending as part of its strategy of supporting economic growth. Like most governments around the world, the French administration has been willing to use spending increases to maintain its popularity in difficult periods.

1992 was a tough year politically: first the farmers blocked the roads, then the lorry drivers did the same. Their protests were parochial and their methods petty. That was the point: a rude reminder to François Mitterrand that his grand design for Europe is only half the political equation.

Political unrest at home and worries about the Maastricht referendum hurt the exchange rate in 1992. Any repetition in 1993 could hurt the government's attempt to show that Germany is not the only source of economic stability in Europe.

Imports look as though they will increase in 1993. Even so, inflation of less than 3% and a current-account deficit of just $4 billion next year make the outlook brighter.

If the Bundesbank decides to stay tough and keep interest rates high for another year, then the French government will probably do the same. If the electorate starts to complain, then the Germans can always be blamed.

KEY INDICATORS

	1991	1992	1993
GDP growth (% pa)	1.2	1.8	1.9
Inflation (%)	3.2	2.9	2.8
Prime rate (year end %)	10.8	11.4	10.0
Exchange rate			
FFr per DM	3.40	3.39	3.38
FFr per $	5.64	5.29	5.48
Current account ($ bn)	−6.1	−1.0	−4.0

EIU GLOBAL FORECASTING SERVICE

GERMANY

1993 ECONOMIC FORECAST

The Germans do not go to the polls in 1993. But it will surely not be a quiet year politically. Chancellor Helmut Kohl learned in 1991 how unwilling the west Germans are to pay higher taxes to fund the reconstruction of eastern Germany; the consequent rise in government borrowing means that the Bundesbank is now on the offensive.

To placate the central bank, the 1993 federal budget deficit is planned to be DM38 billion ($25 billion), or a little below the 1992 figure. Slower growth would change that, reducing tax revenues and raising spending costs.

The Bundesbank is facing a technical problem which all central banks encounter eventually: what meaning to place on an accepted definition of the money supply when the society, and hence the economy, is changing rapidly. All-German inflation will probably decline, to 3.9% in 1993 after 4.6% in 1992.

Even so, the central bank has been proved right on the major issue: unification is taking longer and is involving a much larger collapse in eastern Germany than the government predicted.

There are signs, nevertheless, that the collapse is bottoming out, thanks to huge financial inflows.

Worryingly, most of the finance has gone on consumption and not capital goods. It is generating plenty of demand for new cars and consumer goods but not much in the way of investment.

Amid all the domestic doubts the foreign-exchange markets will stand firmly behind the D-mark. This is because the markets cannot remember such high German interest rates before and want to lock in, especially to the long bonds which the government is issuing heavily.

Nothing is without risk. Two million ethnic Germans might yet be driven out of the former Soviet Union by food shortages or civil war. Their impact on the German budget deficit, should they move there, would be alarming. No wonder the Bundesbank is determined not to be a soft touch.

KEY INDICATORS

	1991	1992	1993
GDP growth (%)	1.1	1.5	2.0
Inflation (%)	5	4.6	3.9
Prime rate (year end %)	11.3	10.5	9.3
Exchange rate DM per $	1.66	1.56	1.62
Current account ($ bn)	−20.7	−14.0	−10.0

EIU GLOBAL FORECASTING SERVICE

Germany: a new policy mix?

Horst Siebert

In 1993, just three years after unification, self-sustained economic growth will get under way in eastern Germany. The success and the expense of that remarkable achievement mean that Germany's wage policy, as well as its fiscal and monetary policies, will have to be starkly reviewed. In 1992, the GDP of the old communist country was down to one-half of the 1989 level; industrial production was at just one-third. More than 4m jobs had been lost. Yet productivity was only at one-third of the west German level.

Investment in 1993 will reach DM120 billion ($80 billion), after DM110 billion in 1992. This amount will, if continued for the next ten years, be roughly sufficient to rebuild the capital stock of the new *Länder*. The growth rate of GDP in eastern Germany is estimated at 7%. There are still problems, especially the duration of governmental approval or licensing procedures for private investment projects. For example, DM30 billion investment in the energy sector has been stalled for these reasons. Another obstacle is the continuing uncertainty stemming from unresolved property rights.

The best sign of how well the adjustment process is going is to be seen in the Treuhand. Out of 12,000 industrial firms, 10,000 will have been privatised by the

Horst Siebert: president, Kiel Institute of Economics; member of the German Council of Economic Advisers.

end of 1992. Employment in the Treuhand firms is down to 600,000—from 4m originally. In 1993, the Treuhand will complete its privatisations, wrapping up a process that Russia and most of Eastern Europe will scarcely have begun. In these privatised firms new entrepreneurial concepts are being introduced with success, though it will always be the problems that catch attention. The ground for an adjustment process is well prepared for a more prosperous 1993.

In addition, 550,000 people are self-employed. Employment pledges of 1.4m jobs and investment guarantees of DM160 billion by the privatised firms indicate the extent of the possible rebound. And there is plenty in the pipeline waiting to come on stream, such as the new Volkswagen plant in Mosel, which should start production in 1994.

These very real signs of hope will only reinforce current German economic policy throughout the next 12 months. But there are three risks, each of which could bring down the whole edifice with disastrous domestic and international political consequences.

The first is wage inflation. Nominal wages in eastern Germany will reach 80% of the west German wage level in 1993 even though productivity will still trail at 30-40%. Unit wage costs in eastern Germany were 177% of the west German level in 1992. Unless wage contracts are

Capitalism makes you work

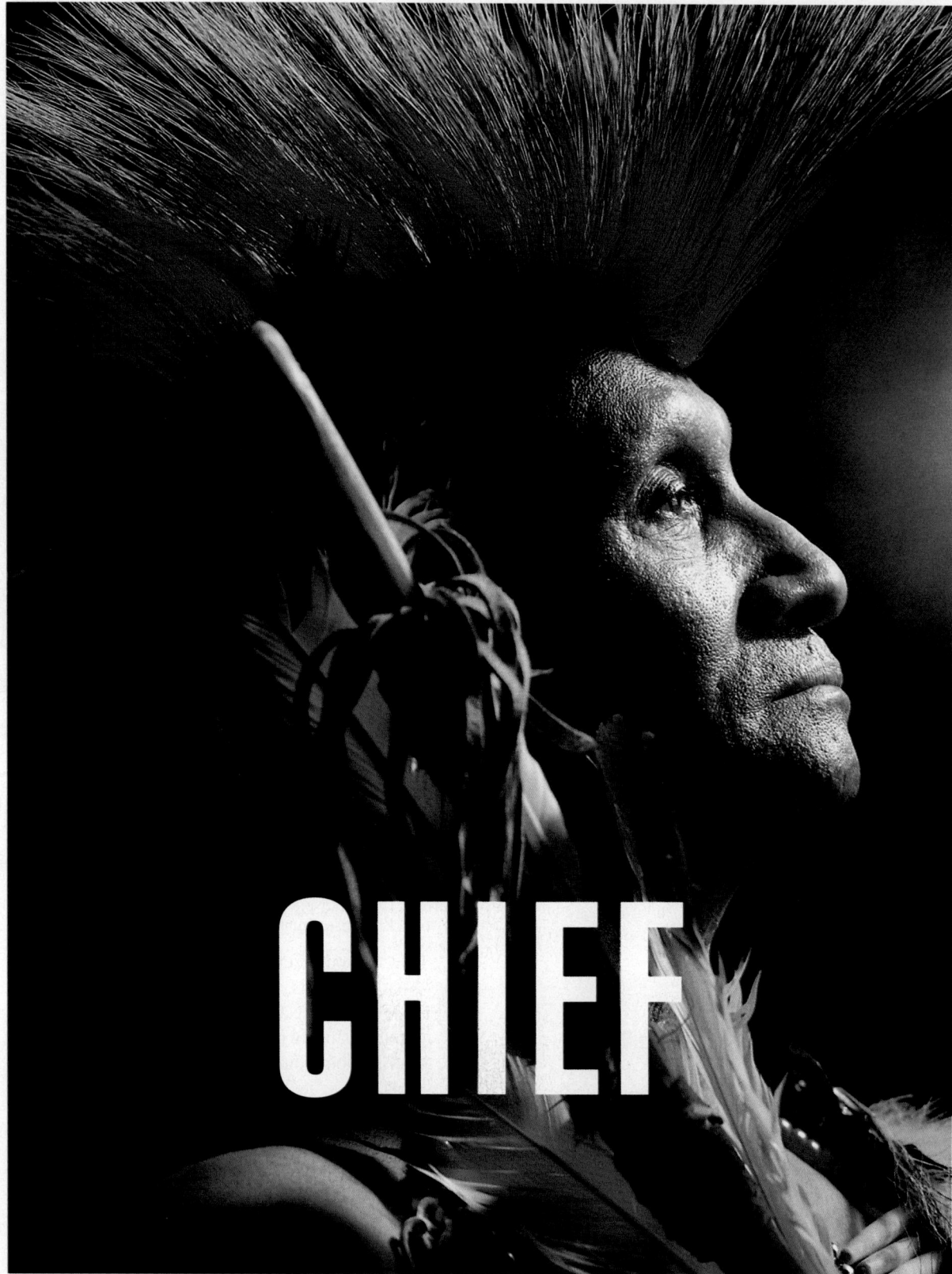

CHIEF

Are we really living in the age of personal development, or does it only seem so? Can we really afford to be different in today's society, behave differently, think differently?

Or can we only distinguish ourselves by what we earn and how we spend it? And has our individualism degenerated to a level at which we know how to take but not how to give anymore? Perhaps it would do no harm to expose western society a little more to the views of other cultures: cultures which often succeed in combining community interests with individual development and expression.

As Origin, we ourselves operate at the center of modern technology. We are an international full service supplier in the field of information technology.

Our 3,500 specialists operate from 85 offices in 14 countries.

Origin: Amsterdam, Barcelona, Bombay, Brussels, Cambridge, Chicago, Cincinnati, Columbus, Dallas, Dortmund, Eindhoven, Hamburg, Kaohsiung, London,

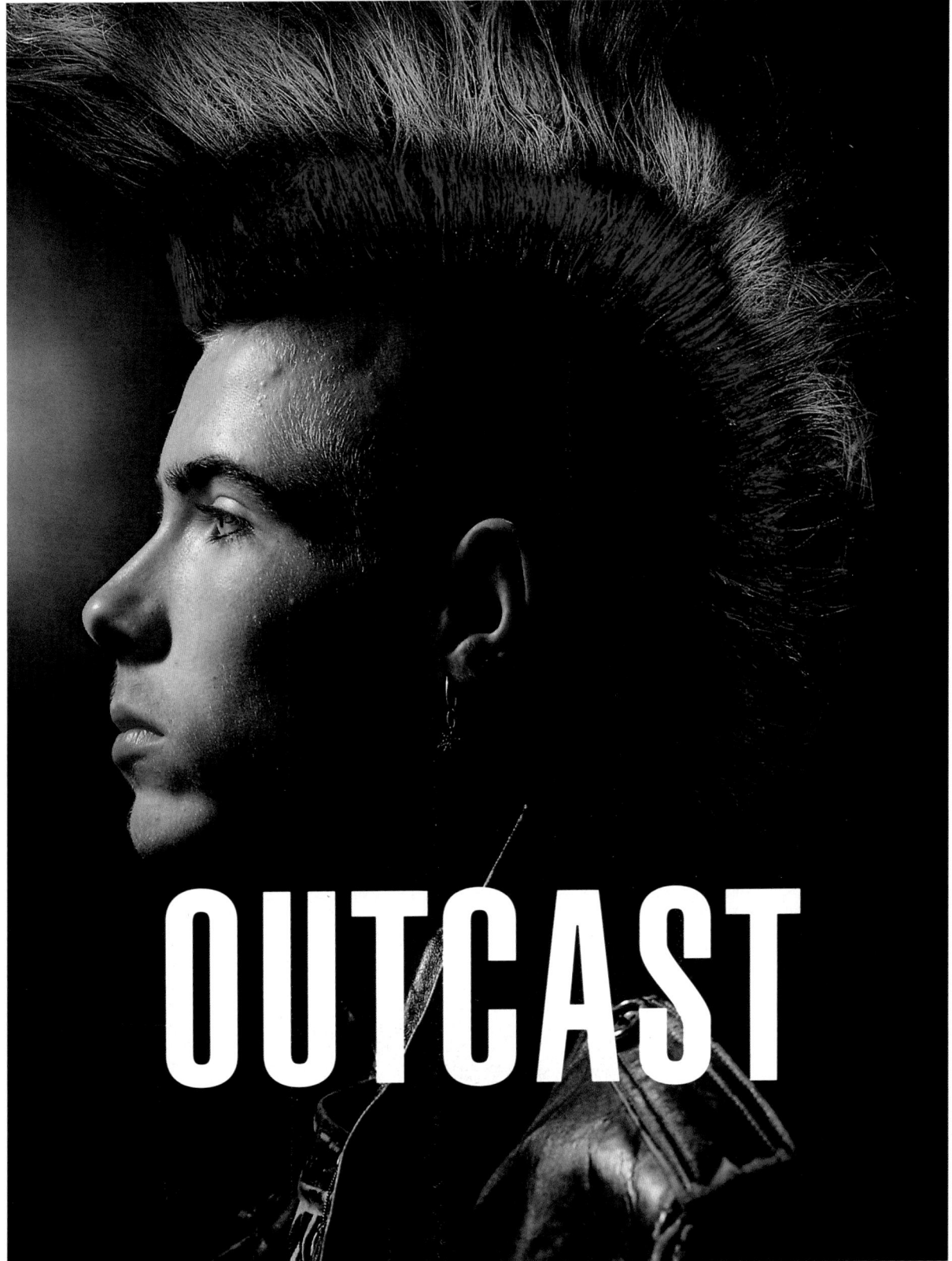

OUTCAST

We have not opted for the traditional pyramid hierarchy, but for 'federal' collaboration between smaller units, in which people know and support each other and which therefore allow more scope for personal development than for career hunting.

This means that our staff do not waste their talents on competing with each other, but devote them to finding creative solutions for automation issues.

Entirely in keeping with the spirit of the company, technology is not seen as an end in itself but as a means to an end; the main focus lies on the users.

This, in turn, leads to systems which do not limit personal opportunities, but in fact stimulate them. If this is an approach which appeals to you, call us in The Netherlands: +31 30 911911.

ORIGIN

Luxemburg, Mechelen, Milan, Mulhouse, New York, Paris, Recife, Redhill, São Paulo, Singapore, Solothurn, Taipei, Tampa, Turin, Utrecht, Whyteleafe, Zurich.

stretched over time and unless wages in eastern Germany are differentiated according to the productivity of individual firms, unemployment will not improve; it will become a permanent running sore.

In western Germany, real wages have risen at a higher rate than productivity in the past two years to the hushed delight of British and French competitors. Both in eastern and western Germany, a different course of wage policy is necessary.

The second risk relates to fiscal policy. Roughly 5% of the west German GDP will have to be shifted each year (and for some time) to eastern Germany—double the size of the transfer of real income in the two oil shocks. The decisive question for Germany's economic future is to what extent these transfers of DM150 billion can be financed without disturbing western Germany's economic machine.

One-third of these transfers are already being financed by additional taxes and social-security contributions. The second third can be financed by credits; after all, German unification is a special historical event and an increase in national debt of DM50 billion a year is acceptable. But how to finance the last third will be 1993's question. By additional taxes, or by reducing government spending? An additional tax rise would certainly damage the international competitiveness of the west German economy.

All this means that the chance to find a new policy mix—among wage, fiscal and monetary policy—is small. What the Bundesbank can do in monetary policy will depend on a restrained wage policy in eastern and western Germany, and on the success in reducing the budget deficit.

Besides wages and fiscal policy, the third risk factor in the pre-election year of 1993 will be the impatience of the people. If east Germans do not see convincing signs of overall improvement, and become even more dissatisfied than in 1992, life for the ruling coalition will be unpleasant. This also holds true if west Germans tire of the need to make sacrifices now so as to invest in their east German future. However, 1993 is not an election year, and there is time to take politically unpopular decisions.

None of this has altered Germany's willingness to give up political autonomy and to anchor itself institutionally in the European Community. Germany's political leaders are determined to stand by Maastricht and to shift monetary authority to a European central bank. Although the institutional arrangements of a European central bank may not be sufficient to produce a stable currency in the future, Germany's commitment to the project will not disappear in 1993.

Italy's designer chaos

Haig Simonian

A Mafia assassination, the fall of the government, secession in the rich north, or the further devaluation of the lira; any of these may happen in Italy in 1993. Seldom has the country, faced with Europe's biggest budget deficit and probably the world's highest number of tax evaders, been faced with such potential volatility.

Politically, the death of communism and transformation of Italy's Communist Party into a social-democratic movement will continue to mean ripples on previously established certainties. Long the butt of embassy jokes about its vaudeville governments—Italy is on its 51st since the second world war—domestic politics have been astonishingly stable under the domination of the Christian Democrats, the biggest political grouping.

The return of 16 parties to parliament at the April 1992 elections showed the sands were shifting. Leading the unpredictability stakes are the autonomist northern Leagues, which managed to push the Christian Democrats into second place in Lombardy, Italy's richest region.

The Leagues are now hungry for power. That will come first in the northern cities, where a string of corruption scandals has severely tainted the established parties, above all the Socialists in their Milanese stronghold. But the Christian Democrats have also been damaged, as have even the "clean" Republicans.

Haig Simonian: Milan correspondent of the *Financial Times*.

Paradoxically, this unprecedented weakness of the parties has offered a chance to reform the state's finances. This is vital if Italy is to work, however slowly, towards monetary union with its EC partners. Slashing public spending and raising revenues by novel means like privatisation is the only way the country can tackle its public-sector deficit, now running at over 100% of GDP. Interest payments on the debt account for almost all the government's budget deficit, which exceeds 10% of GDP.

The government of Giuliano Amato has shown the way. Steps have been taken towards reforming the greatly abused state-pension system. Privatisation should play a big part in raising revenues. No longer can politicians automatically expect to use bloated state-sector companies for patronage and placing the party faithful. IRI, ENI, ENEL and INA, the four biggest state-sector groups, have been transformed into joint-stock companies as a first step towards flotation or radical restructuring. EFIM, the most notorious of the state's industrial loss-mak-

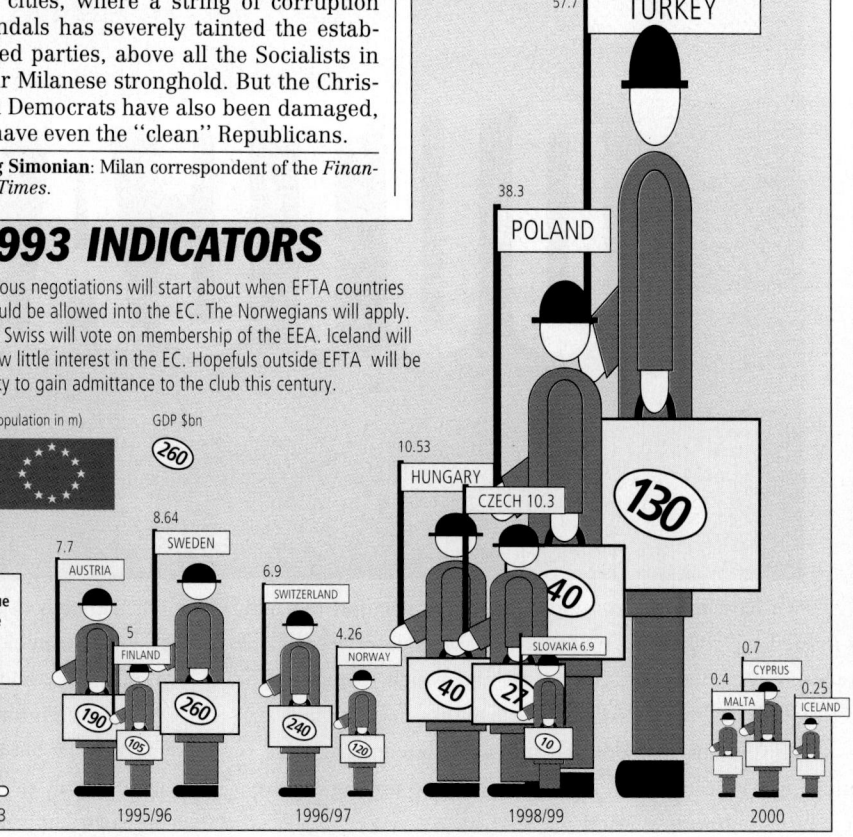

1993 INDICATORS

Serious negotiations will start about when EFTA countries should be allowed into the EC. The Norwegians will apply. The Swiss will vote on membership of the EEA. Iceland will show little interest in the EC. Hopefuls outside EFTA will be lucky to gain admittance to the club this century.

(population in m)   GDP $bn

Queue here for EC

AUSTRIA 7.7 · 260
SWEDEN 8.64
FINLAND 5 · 190 · 105 · 260
SWITZERLAND 6.9 · 240
NORWAY 4.26 · 120
HUNGARY 10.53 · 40
CZECH 10.3 · 40
SLOVAKIA 6.9 · 10
POLAND 38.3 · 130
TURKEY 57.7
MALTA 0.4
CYPRUS 0.7
ICELAND 0.25

1993   1995/96   1996/97   1998/99   2000

The mafia won't be Italy's only problem

ers, has been closed down altogether.

Rolling back the public sector will start in banking and insurance, telecommunications and food. Municipal services like electricity and gas will be sold off at the local level. But privatisation will require measures to stimulate Milan's pint-sized bourse, where long-overdue reforms have failed to stave off plunging prices and dismal turnover.

It will take bold tax incentives to persuade investors to buy more shares. But ministers will have to be careful to avoid over-stimulating demand: switching too large a proportion of private savings into equities could staunch private purchases of the short-term government bonds which finance the lion's share of the deficit. Privatisation issues, offering investors the chance to swap their government bonds for shares, is one deficit-cutting gimmick likely to be seen in 1993.

A weak economy will keep up the pressure for reform. The lira's devaluation against other European currencies in the exchange-rate mechanism and embarrassment over the downgrading of Italy's international-debt rating should help to maintain the external discipline.

But the government will remain on a knife-edge. Ministers will continue to use special decree laws to by-pass lengthy parliamentary debates, as with the 30 trillion lire ($24 billion) emergency budget rushed through to bring the soaring 1992 deficit into line. Cuts of at least 93 trillion lire will be needed in 1993.

But raising taxes and keeping the lid on consumption risks plunging the economy into recession. Well-planned, pump-priming public investment projects to improve Italy's often abysmal public services and patchy infrastructure could counter the risks of a downward spiral.

The threat of another run on the lira and higher interest rates will remain a potent weapon for reformers anxious about the risks of their measures being sabotaged in parliament. Moreover, new elections will be unattractive for the big parties, tainted by scandals and hit by the rise of the Leagues. And tighter controls on public-sector contracts, an engine for illicit electoral funding in the past, will make financing campaigns more difficult.

The Mafia and its sister organisations could still produce some nasty surprises. But it will remain hard to decypher whether possible assassinations of prominent policemen and judges represent a cry of pain from criminals suffering under stringent policing, or a warning to the state to back off.

Italy will have to streamline the cumbersome relationship between its three police forces and make sure that co-ordination does not just mean bureaucracy. And the presence of soldiers on the streets of Sicily and hills of Sardinia could become commonplace.

Constitutional reform to speed up decision-making will remain on the agenda as parliament debates the merits of changing the electoral system to reduce the number of splinter parties and the risk of electoral fraud. Yet with the focus firmly on the economy, the main effort in 1993 will be to tackle the deficit and prevent Italy slipping into a "second division" of EC countries, or worse.

1993 ECONOMIC FORECAST — ITALY

High interest rates and austerity policies will keep Italian growth in check. Anything over 1% growth in 1993 would be lucky. Consumer spending will be slow as wages, at last, are being controlled. Fixed investment will grow more strongly, however, partly because of extra house building in response to the deregulation of rents.

The inflation rate sticks above the European average as the impact of the lira's fall from the ERM feeds through to consumer prices. This effect will prove more powerful than the government's tight control over many prices and its self-denial in not using petrol-price rises to improve government finances.

The rate of 6% in 1993 will be above the 1992 figure of 5.5%. Even before the lira's departure from the ERM the Italians realised that their inflation rate would not fit with the new Europe.

So a dramatic step has been taken. The *scala mobile* system of indexing wages to inflation has been broken. Introduced in 1945, the system was cursed by Italy's business leaders.

The ending of the system was achieved in July 1992 by the new government, headed by Giuliano Amato. Like the new president, Luigi Scalfaro, the prime minister has a high reputation for probity.

Of course, Italy is still Italy. The *scala mobile* may be gone but it could come back in 1994. In the meantime, workers receive agreed monthly pay rises. That should mean low increases in unit-wage costs, especially since productivity trends look favourable.

It will take time to convince the foreign-exchange markets that much has changed. The lira will rejoin the ERM in 1993 at L850 per D-mark. But faster growth in imports than in exports implies that Italy's current-account deficit will remain worryingly high. Interest rates will therefore also have to be kept high, only falling to 14% by the end of 1993. Threats of a fresh run on the lira leading to higher interest rates will focus the government's mind on the need for discipline.

KEY INDICATORS

	1991	1992	1993
GDP growth (% pa)	1.4	1.5	1.0
Inflation (%)	6.4	5.5	6.0
Prime rate (year end %)	12.5	17.0	14.0
Exchange rate			
Lire per DM	747	782	850
Lire per $	1,241	1,220	1,377
Current account ($ bn)	−21.1	−25.0	−27.0

EIU GLOBAL FORECASTING SERVICE

The Specialists
to Spain
and Latin America.

From Heathrow, Manchester and Dublin.

Daily departures direct to 6 destinations in Spain with onward connections to a further 23 destinations in the rest of Spain, as well as 19 cities throughout Latin America. Combining a first rate in-flight service with one of the best on time records, Iberia provides the best and only way to travel to Spain and Latin America.

IBERIA

Was the party worth it?

Spain's year of penitence

Juan Luis Cebrián

When Spaniards go to the polls in 1993 they will take a heavy hangover into the voting booths with them. Those sore heads will come from a 1992 party that could not pay for itself: the pomp and ceremony of the Quincentenary—the Olympic Games, Madrid's European Cultural festival, and the Expo in Seville.

For the second year in a row the Spanish government has had to revise its budget, undermining confidence and causing disbelief among foreign investors. Signs of instability have grown in an atmosphere charged, moreover, with accusations of waste and corruption in public administration.

The government is showing symptoms of exhaustion. Caught up in internal struggles between supporters and opponents of the former vice-president, Alfonso Guerra, the Socialist Party is readying itself for the general elections in 1993 with a feeling of frustration and perplexity. The entire legislative body has been marked by two unshakable curses: confrontation with the labour unions, crystalised in the general strike of December 14th 1989, and the resignation of Mr Guerra, whose brother was accused of corruption and influence peddling.

These two events have also fanned rumours of Felipe Gonzalez's possible with-

drawal, stirred up by doubts he himself has expressed about running again in the elections. Those who know him closest insist in the absolute sincerity of his gestures of frustration, which they say are those of a man who has spent his prime of life in service to politics. But they also describe him as a man who is tired and disillusioned, or at least bored, who has his sights focused more on the European Community than on the problems of governing his own country.

The uncertainty of Mr Gonzalez's candidacy underlies the greatest political enigma Spain faces. The outcome of his decision could determine whether the Socialist Party remains in power or not. Even though the conservative alternative, the Popular Party, is still weak, opinion surveys have thrown a permanent shadow over the future of socialism.

The possibility of a future coalition government between the Gonzalez party and the Basque and Catalan nationalists does not necessarily improve the chances of preserving an economic model which seems to be on its last legs.

Disillusioned by the results of 1992, Mr Gonzalez has inaugurated a European "New Frontier", attempting to bolster popular aspirations. 1997 is the mythical target towards which all Spaniards are now asked to look, as they concentrate and justify their sacrifices and efforts. By

Juan Luis Cebrián: CEO and publisher of *El Pais*, Spain's national newspaper.

1993 ECONOMIC FORECAST

Spain was stuck in the slow lane in 1992 with GDP growth of 1.6%. A delay in interest-rate cuts, slow growth in Europe and a stagnant construction industry held things back, though consumer spending grew. Look for much the same in 1993.

The government plans to reform the income-tax system so as to levy lower taxes on individuals. Any backsliding might damage confidence but would be necessary. Persistent inflation and lower-than-forecast tax revenues both argue for a policy tightening. The Maastricht conditions, as in other parts of Europe, cast their shadow forwards. So expect disappointments.

Increases in VAT and other indirect taxes are already scheduled. These will give a twist to inflation, at least in the short term. However, the government is pushing through policies to liberalise markets, reduce tariffs and prevent restrictive practices. That should help keep the lid on prices.

So confident are the authorities that they are even modernising the consumer-price index, which has long underestimated inflation in Spain: 5.5% is in prospect for 1993, after 6.4% in 1992, under the old system.

The government must reduce its own spending. This will happen anyhow now that the Olympic athletes have left Barcelona and the exhibitors have packed up their stalls at the Seville Expo.

Much will depend on the resolution, sometimes in doubt, of the prime minister, Felipe Gonzalez. 1993 is election year.

Inside and outside the government, most people in Spain look to European convergence and monetary union. There is no rush to put the peseta into the narrow band of the ERM. If inflation is falling in the summer of 1993, that might be the time.

Spain has problems with its balance of payments. Tourism earnings are sliding. As a share of GDP the current-account deficit is 3.4%. EC transfers will help it edge down in 1993.

KEY INDICATORS

	1991	1992	1993
GDP growth (% pa)	2.4	1.6	1.3
Inflation (%)	5.9	6.4	5.5
Prime rate (year end %)	16.2	14.0	13.3
Exchange rate			
Pta per DM	62.6	67.0	70.0
Pta per $	103.9	104.5	113.4
Current account ($ bn)	-16.0	-18.7	-18.0

EIU GLOBAL FORECASTING SERVICE

A FIRM POSITION ON FINNISH FINANCIAL MARKETS

Speedy international transactions.
Efficient service in all leading
financial centres.
The foremost expertise of Finnish
financial markets.
Get in touch with Kansallis, your
guide to the Finnish market.

KANSALLIS BANKING GROUP

The Finnish Market Maker

WE HAVE A LOT TO OFFER

OPTIONS

Custom-tailored options, especially those denominated in Finnish marks, and currency trading in general, such as spot and forward rates. All come within the Kansallis scope.

FIM BONDS

We can guide your entry into the FIM bond market, which offers attractive yields.

A BALANCED PORTFOLIO

To give balance to your portfolio in Finland, we can also offer equities, interest rate swaps, forward rate agreements, and interest rate options.

AROUND THE WORLD

Kansallis Banking Group, with fourteen international branches, subsidiaries and representative offices, operates in all leading financial centres. We watch over your interests around the world and around the clock.

ECONOMIC OUTLOOK

Kansallis Banking Group, one of Scandinavia's leading commercial banks, publishes special economic surveys of trends in Finland and throughout the Nordic region.

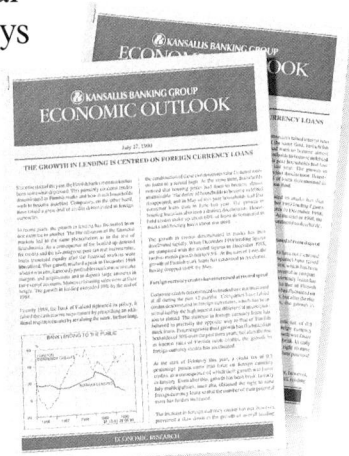

The biggest hole

Jack Grimston

François Mitterrand and John Major will open the Channel Tunnel around Christmas time. But despite the cheesy smiles, the talk of great moments in history and the loss of Britain's island virginity, the tunnel will remain a hole.

Eurotunnel, the Anglo-French consortium which ran the digging and will run the tunnel, will feel the hole in its pocket well into the next century: it will have spent £3.6 billion ($5.8 billion) over its original estimate. (So they spent a penny or two more than they said they would and will finish a little late, as all builders do. But they will still have plenty to congratulate themselves about.)

Eurotunnel's partners, however, may be too ashamed to show up to the party. British Rail and Whitehall, working together to bring you fresh delays, will only make their decision on where to build the rail-link between London and the Chunnel sometime in the spring of next year: a line on the map, nothing more. The tracks themselves will not be useable this millennium.

The tunnel itself will be somewhat short of trains. Eurotunnel's own shuttle trains, which will take cars and lorries from one end of the tunnel to the other, will have no engines for opening day and tarted-up SNCF engines will have to be used. Special long-distance trains, which will do the London-Paris-Brussels routes, will not be ready before the summer of 1994. British freight trains will only be able to get through thanks to SNCF engines coming through the tunnel to give them a pull: British Rail's special freight engines will not be ready.

By 2013, when Eurotunnel expects more than 55m people to go through the Chunnel, these troubles will have long been forgotten. Paris to London will take two and a half hours of smooth-as-ice travel; no waiting in the rain at Ashford; a choice of half a dozen clarets on the wine list. But for 1993 (and a good deal of 1994), take the ferry.

All dressed up with nowhere to go

that time, Spain will have to comply with the requisites of harmonisation imposed by Maastricht if they are to be maintained and if they want to avoid missing the European train, or at least failing to get a first-class ticket.

However, the depth of the current economic crisis casts serious doubt on these aspirations. The devaluation of the peseta, coming in the middle of the overall crisis of the European exchange-rate mechanism (ERM), meant a return to reality—late and sparse as it was. And it did away with what remained of any credibility in the economic policy of the cabinet. 1993 will be yet more rough and difficult than the current year, with a growth rate down to 1.3% and an increase in unemployment.

Given this situation, the new governor of the Bank of Spain will need to use to the full all the instruments of monetary policy. Governor Rojo, in fact, is the economist who has had the greatest influence on Spanish economic policy over the past 25 years. His recent appointment as head of the central bank shows an absolute, if rigid, adherence to the course that Spain has set itself. So in 1993 interest rates will remain high, unless the readjustment of the ERM softens them, constraining the possibilities of expansion.

When Spaniards go to the polls, probably in late 1993, there will be a strong awareness that a period of Spanish history is coming to an end.

Poland, Hungary, Czech 'n Slovakia

Radek Sikorski

Constitutional crises will recur in Eastern Europe throughout next year, just as its economy starts to look brighter. The legacy of communism will continue to haunt the region. Constitutions inherited from the old regime will prove inadequate; petty nationalism will be on the rise; new security problems in the field of foreign affairs will worry every country; the public will confuse democracy with elections, with too many of the latter and not enough of the former.

Czechoslovakia will divide into separate Czech and Slovak republics on January 1st 1993. But the two countries will bicker just as much as they did when united: over currency, the division of the debt, the relations between different branches of former Czechoslovak companies. Still, the Czech republic, freed of the burden of subsidising Slovakia, will begin to surge ahead in 1993.

At the same time, Slovaks will wake up to the fact that their country's independence comes with a price tag: living standards in the Slovak republic will drop, reform will slow down, unemployment will grow. The West will remain wary of Slovakia, and very little investment will go there. By the end of the year, belatedly and grudgingly, the Slovaks may well seek a stronger relationship with the Czech republic.

Poland will struggle with its reputation for political instability. Saddled by the departing communists with an extreme version of proportional representa-

tion, the country has too many parties in parliament to allow a stable coalition to emerge. Bold solutions will be stifled by wrangling between incompatible coalition partners. The power struggle between the president, Lech Walesa, and the government will also come to a boil. Mr Walesa already controls the central bank, foreign affairs, internal security, the army and state television—but he wants more power. The more discord he sows between Poland's disparate political parties, the more grass-root pressure there will be to end the political deadlock. His desire to impose presidential rule may come into conflict with his sagging popularity.

Hungary will not face constitutional problems, but its governing coalition, led by the Democratic Forum, will become still more unpopular. With an election due in 1994, the government may try—quietly—to boost the economy by loosening the monetary screws. The party to watch next year is Fidesz, the Hungarian youth party, which is rapidly growing more popular.

All East European countries will be haunted by arguments over "decommunisation". None has successfully resolved the problem of what to do with former communist-party officials, secret police, army generals or public prosecutors. In most countries right-wing parties have called for the banning of former officials from public life—but only Czechoslovakia has done so.

In 1993 Poland, Hungary and Czechoslovakia will begin to fear the re-emer-

Radek Sikorski: former deputy minister of defence in Poland.

Poland has its headaches

gence of Russian imperial ambitions. With the West's tacit consent, Russia will stake a claim to strategic pre-eminence on the territory of the former Soviet Union. Ukraine and the Baltic states will be offered treaties, similar to the one already signed by Belorussia, limiting their sovereignty.

Central Europe will feel squeezed by this process. The countries will speed up efforts to transform their post-Warsaw Pact military establishments; western defence industries should expect new clients. Most Polish, Hungarian, Czech and Slovak officers are Moscow-trained and the military intelligence of Poland and Hungary in particular has not been cleared of bad apples. If security integration with the West is to be sought, thorough vetting is imperative.

Now the good news: Central Europe's recession will end in 1993. Poland, Hungary and the Czech republic will all experience economic growth. Increasing numbers of people will realise that the sacrifices of the previous three years have been worthwhile. Expanding islands of visible prosperity will emerge. Capitalism will have arrived for good.

Nosediving production curves will begin to level off. In Poland and Hungary, exports to the West have already begun to replace the old Soviet market. Thanks to semi-convertible currencies, Poland, Hungary and the Czech republic will also begin trading with one another. As governments become more comfortable with capitalism, more industries will be opened to private entrepreneurs and foreign competition. As communications improve and western-style office space becomes available, foreign investors will find business less troublesome.

The dismantling of small state industries will proceed apace. The privatisation of retail shops, small distribution networks and newspaper publishing will be completed by the end of 1993. Central-European shopping malls will begin to look more like their western counterparts. Large privatisations are taking longer because the politicians become involved.

An important watershed will be crossed next year: for the first time, the majority of Hungarians, Czechs and Poles will work in the private sector; a minority in the state sector. This will produce a change in business mentality as well as in political behaviour.

None of the three countries has yet dealt successfully with the pre-war owners of land and businesses who are making claims on them. Property rights are still unclear; until this problem is solved, privatisation of disputed property will be slow. Privatisation itself will bring in far less cash than anticipated. Eastern Germany's Treuhandanstalt, which is selling all eastern Germany's state companies, expects merely to break even, once their old debts are paid; few Central-European state sectors are much better. Some of the larger privatised companies will not be able to change as quickly as expected. There will be failures, creating more caution about the process.

At the same time, expect ever-stronger resistance from those who work in state enterprise. They feel themselves to be second-class citizens earning much less than their counterparts in the private sector. Ostentatious consumption by the new rich will contrast ever-more sharply with the fallen living standards of those whom the free-market revolution has passed by. Expect destabilising strikes.

The private sector is already providing most of the growth. Eastern Europe's entrepreneurs are ambitious but not very law-abiding. High taxes, a legacy of the past, encourage most to operate semi-legally. Bad practices, learnt in the early years of capitalism, will be hard to let drop later—and will discourage foreign investment.

Nordics know what's best— and hate it

Robert Taylor

The Nordic people, given to bouts of depression, have every reason to feel unhappy about the prospect of 1993. It will be a year of confusion and uncertainty. Their fate will not be in their hands but will lie in greater happenings outside their borders both to the east in Russia and to the south in the European Community.

The end of the cold war has unfrozen the geopolitics of northern Europe, and all the old shibboleths, over the past two years, have become an obsolete word. The traditional balance between east and west has lost all meaning in Sweden and Finland. Indeed, expect to see the

Nordics outside NATO reassessing their attitude to collective western defence. Finland will move the fastest, as it ponders joining the Western European Union. Sweden will also drop its last doubts about closer involvement in wider European security.

This does not mean that the Nordics will adopt an anti-Russian foreign and security policy. They are keen to maintain friendly relations with Moscow. But this year they will also be anxious to act as a calming influence over the Baltic states of Latvia, Lithuania and Estonia. Those newly independent nations, which were annexed by the Soviet Union in 1940, look now to the Nordics for material help and encouragement. They will get it. How-

Robert Taylor: correspondent for the *Financial Times*, based in Stockholm.

The new HP LaserJet 4. Just launched.

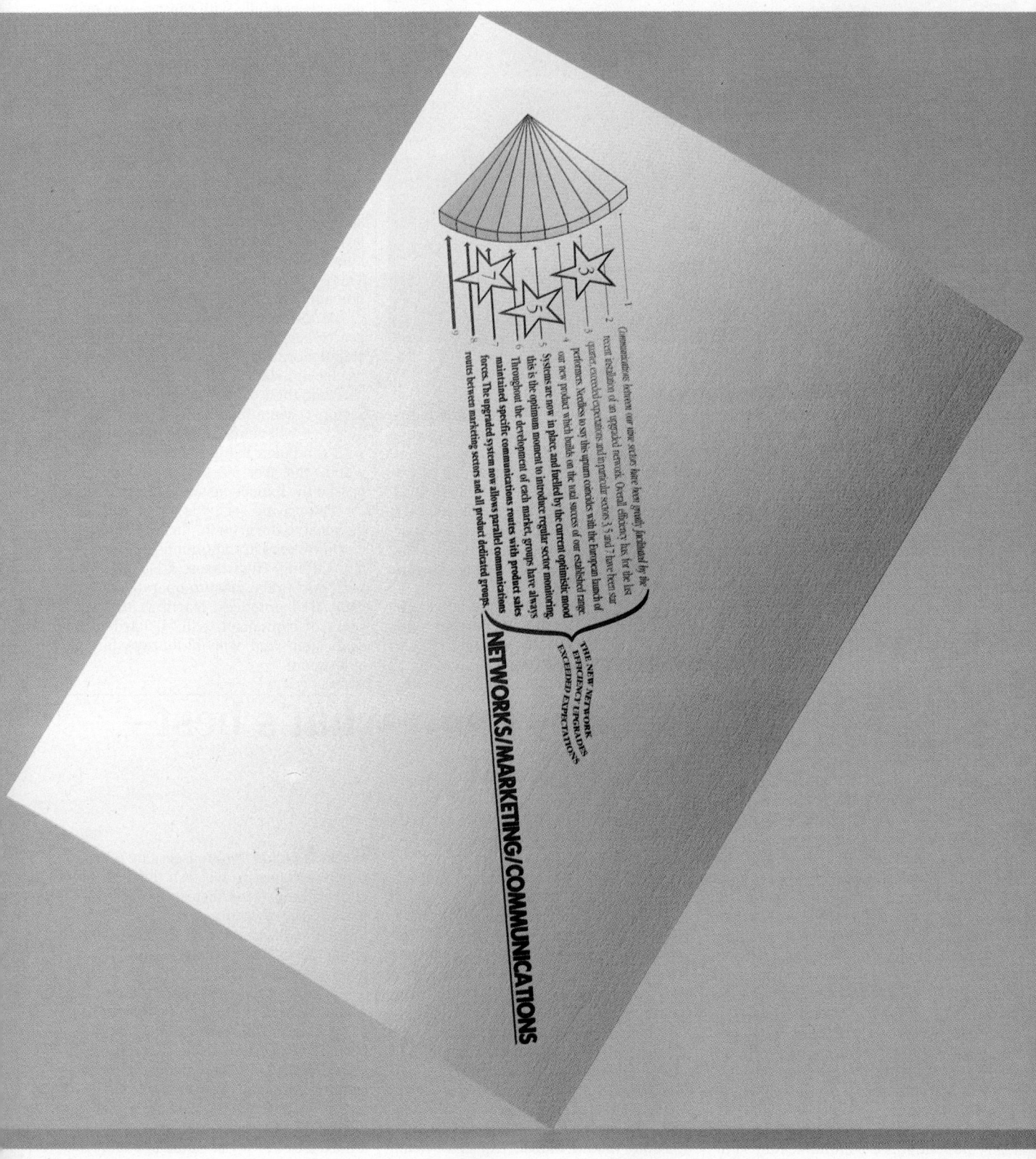

From today you can make every presentation and every document really go with a bang.

Because from today you can get a new standard of laser print quality.

The revolutionary new HP LaserJet 4 printer now packs an incredible 600 dots into every inch. Combined with advanced micro-fine toner and our Resolution Enhancement technology, text and graphics now leap off the page with astonishing clarity in 45 different built-in typefaces.

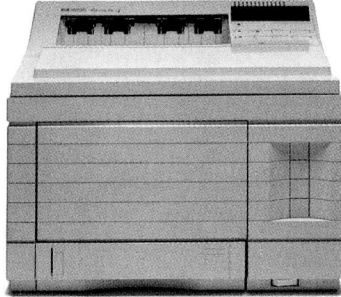

And when you give the command to print, you won't have to wait long for your output. With an Intel RISC processor the HP LaserJet 4 is designed to process even complex documents faster than ever before.

So what price print perfection?

Less than you would imagine. Even less than our previous world beater, the HP LaserJet III.

Ring us now and, along with the HP LaserJet 4, you'll soon see your documents and presentations really start to take off.

4th dimension laser printing.

My dear, they say we're Europeans now

ever, the refusal of the Baltic states to grant full civil rights to the large ethnic minorities who live within their borders will arouse growing concern inside Scandinavia, where abuses of civil rights are abjured. The substantial Russian populations in Estonia and Latvia do not have the vote and they suffer from other forms of inequality. There may be no question of ethnic cleansing, but the way the Baltic states treat their minorities will determine whether they can create social and political stability.

Russian troops are due to leave all the Baltic states by the end of 1993. But this may not happen as planned if no agreement is reached on full protection for civil rights for their own people who wish to stay behind. The dangers of outbreaks of ethnic violence are serious. The Nordics will do their best to persuade their small neighbours across the Baltic that they must compromise or face the terrible prospect of Russian revenge.

At the same time the Nordic region will throw its remaining political semi-isolation from Western Europe to the winds. Next year they will play a full part in the 19-nation European Economic Area, the single market stretching from the Arctic to the Mediterranean that starts on January 1st 1993.

Sweden, Norway and Finland will each spend next year negotiating their membership to the EC. All three countries see their prosperity and security as inextricably linked with the EC. But don't expect those entry talks to be completed by the end of the year or without tears.

Much depends on what will happen in Denmark. The narrow but decisive no-vote against the Maastricht treaty by the Danes in their referendum in the summer of 1992 must be reversed if the EC hopes to move on towards ever closer economic and political union. And it is not to be expected that other Scandinavian countries will sign up to Maastricht if Denmark cannot see its way to doing so.

But unless Denmark can secure exemption from involvement in any common European defence policy or the emergence of a common currency, it seems unlikely that a majority of Danes will change their minds and vote for Maastricht in a second referendum.

These Danish doubts reflect popular hostility towards the EC throughout the Nordic region, especially in Norway, where nationalism remains a potent factor. In Sweden the main political parties face a hard task in convincing the voters that EC membership is vital for their own future well-being.

Popular attitudes will be more sympathetic in Finland, where many people see entry into the common market as essential if the country is to become fully westernised. The longer the delay in satisfying Denmark, the greater the danger that a substantial majority in the other Nordic countries will turn against the idea of EC membership.

As all of them are to hold referendums once the terms for entry have been agreed, no Nordic government can ignore the shifting moods of its own electorate. So a great deal of public persuasion will be seen next year.

Fear of Russia

But the Nordics will be keeping a wary eye on their giant neighbour Russia. Outwardly, relations between them will remain friendly and supportive. But anxieties about the durability of Boris Yeltsin and his democratic reforms will grow. Many Nordics fear his overthrow. Worse, they can envisage his replacement by a nationalistic dictatorship which would stoke up territorial claims in northern Europe. Traditional fears in the region about Russian intentions are never far from the surface—and with good reason.

But a change in Moscow would not force back the Nordic region into its old semi-isolationism from European affairs. Rather the opposite. Since the collapse of the former Soviet Union a sweeping reappraisal of security policy has taken place across the Nordic countries. Any upheavals in the east would accelerate the region's integration into Western Europe.

What will certainly trouble the Nordic region throughout the year will be the slowness and fragility of its economic revival. The turbulence of the international exchange markets in the autumn of 1992, that brought about the floating of the markka in Finland and record high interest rates in Sweden, revealed just how vulnerable the Nordic countries have become to the ups and downs of foreign pressure, since they recently liberalised and deregulated their financial systems.

The volatility of the region's currencies can be expected to persist throughout 1993. This in turn will force central banks to maintain high market interest rates. And these will handicap economic recovery. An additional concern exists over the well-being of the shaky Nordic financial system. No Nordic country has emerged unscathed from the heady days of cheap credit. Mountains of bad debts and non-performing loans have undermined the financial strength of a growing number of commercial banks across the region.

Governments will continue to come to the rescue with loans and guarantees. But the price of saving the financial sector from collapse will be enormous for the long-suffering Nordic tax-payers. The fragility of the banking sector will inhibit the investment plans of many companies and delay a return in business confidence.

So expect no sustained economic upturn until 1994 at the earliest. Since all Nordic governments accept that their days of economic isolation are over, they can no longer use devaluation as an easy option to improve competitiveness. Under the merciless pressure of the international markets they are being forced to cut their budget deficits by rolling back welfare spending. This means that unemployment must remain at levels not known in the Nordic countries since the early 1930s. The end of isolation will go on forcing painful changes as the Nordic model adapts to the demands of the outside world. But adapt it will.

Time to do less, better

Leon Brittan

"When it is not necessary to make a law it is necessary *not* to make a law"
Montesquieu

That ugly word subsidiarity entered the European debate some years ago. It registered in the public consciousness in 1992. The job in 1993 is to define and to apply it.

By "define" I do not mean learned disquisitions on the papal origins of the word. Nor do I mean the famously sesquipedalian formulation of the principle in Article 3b of the Maastricht treaty which states that: "In areas which do not fall within its exclusive competence, the Community shall take action, in accordance with the principle of subsidiarity, only if and in so far as the objectives of the proposed action cannot be sufficiently achieved by the Member States and can therefore, by reason of the scale or effects of the proposed action, be better achieved by the Community".

I mean, practical procedures. Checks and balances. A plan of action to give effect to the principle. The many people who are alarmed by the lurid picture of "Brussels" so often painted in the national presses are wrong to be so. In 1993 that error needs to be made self-evident.

"Brussels" is not some Frankenstein monster created by mad federalists which has broken out of the laboratory and is now lurching about the continent out of democratic control. It is shorthand for the structures of joint decision-making between nationally-elected ministers in Europe. It is political shorthand for the system that has replaced the distrust and hostility of centuries. We need those structures to secure our economic future. We need them for our political cohesion too. Aggressive nationalism is stirring again on our borders. It must never return to Western Europe.

Most people accept that. But they are also rightly concerned about the limits of European integration. Is it intruding detrimentally on national life? The member states may have chosen, for sound practical reasons, to pool certain powers and decisions—but where does the process end? Can it be reconciled with an equally powerful determination to defend national identity? Does it allow independent action?

This is the crux of the subsidiarity debate, which I prefer to call the "best-

level" question. The test is both practical and political. What is the best level for deciding a given policy? And in so far as a "European" solution will introduce Brussels into another corner of national life, is that a price worth paying for the expected benefit?

There are many areas in which it makes sense to use Community procedures in the common interest. The single market is an obvious case. In 1992 the Community broke down barriers to cross-border insurance business. That was not achieved without treading on the toes of some countries which have traditionally controlled both policies and premiums within their borders. Yet it will bring benefits for all.

Economic and Monetary Union (EMU) is one of many examples of an area in which it makes sense to use Community procedures in the common interest. EMU may not be necessary for a single

"Aggressive nationalism is stirring again on our borders"

market, but it has its own logic and will generate real value-added for us all, provided it is established on the right basis, and with tough conditions attached. John Major has left Britain's options open, but I have no doubt where the national interest will be seen to lie.

If, however, the Community is to contribute effectively in areas such as this, where it really matters, it must be prepared to step back where the case for EC involvement is less evident. When the Community was young and fighting for recognition it was natural enough that it should develop its role wherever possible. And the drive to create a single market has inevitably given rise to a welter of new legislation. As the Community matures, however, it needs to demonstrate that it is not a ratchet, taking on ever more powers, and never releasing them.

Where "harmonisation" was the cry of the 1970s, the preference now is for

mutual recognition of national systems. Where once the natural reflex was to set European standards centrally, the aim now is to leave choices to industry itself wherever possible.

As in a conglomerate company, deciding the appropriate level of decision-making involves a functional choice. What would be most effective at a given stage in a company's development? The debate about the "best level" of decision-making in the Community has too often been ideological. In 1993 it should be rigorously practical.

When it comes to education, health, culture, or social policy, for example, there is no practical advantage in taking decisions at a European level. Yet this should not exclude co-operation where national ministers see advantages in particular schemes.

By contrast, the whole logic of competition policy, which has been one of my primary responsibilities over the past four years, is that the member states need a referee to see fair play between them. It is no good asking a member state to judge for itself whether it is giving its companies an unfair advantage over competitors elsewhere in the Community.

Even here there is room for the exercise of pragmatic judgment about decisions which do not need to be taken centrally. I recently proposed, for example, that the commission should not intervene in questions of state subsidy below a certain threshold, because these were unlikely to create distortions in the European market. We are now implementing that policy. In the same spirit, the commission needs to judge carefully where it might shift some of its current responsibilities without damaging its underlying purpose.

My hope is that the subsidiarity debate will lead to a clear programme of action. The Community should proceed confidently where it can bring real added value. But in 1993, with the single market in place, it should try to reduce the ambit of its work. It needs to review its procedures, too. More can and should be done, for example, to increase openness in the working of the council and the commission; to develop the role of the European Parliament; and to find more satisfactory ways of bringing national parliaments into the Community process. This will be the task for 1993.

The Rt Hon Sir Leon Brittan QC: vice-president, Commission of the European Communities.

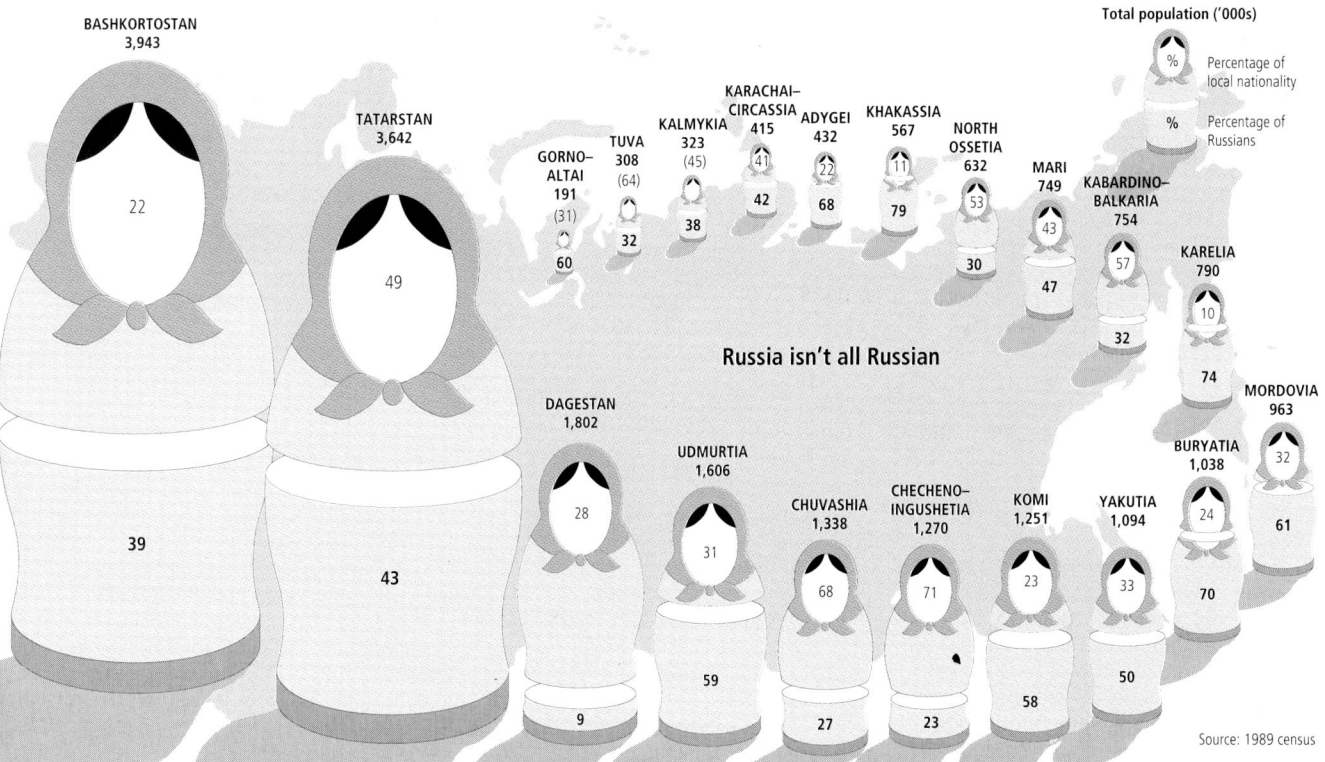

Russia isn't all Russian

Total population ('000s)

% Percentage of local nationality

% Percentage of Russians

BASHKORTOSTAN 3,943 — 22 / 39

TATARSTAN 3,642 — 49 / 43

GORNO-ALTAI 191 (31) — 60

TUVA 308 (64) — 32

KALMYKIA 323 (45) — 38

KARACHAI-CIRCASSIA 415 — 41 / 42

ADYGEI 432 — 22 / 68

KHAKASSIA 567 — 11 / 79

NORTH OSSETIA 632 — 53 / 30

MARI 749 — 43 / 47

KABARDINO-BALKARIA 754 — 57 / 32

KARELIA 790 — 10 / 74

MORDOVIA 963 — 32 / 61

BURYATIA 1,038 — 24 / 70

DAGESTAN 1,802 — 28 / 9

UDMURTIA 1,606 — 31 / 59

CHUVASHIA 1,338 — 68 / 27

CHECHENO-INGUSHETIA 1,270 — 71 / 23

KOMI 1,251 — 23 / 58

YAKUTIA 1,094 — 33 / 50

Source: 1989 census

Russia writes itself a constitution

John Parker

John Parker: Moscow correspondent for *The Economist*.

Russia will spend 1993 trying to set up a political system to match its new status as a sovereign state. Since Russia has never before existed inside its current borders, history is of no help.

There is little consensus as to what Russia's national interests are. And there is a great deal of doubt as to whether the country will become a liberal-democratic state within Europe or a modern version of tsarism's Eurasian autocracy. Not surprisingly, therefore, the question as to which political institutions to create is still an open one—within a year, however, it will be settled.

In the first year after the collapse of Soviet power, Boris Yeltsin bravely attempted to build a market economy—a rare example in a newly independent country of putting economics before politics. Now he can postpone political reform no longer. Russia's political system is breaking down even faster than its economy. Unless it is reformed in 1993, Russia will fall to pieces.

There will be two political forces at work on the Russian president next year.

The first is that of the "national-patriots", exemplified by his vice-president, Alexander Rutskoi. They stand for a "Great Russia" with a large army, an interventionist foreign policy (not necessarily to the West's liking) and extensive government control over the economy during a gradual transition to capitalism. The second force is the democrats. They stand for the rule of law, a political system of checks and balances and a big-bang approach to economic reform designed to move smartly towards free enterprise.

Neither side is strong enough convincingly to defeat the other. True, as the economy contracts further and economic reform runs into trouble, the nationalists will increase their power. This will give them enough authority to dictate Russian policy in two areas: the republics of the former Soviet Union with large Russian-speaking minorities—25m ethnic Russians live outside Russia—and foreign policy generally.

So expect further Russian intervention—possibly military—in neighbouring countries of the former Soviet Union. (Like, for example, the Baltic states, where Russian speakers have been de-nied the vote in parliamentary elections, or Moldova, where Russian "peace-keeping" forces have been sent into battle to support Russian-speaking secessionists.)

Expect, too, disagreements with the West over Russia's relations with some former Soviet allies. There will be quarrels over ex-Yugoslavia, where Russian patriots support Serbia; Islamic countries, with which they want closer ties than the West would like; and India, to which Russia has already sold high-technology goods in defiance of American sanctions.

Both nationalists and democrats are motley and disorganised. Neither has any proper party discipline. Russian politics is organised (if that is the word) either into "movements"—which one politician has likened to a train which moves towards a fixed destination but whose passengers are free to get on and off at will—or into "taxi-cab" parties, which have a handful of members hopping in and out while the party drives round and round in circles.

With neither side able to stamp its authority decisively on the other, politics in 1993 will centre on the conflict between parliament and government. For an Englishman or American the tension between the legislature and the executive was resolved (bloodily) centuries ago: for a Russian this central constitutional question remains quite unresolved.

Russia's government and parliament are certain to remain in conflict. The majority of Mr Yeltsin's government in 1992 were young radicals passionately committed to overthrowing communism. The parliament, on the other hand, was elected in 1990 only six weeks after the Communist Party had eschewed its constitutionally-guaranteed monopoly on political power. It is dominated by conservative state-factory managers who used the Communist Party's local authority to have themselves elected. They have much in common with the nationalists.

Mr Yeltsin will try at first to co-operate with parliament in 1993—as he did during 1992. But he cannot give in to parliament altogether because that would mean allying himself with nationalists against reformers. Mr Yeltsin was elected president on a platform of reform. His power, prestige and popularity depend upon it.

So Mr Yeltsin will introduce a new Russian constitution. Everyone agrees that the old one, inherited from Soviet practice, needs to be abolished. It has already been amended hundreds of times. The new one would abolish the present nonsense of a permanently-sitting parliament which reports to an occasionally-sitting supreme legislative assembly, the Congress of People's Deputies. Instead, it would introduce a scheme modelled on America's bi-cameral arrangement.

This will cause the biggest political battle of 1993. Expect one of two outcomes. Either the parliament will bow to the president and accept a new constitution in return for several years' continuation in their present jobs and the postponement of parliamentary elections. Or Mr Yeltsin will appeal to the population for a referendum on the constitution, which is likely to pass. In either case, the result is likely to be approval of a new constitution.

But that will not solve Russia's other constitutional problem: the animosity between the federal and local governments—and the lack of any ground rules governing their behaviour. Though Russia signed a treaty between the federal and local governments in 1992, economic reform soon shattered it. Local governments reacted to the reduction of subsidies from the federal government in Moscow by illegally withholding taxes that they were required to pay to federal coffers.

The weakening of Moscow's authority as a result of battles between parliament and government will encourage these centrifugal tendencies further because Mr Yeltsin will need the support of regional leaders in order to force his new constitution through. So the break-up of Russia, as geographically defined for the past year, cannot be ruled out.

Collapse ain't all bad

John Parker

The Russian economy will contract alarmingly in 1993—perhaps by more than 25%. In 1992 its GDP dropped by around 20%, in 1991 by 13%. By the end of next year the economy will be little more than half as big as it was at the start of 1991. Now for the bad news. The budget deficit, which has been under control, will grow hugely. So monetary policy will be loosened. Not that it was tight in 1992: money supply increased more than ten times in the year.

Moreover, oil prices in 1993 will have to rise to, or near to, world-market prices. That means they will more than double. If they do not, the all-important oil and gas industries, which account for more than 60% of Russian exports, will go bust. Both will increase inflationary pressure.

But, worst of all, the insatiable demands of state companies for credit to finance losses will send the money supply into orbit and tip the economy into hyperinflation. This will destroy the first fruits of economic reform, wreck thousands of firms and cause an attempt to reintroduce price controls. These will not work because no government has enough authority to enforce them.

And yet, surprisingly, there are grounds for optimism. Had Russia's collapse been slower, it would have lasted longer: the old lies would have lingered.

As Russia picks through the wreckage of hyperinflation, it will find that not only have the first attempts at reform been destroyed, but so has the attempt to reimpose central planning.

The Russian government will auction 5,000 medium-sized and large state-owned companies for a combination of cash and vouchers during 1993. These targets are immensely—probably impossibly—ambitious. Managers of many state-owned firms oppose them. Nevertheless, privatisation will not be stopped. The vouchers are the only popular part of Boris Yeltsin's economic programme.

In parts of the economy, this will suck in the foreign investment which has dismally failed to flow into Russia during 1992. Managers and workers in those companies most immediately attractive to western firms—especially factories making consumer goods—will sell their newly privatised stakes at a huge profit to foreign firms. Foreigners, despite this mark-up, will thereby acquire a cheap option on a market of 150m people ill-supplied with consumer goods.

Eventually, lower inflation will mean that the spending power of those in work will rise (after nearly halving in 1992). So the collapse in output will not turn into a further collapse in living standards. This should make it easier to redeploy re-

You can look but you better not touch

sources—oil, capital and labour—away from unprofitable firms and towards new industries. This is the necessary condition for the restructuring of the Russian economy.

Moreover, as weak companies go out of business, the raw materials they now use inefficiently will become available for export. This should mean Russia will be able to run a trade surplus next year. That would ease Russia's difficulties with financing foreign debt and enable it to cut its punitive taxation on export earnings.

Lower export taxes, together with lower inflation, will in turn mean Russia should attract back some of the capital that fled the country in 1992. Estimates for capital flight—the amount of foreign currency illegally stashed abroad in 1992—run up to $30 billion. Attracting that back will do at least as much for Russia's international financing problems as the promised amount of aid from western countries.

The benefits of more trade with the West will be offset by a collapse in trade with other republics of the former Soviet Union. The rouble zone—an unstable compromise in which republics use the Russian currency but run separate, though supposedly co-ordinated, monetary policies—will collapse in 1993. Russia will no longer accept the roubles issued by other central banks as payment for Russian goods.

This will force the other countries of the rouble zone to choose between introducing their own currencies (and shouldering responsibility for monetary policy) or continuing to use the rouble, while giving up sovereignty over monetary policy to Russia. Some countries—Ukraine, Belorussia and possibly Kazakhstan and Uzbekistan—will choose to introduce their own currencies. But Russia is then likely to insist that much of the trade between them and Russia is conducted in dollars.

Because they will find it hard to earn those dollars, they will be unable to finance the same volume of trade with Russia that was achieved in 1992, which itself was far lower than in 1991. Trade between Russia and the other republics of the former Soviet Union will therefore collapse.

This will harm the other countries greatly because they all run large trade deficits with Russia, even though in 1992 Russia was subsidising oil exports to them. It will harm Russia less because its main export is oil—which can be sold on world markets. So, though the slump in Russia next year will be substantial, it will be minor compared with the problems of the other, unreformed, republics of the former Soviet Union.

Water and religion

John Parker

Who pulled the plug on the Aral Sea?

Water and religion will combine to make Central Asia the least stable part of the former Soviet Union in 1993.

The region is desperately poor and, without the subsidies that Moscow used to provide, it faces unsustainable budget deficits ranging up to 60% of GDP. Water is the main economic resource of this arid region, tumbling down from the Himalayas to the Aral Sea. Even to prevent a worsening of the already catastrophic rate at which the Aral Sea is drying up, governments must limit the amount of water used by farmers.

Yet the amount they use is already too small for rates of farm output—and the population will double in 20 years. Five republics share two river systems. Arguments over how much water each republic uses are inevitable—and will add to an already alarming ethnic fragmentation which has already erupted into numerous clashes.

No government can maintain stability in these circumstances, least of all those that Central Asia has. Except in Kirgizstan (whose president was elected in 1991) and Tajikistan (whose president was overthrown after an anti-communist uprising in 1992), all are like one-party states run by communists-turned-nationalists.

None has proved capable of convincing local nationalists that they really have changed their spots. In Uzbekistan, the most populous country in the region and the one that will come under the greatest strain next year, an opposition leader says, "If the leadership refuses to begin a dialogue with the democrats, the power vacuum may be filled by a third force."

This force is Islam. Islam in Central Asia comes in two forms: the radicals, represented by the Islamic Renaissance Party (IRP), which is strong in Tajikistan and which wants to set up an Islamic state there, and the moderates, who have been able to run mosques and schools under the watchful eye of the secular authorities.

It is sometimes thought that the radicals are too weak to mount a serious challenge to the governments while the moderates, though they are stronger, will not do so. This is wrong. The IRP was the spearhead of the opposition that overthrew the president of Tajikistan in 1992, while the leaders of the moderates both there and in Uzbekistan have gone into open opposition.

The former communist leaders can no longer rely on force if things go wrong, even though the local detachments of the former Red Army have fallen into their hands. In Tajikistan, the national guard's defection to the opposition made the communist president's position untenable.

In these circumstances, the fall of one domino could push down the others. After the overthrow of the government in Tajikistan, Uzbekistan is next in line because there are 1.2m Uzbeks in Tajikistan and 1m Tajiks in Uzbekistan.

Moreover, the collapse of the Tajik government was accompanied by civil war in the country. The former communists in Central Asia not only cannot hold on to power much longer. Worse, it may no longer be possible to remove them without bloodshed.

MARTHA LIVES BY THE
CREDO THAT THE OUTCOME
OF YOUR DAY MAY INDEED
HANG BY A THREAD.

Martha, Seamstress
The Pierre, New York

She knows in her heart that an impeccable appearance can be one of your strong suits. A sentiment shared by those she works with. From the valet who launders your shirts and presses your trousers, to the individual who collects your shoes each night and returns them at dawn, polished to perfection. At The Pierre, we believe that you, as well as your room, should be beautifully appointed.

Fifth Avenue at 61st Street, New York, N.Y. 10021 In London, phone (081) 941-7941. Elsewhere contact Leading Hotels of the World.

©1990 Four Seasons Hotels Ltd.

Four
Seasons
The Pierre
NEW YORK
one of
The Leading Hotels of the World®

New people, new vigour, old ideas

Mike Elliott

Since the inauguration of Bill Clinton as the president of the United States on January 20th will bring to an end 12 years of Republican control of the White House, it is natural to see 1993 as a watershed in American life. Mr Clinton had, after all, campaigned with single-minded determination on the simple proposition that it was "time for a change". Ross Perot, the independent candidate from Texas who garnered an astonishing 19% of the popular vote, had implicitly campaigned on the same grounds. Yet what will be most striking about America in 1993 is how little will alter.

Naturally, thousands of patronage jobs will now change hands. Yet at the most basic level, a mere switching of control of the executive branch from one party to another has far less significance in America than it would have in most other countries. The essentials of American life remain unchanged. The country is, by the standards of any other industrial democracy, God-fearing, patriotic and unstinting in its gut identification with the "free-market system". Political theories or the desire to push through novel dogmatic ideas form little part of American political life. Mr Clinton will steer well clear of them.

Even in politics, the change of control of the White House will not mean that the system will be turned upside down. The Democrats have, after all, controlled both houses of Congress for the past six years of Republican rule, and one of them—the House of Representatives—for the whole 12-year period. On the eve of the election they controlled most of the important governors' mansions.

True, the Supreme Court has only one member—Byron White—who was appointed by a Democratic president. But confounding those who like to think of the members of the court in the simplistic

Fresh, not radical

terms of "conservatives" and "liberals", a pragmatic, legally cautious, block of Republican-appointed justices has made it plain that they are not prepared to overthrow the constitutional jurisprudence of earlier, more activist, courts just for the hell of it.

Indeed, despite the rhetoric of "change", one of the most striking aspects of Mr Clinton's rise to power is a certain continuity of ideas. In large measure, Mr Clinton's "new Democratic party" draws from the same intellectual wellsprings as many 1980s Republicans. Like those Republicans, Mr Clinton believes that the market is a more efficient way of ordering human events than the state and that high taxation stunts economic growth. Like them, he is enthusiastic about the power of the entrepreneur. He does not think that the way to resolve the manifold and shaming crises of America's cities is merely to throw money at them.

In all these beliefs, Mr Clinton has shown himself to be not quite the "modern southerner" that he is usually described as being—southern Democrats

tend to like Big Government, which has given them lots of military spending and pork-barrel projects. His ideas actually are most advanced in the western states, whose fiercely independent people have always been suspicious of government even while they have been socially liberal. It was western governors like Bruce Babbitt of Arizona, Roy Romer and Dick Lamm of Colorado, and indeed Jerry Brown of California, a bitter opponent of Mr Clinton in the Democratic primaries, who first put into practice the idea of a limited-but-active government that is at the heart of Mr Clinton's politics. As if to prove the point, the area of his greatest success on November 3rd was not in the south but the west, although Mr Clinton and Al Gore, a senator from Tennessee, are both southerners. In the west, Mr Clinton won eight states, including California.

As the Clinton administration readies itself for power in 1993, a central question is whether these western, "new Democratic" ideas will be able to move from theory into the practice of government. Much will depend on whether the new president will be able to make the American business community his ally.

The Arkansan comes into office with more endorsements from respected business leaders such as John Young, of Hewlett Packard, than any Democrat in memory. Nonetheless, where businessmen are gathered together, it is common to hear the refrain that however sympathetic to their agenda Mr Clinton himself might be—however suspicious of government regulation and high taxes—there is not a sufficient number of Democrats of his persuasion to staff all the jobs of interest to business.

Businessmen are particularly concerned (probably wrongly) about the influence in a Clinton administration of Mr Gore. Something of a moderate environmentalist, increasingly interested in the use of economic incentives to reduce pol-

Mike Elliott: bureau chief of *The Economist* in Washington, DC.

lution, Mr Gore is thought by many in the business community to be a far-out tree-hugger, who will regulate them to death.

Of all this class of concerns about the depth of commitment of a Clinton administration to "new Democratic" policies, the most pervasive centres on Mr Clinton's likely relations with Congress. Washington has a long memory; it remembers that unco-operative congressional Democrats were almost as responsible for Jimmy Carter's political demise as was Ayatollah Khomeini. Though the folk around Mr Clinton insist that he will not make the same mistakes as Mr Carter (just as, during the campaign, he did not make the same mistakes as Mr Dukakis) the risk is a real one. He has not gone out of his way to curry favour with Congressional Democrats, and it is a fair bet that some of those to whom he is closest will leave the Hill for positions in his administration.

Yet there is on the Hill 12 years' worth of frustration on the part of influential committee and sub-committee chairmen, who will want their own pet schemes put into law rather than those of the new Democrats. Moreover, although Congress itself is changing fast (the 1992 elections saw more than 100 new members of the House) much of the Democratic caucus remains resolutely "old" Democrat. If Mr Clinton thinks that he is going to be able to push western ideas like deregulation and privatisation through Congress easily, he is in for a shock.

Mr Clinton's domestic policies in 1993 will be typified by what might be called Euro-supply side ideas. The central message of Mr Clinton's campaign, though rarely spelt out clearly, was that the American economy is in a state of transition. As the factors of production—particularly labour—have become globalised, so the low-skill high-wage jobs that propelled a generation of Americans to unheard-of prosperity in the years from 1945 to 1973 have gone. They will not return. Mr Clinton's programme is predicated on the assumption that the new American economy must be export-driven and high-value added. He is right. America enters 1993 keenly competitive. The vast productive capacity of middle America, leanly managed and technologically advanced, could knock spots off European and even Japanese competitors, if half the attention was given to exports that those foreign rivals give. The analysis is not controversial; many Republicans share it.

Mr Clinton will inherit an economy where the room for manoeuvre is strictly limited. Notwithstanding a decade's worth of measures such as "caps" on spending and supposed automatic cuts, the federal budget deficit continues to balloon; in fiscal year 1992 it came in at $292 billion, a new record. The immediate damage comes in two forms. First, an ever-growing share of the federal budget is appropriated not for productive purposes but simply to pay interest on $4 trillion of debt; second, long-term interest rates are higher than they should be.

As the transition to a new administration starts, members of Mr Clinton's entourage are split between those who want an immediate programme of deficit reduction and those who want to press ahead with the development of costly new programmes—whatever their effect on the deficit. The terms of the debate have been sharpened because the country is emerging from the recession steadily, but terribly slowly. America enters 1993 with inflation and interest rates at record lows. In other words, those who want to press on with the new programmes think that conditions are uniquely propitious for the fiscal stimulus they would provide.

Yet when such talk was heard from Mr Clinton's friends in the month before the election, the markets responded by dumping shares and raising bond prices. The battle between the markets' horror of the deficit and the Clinton administration's understandable desire to put its economic programme into practice will dominate the early part of 1993.

Internationalists all

One crucial area where the new Democrats' theory may be difficult to put into practice concerns trade policy. New Democrats are free-traders (this, above all, is where the influence of the west on the new party is seen most sharply). Given the historical nature of the Democratic coalition, and the place that organised labour has in it, Mr Clinton's endorsement-with-reservations of the North American Free Trade Area (NAFTA) before the election was about as unequivocal as any Democrat could afford to be. Yet he will come under intense pressure to renegotiate the NAFTA to "protect" rustbelt jobs (in reality, low-skill jobs are going to Mexico with a NAFTA or without it).

In a way that Mr Clinton's men have perhaps not yet grasped, free trade matters for more reasons than the economic boost it gives the economy. The Republican administration's rhetoric (not always matched by reality) on trade served a political purpose too. Specifically, it underpinned the important relationship between America and Japan. That relationship is close and complex; it encompasses security and cultural matters as much as economic ones. It has its bumpy patches, as all close bilateral relationships do, but in a way that Europeans often fail to understand, it is basically healthy.

Yet its health depends at the limit on an implicit guarantee by successive American administrations that they believe in open trade between the two economies. Without that guarantee, there is enough potential rivalry in the relationship—and enough nervousness in East Asia that America is abandoning the region to a contest between Japan and China—to cause serious problems in the future.

The same argument can be made in respect of relations between the United States and the countries of Latin America. An improvement in those relations (especially with Mexico) was the unsung success of the Bush administration. Yet there, too, the guarantee of free trade, and hence access to the American market for Latin American goods, was the essential component of a political opening. NAFTA, and the Enterprise for the Americas Initiative (which has a long-term goal of free-trade agreements with other countries of the continent), have been vital economic tools without which the new and friendlier politics of the continent would not have been possible.

The Democrats will probably be mildly more determined to cut American forces in Europe quicker and deeper than Republicans were, but there is so far no sign that this will be anything other than a change of degree. They will be no less committed to the Middle East peace process than were the Republicans, and (despite fears in the Arab world) will probably turn out to be no more pro-Israel than America is always inclined to be. There will be some huffing and puffing about conditions in China, but, try as they may to avoid it, the world's sole superpower and most populous country will start to speak to each other more fruitfully in 1993.

In other words, if Mr Clinton's new Democratic ideas are implemented, the country will, in a host of areas, see interesting changes of policy—but ones that are really changes at the margin. But there is one change that will be palpable: Bill Clinton will bring to the White House a love of the job, an attractive vigour, if not a sophisticated style. Bill Clinton really wants to be president, really wants to put his ideas into practice, really wants to scrub and swab the decks of the ship of state even if in the grand sweep of things he is not altering its course. After four years of George Bush, such enthusiasm for the task at hand is welcome. America as a whole will benefit from it in 1993.

Kaleidoscope America

Bill Bradley

The ethnic and racial landscape of America is undergoing a rapid and unmistakable transformation. In the 1990 census nearly 30% of the population identified itself as either non-white or Hispanic. By 2000 only 57% of Americans entering the workforce will be native-born whites. During the 1980s the Asian-Pacific American population more than doubled; the number of Latin Americans rose by over 50%.

Americans are a different people now: literally. In schools, parks, hospitals, restaurants and work-places Americans deal increasingly with people who look different from the white majority, who come from different parts of the world, who often practise different religions—but who share a unique optimism about their prospects. America is becoming a world society.

It is no longer a matter of white Americans "allowing" non-white Americans entrance into "their" society, if they meet certain criteria. When politicians such as David Duke say our economic problems are caused by blacks and Jews or Pat Buchanan implies that they are caused by foreigners, they reveal ignorance about their country.

The reality is that African, Asian, Latin and native Americans are at the heart of what America has been and increasingly is. Together all Americans will determine what America will become. That optimism about finding unity in our diversity—even against the backdrop of tribalism sweeping across the world from Yugoslavia to the Indian sub-continent, from Somalia to the republics of the former Soviet Union—offers a unique opportunity for America to lead by example. Yet it will be America's trickiest task.

The potential for insularity and violence is great. Racial tension invades many aspects of American life, from competition for jobs to controversy over a school's curriculum, from the unthinking use of stereotypes to battles over electoral district boundaries.

Many white Americans will not relinquish the sense of entitlement skin colour has given them throughout their lives and the nation's history. The "anglo club" attitude, which emphasises non-whites as "the others", still persists even among whites who themselves have much in common with the economic interests of most non-whites.

On the other hand, some non-whites consciously reject much of American history. This is partly because they see themselves as excluded from it and partly because they believe that America, even at its best, is incapable of accepting a role for them in shaping a common future. Even though common sense says we must find common ground, people of all races often fail to make the effort.

So race will remain at the centre of America's domestic turmoil. The events in Los Angeles in 1992 remind us of how far we have to go. They were not black disorders alone. Over half of the looters were Latin. The victims were often Asian-American. Few of the victims and none of the perpetrators were well off. The actions of the looters were clearly self-destructive, a testament to the

"Race will remain at the centre of America's domestic turmoil"

absence of meaning in countless lives, surfeited daily by violence on television and in the streets, and burdened with persistent poverty in the public institutions of the community and in their homes.

The task at hand is for us to diffuse the potential for conflict, isolation and hopelessness with candour, effort and resources. The fact that racism exists does not mean that democratic institutions, properly used, cannot help to blot it out.

Being an historical outsider must not provide an excuse for opting out of the American ethic that rewards initiative, hard work and self-reliance. These remain imperatives in the successful pursuit of the American dream. National leadership, which is at core moral, can encourage each American to see why diversity is a strength and why it can enrich all Americans' lives.

Popular culture has already begun to make the transition. From food to music, America's diversity strengthens the country; it appeals to Americans and envious foreigners alike. What people don't yet see is the importance of diversity on an economic level. For example, in the next decades world corporations will evolve. Their managements will increasingly reflect racial diversity to accommodate and mirror the world markets.

Advantage America

America, by developing its natural diversity, could very well obtain an advantage. Imagine a stable and growing multiracial South Africa with African-Americans leading American corporations. Imagine a China or an India finding partners in American companies that deliver quality goods and multiracial American managements that feel the cultural rhythms of the society.

By having corporate leadership more of a reflection of our own increasing diversity, we will also have a more open and freer society. If we have worked out these conflicts first, we will not only gain a competitive advantage and improve our own living standards, but we will be one step closer to realising the promise of America for all of our own citizens.

The media will be central in creating a new pluralistic ideal. Firms that succeed in part because of their diversity should be newsworthy. Instead of focusing on violence and hedonism, the media has a responsibility for conveying our new society's rich potential.

Stories about successful neighbourhoods, as well as stories about neighbourhoods that have been turned into war zones, can shape attitudes. Just as television advertisements began in the 1970s to reflect racial diversity, so now the story must be told of corporate diversity that leads to profits.

As Rabbi Abraham Heschel said, "We are not all equally guilty, but we are all equally responsible" for building a decent country. The America our children inherit could be a nightmare of ethnic animosity.

Or it could be one where people are judged not by their colour, the shape of their eyes, or the religious rituals they follow, but by how hard they work, and how much they contribute to the collective whole.

Senator Bill Bradley: Democrat, New Jersey.

e to be in.

ower steering as standard.

We've also uprated the suspension make it smoother and more agile, and make the handling more responsive.

And we've built in more safety atures like side impact bars and re-forced structures to help minimize e effect of angled impacts.

The new 16v Escort is clearly a top performer. It's still Britain's No.1 best seller. And it's ready and waiting for you to give it a workout.

For a Cars brochure or Options prospectus, with worked examples, as well as the location of your nearest dealer, call free on **0800 111 222.**

The new 16v Escorts.

Everything we do is driven by you.

1993's Americana

Mike Elliott

What will jolt America next year? Here are four guesses.

• **The shrinking defence industry**. In the late 1980s the defence budget ran (in 1992 dollars) at around $300 billion. On the Bush administration's plans, that figure might be expected to drop to, say, $250 billion a year within five years. But unless the geopolitical changes of the past five years are stunningly reversed—unless, say, Russia decided that at whatever cost it is still engaged in a global struggle with the United States—such a figure is unsustainable. In the mid-1930s, another period when America was at peace, defence spending (at 1992 prices) was less than $20 billion.

It is reasonable to assume that defence spending by the century's end will run at no more (in today's prices) than $150 billion a year. "Defence conversion" will soon be one of the hottest topics of industrial seminars, though some leading companies, like General Dynamics, will probably not choose to convert anything. Rather than try new and risky ventures, they will deliberately shrink.

Defence cutbacks are already being blamed for the unexpected depth of the recession in southern California (where perhaps 200,000 defence jobs have been lost this decade). Yet, luckily, much of the industry is concentrated in areas whose non-defence economy is fundamentally strong: Florida, Connecticut, the Virginia Tidewater; for that matter, southern California itself.

The main social change associated with the shrinking defence budget may be found elsewhere. In many small towns, especially in the south, service in the reserves provides a useful second pay cheque; but the reserves will soon be savagely reduced in size. And there is no doubt that for 20 years the army has provided a quite disproportionate number of high-skill jobs and command positions for black Americans (one of whom, Colin Powell, is chairman of the joint chiefs of staff). As the armed services shrink, so will those opportunities.

• **Instability in the Caribbean**. Ten years ago American policy-makers worried that Mexico, which had just defaulted on its debt, was entering a period of political and economic turmoil. But they congratulated themselves that, by opening the booming American economy to exports from the small nations of the Caribbean through the Caribbean Basin Initiative, they were damping down the potential for instability there.

Now the worries are reversed. Mexico is undergoing political and economic reform; reform that will be locked in by the new North American Free Trade Agreement. But none of the small Caribbean nations has been able to use the Basin Initiative to achieve fundamental economic change.

Is that unemployment ahead?

The political situation in Haiti goes from bad to worse; the Dominican Republic is far from stable and an economic disappointment. And Americans assume that the 1990s will be the decade when they will have to cope with a transfer of power in Cuba. In the long term, a prosperous, capitalist Cuba, 50 miles off the coast of Florida, could be a motor for the whole Caribbean. But in the short term, Americans will see nothing but trouble ahead.

• **The return of New York**. For 15 years New York city has gone through a bewildering cycle of boom and bust. In the mid-1970s the city had a budget crisis that was taken as a sign of its irreversible economic decline. It then saw ten years of unparalleled boom as the financial services industry expanded.

The boom went bust after the stockmarket crash of 1987; it was fashionable to think that the future belonged to "livable" cities like Seattle. Now many of New York's indicators are positive once more. Wall Street firms are profitable again; its law firms are hiring. Violent crime is actually decreasing. In the summer of 1992 15,000 members of the media descended on the city for the Democratic Party's convention.

They found somewhere that was clean, bright and—in a most un-New York way—friendly. At the end of 1992, just as the film "Singles" celebrated Seattle, three massive new night clubs opened in New York. Even the *New Yorker*, venerable symbol of the city's literary establishment, has been woken from its torpor by its new editor, Tina Brown.

• **The peculiar future of American women**. Despite many false alarms in the past, there is little doubt that 1992 was a breakthrough year for women in American politics. Eleven of them stood for the Senate. Hillary Clinton, the wife of the new president, is a "new" kind of political wife, one with a career of her own. She will have more than one job to do next year.

There are plenty like her in the Republican Party too—women like Lynn Cheney, the wife of Dick Cheney, defence secretary to George Bush and a likely presidential candidate in 1996.

And yet underneath the political success there are some nagging qualms. For one thing, as 1992 progressed, women seemed almost to welcome being "ghettoised" in "women's issues" like family leave or abortion. Only Lynn Martin, Mr Bush's labour secretary, has defined a political interest in areas that are not traditional ones for women.

Moreover, there is a danger that—like the Irish a century ago—American women will place too much store by success in politics and the public sector. For all the claims of political breakthroughs, it is noteworthy how few American women have made it to the top of major corporations or founded one themselves. America still has no equivalent of Anita Roddick, who built Britain's Body Shop into a global retail chain. That is puzzling; and disappointing. It is something that may well change in 1993.

Canada's eye off the ball

William Thorsell

Like Bosnia & Herzegovina, Canada spent 1992 pondering its identity as a sovereign state. That the seventh biggest economy in the world, a country renowned for boring pragmatism and decent liberality, should still be messing around in this way is quite dumbfounding—both to its friends and to itself. When will Canada's inability to come to grips with itself as a federation end? Not next year.

A referendum in October 1992 was a barely disguised vote on sovereignty for Quebec. Its outcome means that Canadians have rejected the most ambitious package of constitutional reforms since the Charter of Rights and Freedoms in 1982. It will mean that next year Canada will remain distracted from the one issue that really matters to most Canadians: the restoration of economic growth. The referendum opened as many wounds as it aspired to heal and those many Canadians who hoped that the whole issue had been put behind them have a shock coming in 1993.

October's referendum came after two years of seemingly incessant public forums, commissions and conferences seeking agreement on three major goals: formal recognition of Quebec's place as a distinct society within Canada, reform of parliament to give smaller provinces more influence through an elected senate, and recognition of the aboriginals' inherent right to self-government within Canada. The common theme has been a redistribution of power within the federal government to less populous regions, and from the federal government to the provinces and aboriginals.

These are the kinds of political questions that fascinate 5% of the population and bore the saner 95%. To this extent Canada's political life has been hijacked. The restless provinces of the Canadian west, newly conscious aboriginals, populous ethnic minorities and politicised women make the quest for Canadian unity shrill and complex. It also means that the real question for the country—Canada's rapid absorption into the northern part of the United States—has been going by on the nod.

As the North American Free Trade Area becomes ever more accepted, so decisions of investment, jobs and trade flows are made against the reality of this free market. Yet as Canada's frontier with

William Thorsell: editor-in-chief of the *Globe and Mail*, Canada's national newspaper.

its neighbour almost ceases to exist, a few Canadian politicians will spend next year trying to draw irrelevant lines on a constitutional map that no one will consult.

Canada's prime minister, Brian Mulroney, enters 1993 near the end of his

North America's uncommon market

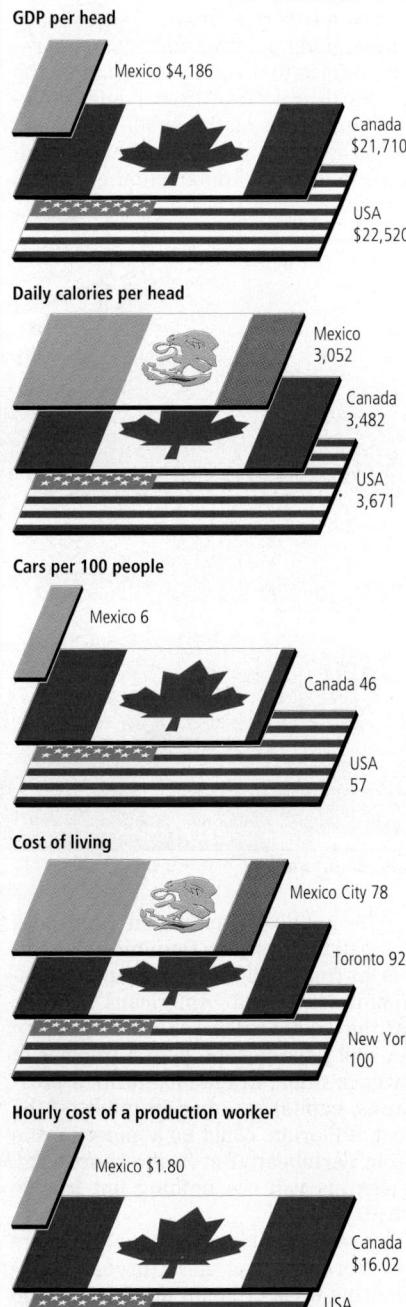

GDP per head

Mexico $4,186

Canada $21,710

USA $22,520

Daily calories per head

Mexico 3,052

Canada 3,482

USA 3,671

Cars per 100 people

Mexico 6

Canada 46

USA 57

Cost of living

Mexico City 78

Toronto 92

New York 100

Hourly cost of a production worker

Mexico $1.80

Canada $16.02

USA $14.77

political life, after eight years in office and with the lowest recorded approval rating of any prime minister in Canadian history. His narcissistic personality and the ceaseless constitutional debate are liabilities he will not shake off.

Although he has undoubtedly scored a number of political successes among the few who follow these things, Canadians of every stripe are more unhappy with the outlook for 1993 than any particular twist to the constitutional debate. The chronically weak economy is making them especially miserable. Canada's recession started in the spring of 1990, dug far more deeply than that in the United States, and has hung on more doggedly.

The cost of servicing Canada's enormous federal debt—now approaching C$450 billion ($360 billion) or 63% of GDP—is going to hang round the economy as it tries to recover in 1993. Higher provincial taxes next year will do nothing to boost consumer spending and everything to bolster inefficient local governments. A zealous monetary policy has driven private-sector inflation below zero. Consumer debt is high and unemployment, 11% nationally, will continue to rise. In 1993 many Canadians will be in the mood to reach out and punch someone.

They will get a chance in the general election that Mr Mulroney must call before the end of 1993. His own unpopularity would seem to doom the Progressive Conservatives to defeat, but for two reasons. Mr Mulroney's opponents—the Liberal leader Jean Chretien and the New Democratic Party's Audrey McLaughlin—are weak. The prime minister retains the advantage in Quebec, despite its sovereigntist mood, and is a formidable campaigner anywhere when he has to be.

More provocatively, the Conservatives are the only national party in a position to change their leader before the next election. (The other parties are committed in this round.) Mr Mulroney senses his time is up. Last year he seriously considered a new job: a run for secretary-general of the United Nations.

Despite a dreary 1993, it is possible to imagine Canada emerging by mid-decade with its constitutional issues resolved, its public finances under control, its currency fundamentally sound and its private economy competitive in a free-trade area that stretches through the United States and Mexico. Throw in the possibility that the longest trough in modern times for the commodity cycle may be ending (energy and food prices are showing signs of recovery) and Canada's future may yet turn out to be worth waiting for. Few would be more surprised at this than the Canadians themselves.

GATEWAY AMERICA ANNOUNCES ECONOMIC AID FROM RUSSIA.

The World Trade Center in New York City has a revolutionary new tenant. By the end of 1993, the Republic of Russia will occupy 74,000 square feet of space which will become the first Russian Trade and Cultural Center in the United States. The center will house exhibition space, an information service, retail stores, administrative offices, and of course, a Russian restaurant.

The Russians picked the perfect place to break bread. Because the World Trade Center is the premier location in the U.S. for businesses engaged in international trade. Currently, it houses nearly 500 firms from 62 different countries. Along with all the support services necessary for those companies to do business with each other, the rest of the country, and the rest of the world.

The Port Authority of New York and New Jersey is completing a major renovation of the World Trade Center, which just celebrated its twentieth anniversary. In addition, we're making important improvements to the metropolitan area's major airports, marine ports, and interstate transportation system. To help our region live up to the title, Gateway America, and fulfill its role as the nation's leader in world trade.

To find out how we can help your company with space in the World Trade Center or any of our other business services, call our London office or drop us a line at our headquarters in New York. We can celebrate with caviar. In London: 44-71-481-8909.

THE PORT AUTHORITY OF NEW YORK & NEW JERSEY
One World Trade Center, MAP 68-S, New York, N.Y. 10048, U.S.A.

BORDERLESS

When the leaders of nations and celebrities traveled to the East, NYK provided the services to help make history. Today, too, on a worldwide scale but in the same tradition, NYK is making extraordinary advances in shipping history with a fleet of some 400 ships including containerships, conventional vessels, tankers and specialized tramp carriers. Now more than ever before, NYK services have expanded to meet the challenge of global economic interdependence.

Borders between nations, between carriers, borders between products and between people and ideas are being dissolved. NYK's integration of global logistics and megacarrier capabilities opens fresh vistas on the borderless society.

NYK LINE
NIPPON YUSEN KAISHA

Head Office: 3-2, Marunouchi 2-chome, Chiyoda-ku, Tokyo 100, Japan   Tel. (03) 3284-5151

Poor Japan

Bill Emmott

For three years, Japan has seemed on the brink of recession. The stockmarket collapse that began in January 1990, followed a year later by falling property prices, looked sure to cause an economic setback. Yet Japan's economy kept on going, like a cartoon character who runs over a cliff and remains suspended in mid-air, legs still pumping away. A few banks and brokers had a problem or two, to be sure, but Japan's industrial powerhouse looked scarcely affected.

Beginning in mid-1992, however, gravity began to take hold. The evidence that recession had come at last was everywhere, from the lines of empty Tokyo taxis to the increasingly shrill calls for reflation from Japanese politicians, to the growing number of well-known companies that announced not merely falls in profits but losses. And, despite the Japanese government's ¥10.7 trillion ($87 billion) rescue package, announced on August 28th, the recession will continue in 1993, possibly for longer than forecasters imagine. It will force changes both in Japan and in the way in which the world views Japan.

Since the mid-1980s the world has thought of Japan as an alarmingly unstoppable bulldozer, but one that is nevertheless driven by men with bulging wallets who are an easy touch for a loan or gift. How nice it would be if the bulldozer stopped but the philanthropy continued; then outsiders might even start to love Japan. Nice, but unlikely: relief at the bulldozer's retreat in 1992-94 will next year be tempered by annoyance at the philanthropist's stinginess.

Foreign direct investment by Japanese firms peaked in 1990-91 but then almost disappeared the following year. Portfolio investment abroad by Japanese pension funds and insurance firms virtually ceased in 1990. And Japan's huge banks, cited incessantly by American hysterics as proof of Japan's growing hold on the world economy, released that grip

Bill Emmott: business affairs editor of *The Economist*. Author of "The Sun Also Sets" (1989) and "Japan's Global Reach" (1992).

and sprinted back home, stopping lending to foreigners and devoting their capital to shoring up their domestic balance sheets. Far from being a supplier of long-term capital to the world, Japan in 1992 became a consumer of it.

It will be at least another year before the outside world celebrates Japan's return as an exporter of capital—and probably two years before it starts bemoaning the fact again. Foreign direct investment will not revive by much while Japan's new multinationals squirm under their newly costly capital and suffer because of their over-investment in factories and machines at home and abroad. Japanese banks may not return as big international lenders for as much as three or four years, so heavily are their balance sheets burdened by bad debts. Portfolio investors might return more quickly if an American recovery began to make overseas bonds and equities attractive again, but they will not soon offer the "walls of money" they

brought with them in the 1980s.

The disappearance of Japanese capital in 1991-92 was disguised in foreigners' eyes by their own recessions (which may have been worsened by the fall-off in Japanese capital exports, but were generally blamed on people closer to home, like governments) and by the continued generosity of Japan's official purse. Overseas aid went on growing in 1992; Japan's payments for the Gulf war remained prominent in both minds and ledgers; and for the first time Japan's parliament authorised the country's troops to join UN peacekeeping operations. So Japan seemed to be more outgoing. It refused to put up money to help Russia, but that could be blamed on the two countries' territorial dispute in the Kurile islands.

Now, however, even official Japan is going to become meaner. In recent years, Japan's central government budget has been in surplus to the tune of 1-2% of GDP, so it was easy to boost spending on aid or

Once I would have bought both

1993 ECONOMIC FORECAST

JAPAN

The 1990-92 slump in Tokyo stock prices has so shaken confidence that Japanese companies will remain reluctant to use the equity market for new finance. Normally that might not matter much: Japan's firms could switch back to bank financing. Unfortunately, lower stock prices have also hurt the banks, whose capital is partly tied up in the equity market. So new loans will be harder than usual to arrange.

The economic slowdown has been the worst since the oil shocks of the 1970s. It is not just capital spending which has slowed to a crawl—the shops are quiet too. Here again the problem is partly one of confidence. People prefer to save. Japan is no place to be unemployed. Nonetheless, expect house-building and consumer confidence to pick up.

A lot of Japan's savings flow abroad in search of high interest rates. With the current account in substantial surplus it could hardly be otherwise. The currency markets favour the yen because they believe the current-account surpluses will continue. They are right: 1993 should see a surplus of $106 billion after a likely $108 billion in 1992.

Many doubt the government's commitment to reducing this surplus. After all, strong export growth and a weak import trend have helped keep the Japanese economy out of severe recession. 1992's growth rate may not have reached 2% but it was still a better figure than in most other major economies. If confidence revives, 1993 could promise 3.4%. Be warned, however: the range of Japanese economists' forecasts for 1993 is unusually wide, so uncertain is the outlook for consumer confidence.

The government sees domestic-led growth as the best source of long-term economic security. To support confidence it has cut interest rates and launched a mildly reflationary fiscal package.

Despite its July 1992 electoral victory, the government knows that the public is disaffected. If necessary, policy will focus once again on boosting the trade surplus still further.

KEY INDICATORS

	1991	1992	1993
GDP growth (% pa)	4.4	1.9	3.4
Inflation (%)	3.3	2.1	2.2
Prime rate (year end %)	6.6	5.1	6.0
Exchange rate ¥ per $	135	126	130
Current account ($ bn)	72.9	108.0	106.0

EIU GLOBAL FORECASTING SERVICE

defence, or to find funds for the Gulf war. In 1993, however, that budget will move into deficit. Recession will depress tax revenues. And the August 1992 spending package will force the finance ministry to become a net borrower for the first time since the mid-1980s.

The finance ministry loathes this idea. It has chosen to run a surplus partly in order to repay debts incurred during the 1970s but mainly in order to prepare public finances for the rapid ageing of Japan's population in the late 1990s. It is storing up savings in the public social security funds in order to finance old people's consumption in a decade's time. Even its 1989 tax reform, which purported to offer cuts in personal taxation, actually resulted in income-tax revenue rising by 14.5% a year, twice as fast as the rise in household income.

That is why the ministry is likely to do everything it can to restrict the rise of its budget deficit. With revenues depressed and spending bloated for cyclical reasons, any public spending that looks discretionary and philanthropic will be vulnerable to cuts. That will be especially true of spending on foreigners. Aid, defence contributions and concessionary lending will not disappear altogether, but at best they will grow more slowly, at worst they will actually shrink.

This will be irritating for developing countries, Japan's Asian neighbours, and certainly for Russia and the former Soviet republics. Japan's foreign ministry has already lost any friends it had in Moscow by being intransigent over the windswept cluster of islands north of Hokkaido which Soviet troops occupied in 1945 and few Japanese care about. Ideas of a "Japan Sea Economic Zone", linking Vladivostok to Niigata on Japan's north-western coast, are just dreams. As the finance ministry's purse-strings draw tighter, such disappointment could even turn into an enmity that will eventually bode ill for the peaceful balance in an Asia dominated by China, Japan and Russia.

Americans and West Europeans will not be fussed, however, about Japan's bout of meanness. Their reaction will be dominated by relief at the retreat of Japan's industrial bulldozer. In 1992 the behaviour of Tokyo's stockmarket already led some American commentators to wonder if the Japanese threat was easing. In 1993 the evidence will shift to industrial competition, and will become overwhelming. It will be a year of cover stories and news bites featuring the successful "defeat" of Japanese rivals by American makers of semiconductors, computers, cars and much else besides.

Despite a Japanese current-account surplus still around $100 billion, news that Ford, Intel and Apple are beating the Japanese is likely to be enough to keep at least the worst excesses of anti-Japanese protectionism at bay. Though a bill or two to tax Japanese multinationals or to punish Japan for not importing rice may be presented to, or even pass, Congress, as far as Japan is concerned trade war will become trade snore.

Down, but not out

Japan's recession will look remarkably similar to those in the United States and Britain in 1990-92, even if it is milder than both. It has begun because of the financial collapse, a rising cost of capital and a huge drop in capital investment by Japanese firms. But it will drag on principally because of the Japanese consumer. Like consumers in America and Britain, ordinary Japanese are up to their necks in debt. So recovery cannot easily be driven by consumer spending.

Justly famed for being prudent savers in the 1970s, in the late 1980s Japanese turned to borrowing and spending in a big way. By 1990 their household debts had risen to 117% of their annual incomes, well above America's 103%. That did not matter as long as household assets such as stocks and property were also rising in value. But since 1990 those assets have plummeted. Now the repayment burden on consumer debt is rising while the value of collateral is falling. In 1991-92 the debt repayment burden of Japanese households grew more rapidly than disposable income for the first time.

That income will come under increasing pressure in 1993. Unemployment remains low, at only a jot over 2% of the labour force. Already, however, disguised unemployment has grown rapidly as companies hold on to millions of workers they no longer have a use for.

In 1993 such unemployment will shed its disguise. Even the biggest Japanese manufacturers cannot carry surplus labour indefinitely. Steel makers and others have already begun to ask for "adjustment assistance" from the government to help with redundancy payments. The shake-out in 1993 could push unemployment past 3% and will pose an increasing drain on public funds.

As the economy sags, pressure will grow for a further reflationary package. Given the weakness of personal incomes and of consumer spending, there may even be a strong push for that most unJapanese of measures: a tax cut. Normally, Japanese consumers are ignored. But soon a powerful group will want those consumers to have more cash to spend: Japanese producers.

Going for prowess or profits?

Peter Tasker

The Japanese always enjoy a good crisis. Time and again over the past decades disruptions in their usually smooth progress to greater prosperity have been taken as opportunities for the next advance.

The cycle should be familiar by now. Over-confidence is replaced, apparently overnight, by a jittery inferiority complex. Self-recrimination spreads from the media to the private sector to the government. Breasts are beaten, scapegoats "outed". Foreigners proclaim, often with some satisfaction, that the "miracle" is over; that the Japanese are finally becoming more "westernised".

Meanwhile, the acknowledged crisis is allowing Japanese companies to put through radical measures that they would never have got away with in the good times. Unit labour costs are squeezed, inefficiencies ironed out of the system, resources shifted from the weaker players to the strong. As the pessimism mounts, quietly but surely the stage is being set for the next turbo-charged surge of growth.

Will the breaking of the "bubble economy", meaning the easy money-powered expansion of 1987-92, prove any different from the previous experience? There are sound reasons for believing that the current slowdown does represent a watershed for Japan in a way in which the previous "crises" did not. Most obviously, it is self-generated, not the result of an external *shokku*.

Peter Tasker: Japanese investment strategist at Kleinwort Benson. He has been based in Tokyo for the past ten years. His book, "The End of the Japanese Golden Era", was a bestseller in Japan in 1992.

The more profound point is that Japan's current economic malaise is not just home-grown, but systemic. Many of the unique features of the "Japanese model", so admired and feared by foreign observers, were directly responsible for the creation and destruction of the "bubble economy" and have been severely weakened by the process. The remarkable events in the financial markets are both the clearest indication of that and also one of the more important causes.

It is axiomatic that Japanese companies pay little regard to short-term profits. Profits are "spent" on maximising market share in key areas, usually decided by reference to what major competitors are doing, perhaps with some bureaucratic nudging. The result has been super-aggressive business strategies, with pricing, product variety and innovation, capital investment, R&D and advertising budgets all aimed at market dominance, not the maximisation of profits.

Unsurprisingly, foreign companies have been unable to stay in the game. A classic example is the memory-chip market, where massive investment programmes have secured a global share of 90% for Japan. This is often cited as the most spectacular triumph of the "Japan Inc" strategy—the domination of the "commanding heights" of technology.

Yet who are the real winners and losers? Japanese companies have poured resources into an increasingly profitless business, smashing against each other like sumo wrestlers in a never-ending battle for supremacy. For the top five pro-

ducers, capital investment rose from being equal to annual pre-tax profits in 1982, to being more than three times annual profits in 1992. Meanwhile, the chips have got cheaper and cheaper, much to the delight of PC makers in Taiwan, Hong Kong and the United States.

Or take beer. The number of brands of domestic beer on the Japanese market grew from nine in 1980 to 75 in 1990. In that time the beer industry's capital investment grew by a multiple of 3.8 and its advertising spend by a multiple of 4.5, but pre-tax profits merely doubled. As with the chip producers, return on equity plummeted.

In "Kaisha", the classic study of corporate Japan, James Abegglen explains that Japanese managers focus on the long-term health of their companies as viewed from the perspective of other lifetime employees. The performance measures that are most important to them are the scale of revenues and assets. Return on capital and profit margin, measures which view corporate health from the perspective of the investor, are not anything like as significant.

If Japanese managements ignored the interest of investors, then how was Japan able to enjoy such a buoyant stockmarket over the years? First, high growth in demand—either at home or in export markets—enabled Japanese companies to provide investors with reasonable growth in profits, even while profitability itself remained low. Now, however, there are doubts whether that growth will ever recover its former speed.

Second, Japanese institutional investors have traditionally operated in the same way as industrial companies. Life insurers, for example, would happily purchase a steel maker's overvalued shares in order to sell more policies to its employees and thereby increase its market share. With around half the float of the equity market "locked up" in the stable shareholding system and individual investors dancing to the tune of the Big Four securities houses, conventional investment hardly existed at all.

Then, from the mid-1980s, the Japanese authorities embarked on the creation of a Frankenstein's monster—a deregulated financial system. The reputation of the monster's inventor—the Ministry of Finance—was one of the first victims of its wrath.

The greater the slowdown in the Japanese economy and the longer the bear market in Japanese shares, the more profound will be the transformation wrought. In the end, Japanese companies will emerge more return-conscious, more agile and much more profitable.

Japan finds a cause

Patrick Smith

The Japanese are turning a singular hue of green. They will address the world's environmental problems in 1993 (and beyond) the way they embraced high-growth-at-all-costs for much of the post-war era: in unison and eventually to great effect. Such a role has long been talked of in Japan; in the coming year it will take hold as one answer to the nation's agonised search for greater global responsibility.

Though its environmental record is mixed, the issue is a natural for Japan. It is uncontroversial; it is universally recognised as a matter of urgency; and it involves no security forces (and hence no messy constitutional conundrums).

Japan already has a fair amount to boast of. It accounts for 14.5% of global GDP but less than 5% of carbon dioxide emissions. Its sulphur dioxide emissions are one-tenth the OECD average. The energy Japan now consumes per unit of national output is the world's lowest. This reflects the oil crises of the 1970s and a popular green movement that gained short-lived influence in the decade preceding them.

That is only half the story. Japan has been a leading offender in controversies over whaling and drift-net fishing. The destruction of South-East Asia's rain forests continues largely in the service of the Japanese housing industry—and because the Japanese think disposable wooden chopsticks (one pair per person per meal) hold rice better than plastic ones.

The private sector is only now seeing the value of good corporate citizenship abroad. A massive wave of low-technology factories migrated elsewhere in Asia in the 1970s, when anti-pollution regulations were introduced at home.

A 1992 survey of manufacturers indicated that a huge 11% of companies were involved in environmental disputes overseas. And it is safe to assume that to be a conservative reflection of the problem. But the export of pollution is becoming a big issue at home. Witness the outcry among Japanese when, in mid-1992, a Malaysian court ordered Asian Rare Earth, a mineral-refining concern in which Mitsubishi Chemical Corp has a 35% stake, to close after a ten-year battle with local activists over radioactive waste. (In the end, a higher court in Malaysia stayed the verdict.)

Local officials are taking the lead in giving muscle to Japan's new mood. This is itself unusual. *Ura Nihon*, or inner Japan, normally counts for little in the national system—most prefectures being akin to developing countries: Tokyo acts as their metropole. But the bureaucrats in Kasumigaseki, the capital's administrative district, ceded the pollution issue to local government when high growth first befouled the nation's shorefronts, rivers and air some three decades ago. Tokyo has done so again, simply because local administrators are better able to see the problem, because large corporations cannot lobby them as they can in Tokyo, and because locals have a genuine interest in improving the quality of life in their communities.

Kyushu, the southernmost of Japan's four main islands, is now also the greenest, partly because it was in Minamata, on Kyushu's southern coast, that organic mercury took hundreds of lives and destroyed thousands of others in the 1950s and 1960s. Tiny Minamata is currently spending ¥16 billion ($130m) to turn itself into an environmentalist's mecca. Kumamoto Prefecture, of which the town is part, has the strictest water-quality standards in Japan, the tightest limits on farm chemicals and golf-course fertilisers, and bans outdoor advertising in its capital.

Kitakyushu, a city of 1m people on the northern coast, is a more graphic example of how effectively the Japanese can change when they choose to. The birthplace of Nippon Steel, it once considered *nanai iro no kemuri*, "the smoke of seven colours", a sign of its good fortune. No more. A 20-year clean-up has cut water pollution and sulphur oxides in the air by 90% each. At the 1992 Earth Summit in Rio de Janeiro, it was Kitakyushu's straight-talking mayor, Koichi Sueyoshi, not a national politician, who was singled out for an award to Japan.

Tokyo is getting the idea. It is considering an environment tax that would enable Japan to pay 10% of the cost of a third-world clean-up (estimated at $70 billion annually through to the end of the century). And by mid-1993 the Environment Agency will raise regulations on chemical fertilisers to a standard approaching Kumamoto's. Keidanren, the powerful industry federation, has already promulgated a Global Environmental Charter, and many blue-chip companies—Sony, NEC and so on—are scrambling to come up with their own. Most feature the

Patrick Smith: *New Yorker* correspondent in Tokyo; author "Nippon Challenge" (Doubleday).

India's tiger gets ready to spring

Roland Dallas

Not all the success stories of Asia are small like Hong Kong and Singapore. Take India, knocked off course by the balance-of-payments crisis following the collapse of trade with its old Soviet export market. The lot of almost 880m Indians will improve next year, even if not spectacularly.

Keeping the reforms on track will be difficult. Bureaucrats, protected businessmen and discontented workers in India will put up obstacles. International bankers will try to jolly things along. The government will stick to its own cautious path, trying to build up public support for each change: spending cuts to get the deficit down to about 5% of GDP; more careful control of the money supply to reduce inflation (M3 grew by 19.5% in 1992, 6.5% above the IMF prescribed dose). Growth of 6% could be on the cards for next year.

Reforms to watch out for include:
• Full convertability of the rupee on trade accounts. Exporters will like this. But the government will need to take care that a falling market rate does not wreck plans on inflation.

• An end to price controls on oil.
• Subsidy cuts. The food and fertiliser subsidies alone swallow up almost Rs100 billion ($3 billion) a year. They will have to be tackled if the deficit is to come down. This will be the most demanding test of faith for the government and will bring the biggest risk of mass discontent.
• Reduction in the paperwork for foreign investors and exporters. But plenty of bureaucracy will remain.

Work on privatisation will start to progress. The worst state firms will be offered in full to the private sector and 49% of slightly better-off ones.

The government has at last accepted the principle of privatisation and it will spend next year trying to build up support to get India through the pain caused.

As Indians look jealously at China's success at attracting investment, Indian Thatcherism, reform and privatisation will become unstoppable. Disputes will be about the pace of change. The Indian tiger may not leap next year, but it will be preparing itself.

popular notion that Japan is uniquely placed to lead honourable Earth towards a new harmony between economic activity and environmental right-mindedness—between man and nature.

Japan's new global initiative is partly the result of *gaiatsu*, or foreign pressure, which has risen significantly since Tokyo's disastrous dithering during the Gulf crisis. And at home, to go green is simply good politics. As a consequence, it is not hard to find cynics as to Tokyo's commit-

ment to the environment, but there are signs it will sink roots. No less a personage than Noboru Takeshita, a former prime minister and still senior in the Liberal Democrats' largest faction, has adopted the green cause as if it were a personal crusade. The Ministry for International Trade and Industry is engaged in (and losing) a publicly-waged turf battle with the small but growing Environment Agency—a sure sign that the territory at issue will be of increasing significance.

The year of the Chinese capitalist

Jim Rohwer

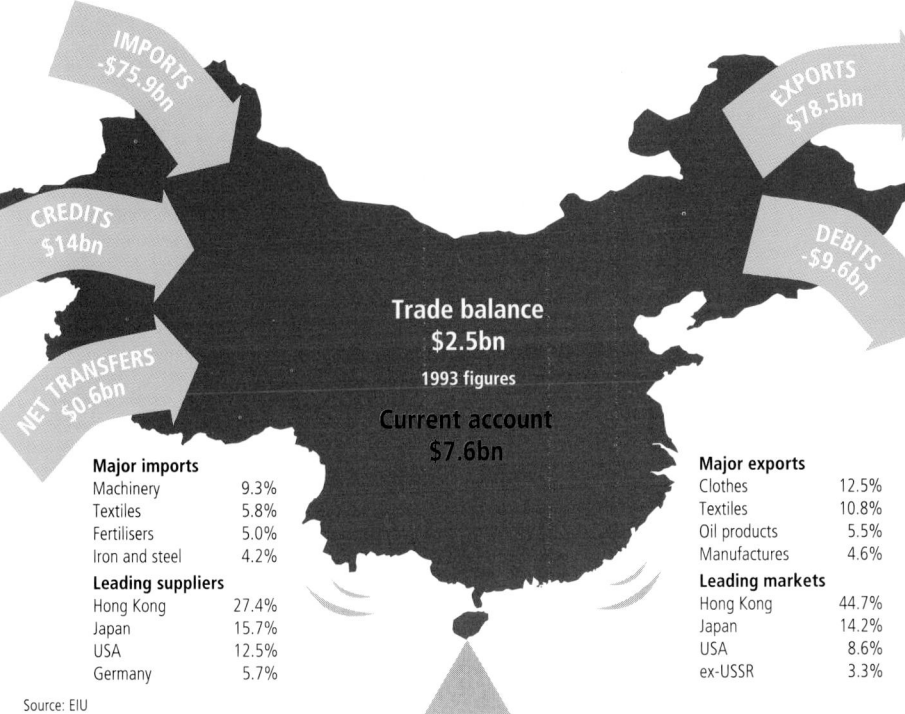

IMPORTS -$75.9bn
EXPORTS $78.5bn
CREDITS $14bn
DEBITS -$9.6bn
NET TRANSFERS $0.6bn

Trade balance $2.5bn

1993 figures

Current account $7.6bn

Major imports
Machinery	9.3%
Textiles	5.8%
Fertilisers	5.0%
Iron and steel	4.2%

Leading suppliers
Hong Kong	27.4%
Japan	15.7%
USA	12.5%
Germany	5.7%

Major exports
Clothes	12.5%
Textiles	10.8%
Oil products	5.5%
Manufactures	4.6%

Leading markets
Hong Kong	44.7%
Japan	14.2%
USA	8.6%
ex-USSR	3.3%

Source: EIU

When the final figures are in, the world's most populous country will prove to have had one of the fastest-growing economies of 1992. That is nothing new for China's 1.15 billion people. In the 14 years since Deng Xiaoping began reforming China's economy, real GDP growth has averaged almost 9% a year, a rate that doubles the size of the economy every eight years.

If China meets the goal it has set for itself, the economy will grow by 10% a year for the rest of the century—and will be six times bigger in 2000 than it was in 1978. That would equal the performance turned in by Japan and Taiwan in the 23 years after 1950. But China's growth would have come in a country not of 20m or even 120m people, but in one that is

home to more than a fifth of mankind. Can this really happen?

It can—but at some point China's government is going to have to tackle the hardest part of the reform task: turning the state-owned heavy industrial companies from cash-devouring dinosaurs into commercial businesses. That will not be easy. It raises the possibility of industrial unrest among the 250m urban Chinese, most of whom depend on state factories not just for a wage but also for housing, health care and a pension.

State-enterprise reform would also destroy nearly all that remains of communism—and raise the ticklish question of why the Communist Party should continue to enjoy its monopoly of political

power. Next year should give a good indication of how far China's government is ready to move down this risky road.

This is because the cyclical boom-bust pressures that China's partial reforms have given rise to will reach a peak in 1993. When, in 1991, the authorities let up on the monetary brakes they had slammed on at the end of 1988, the economy promptly picked up speed. In 1992 it reached double-digit growth. Unfortunately, credit also grew twice as fast in the first half of 1992 as the government had expected it to, and consumer-price inflation in the cities began increasing.

The trouble is not in the private bits of the economy. Enterprises owned not by China's central government but instead by lower-tier governments, co-operatives, foreigners and ordinary folk now account for more than half of industrial production. These outfits are financed either by foreign money or by the huge pool of private Chinese savings, and they enjoy double-digit rates of labour productivity growth. They can easily expand at double-digit rates without pushing up prices.

The state-owned companies, however, cannot do anything without pushing up prices. These enterprises, mostly in heavy industries like steel, petrochemicals and cars, amount to an Eastern Europe or Russia plonked down in the middle of the Chinese economy. Overmanned, inefficient and usually monopolies, they are a drag in two ways. They claim far more than their fair share of raw materials and of scarce energy and transport. And, with their mounting losses (at least two-thirds are in the red), they put a severe strain both on the government budget and on credit.

Last time austerity was imposed, in 1988-90, government conservatives, put firmly in charge by the Tiananmen Square debacle of June 1989, hoped that the squeeze would hurt the non-state companies but give state firms a breathing spell. In fact the non-state firms, indifferent to government financing and much more efficient than their state-owned rivals, were relatively unscathed. The state companies were crushed.

In the relaxation of 1991-92, the government tried tinkering with the state firms to improve them. Old debts were cleared, new management schemes introduced. None of this even grazed the core of the problem: a system that, as in the ex-Soviet block, guarantees that losses of state firms are always funded by the state-banking system and their inefficiencies are never punished.

The new leadership installed in China late in 1992 can use the economy's coming showdown with inflation either to try another austerity programme or to begin demolishing the state sector.

The cautious route—austerity—would hardly be a disaster: some economists think private businesses are coming along so nicely that their gradual dwarfing of state industry would be enough to unleash a Japan-like economic miracle in China. That is a fair bet. Dismantle the state enterprises and it becomes a certainty.

Plenty of puff left

Simon Ogus

The little dragons of East Asia will be as economically successful in 1993 as they have been in the recent past, perhaps more so. Recession is a word to be read about in the papers, not feared down in the factory. Although each of the dragons is growing in economic maturity, each has remained relatively unhurt by the winds that have buffeted their major trading partners. The health of their intra-regional trade and capital flows, and their rapidly expanding domestic consumer markets, have seen them over bad times elsewhere.

Yet speak to your average Singaporean, Taiwanese or Korean, and you will hear stories of economic decline, a waning work ethic and lost competitiveness. The dragons are having to come to terms with structural shifts in their economies away from traditional low-cost manufacturing. Policies to deal with higher inflation and other symptoms of overheating have also led to a cyclical slowdown, adding to the sense of despondency. In reality, however, the dragons are adapting to these changes remarkably well. Growth rates of 5-7% at the trough of the cycle are figures the rest of the world can only dream about.

The notable exception to this regional gloom and introspection is **Hong Kong**, which, perversely, has been the group's laggard in recent years. The Hong Kong people are (understandably) prone to wild mood swings depending on the behaviour of China, and are currently in a euphoric phase. The economy has been rebounding quite nicely since 1990 thanks to a combination of negative real-interest rates—Hong Kong rates are constrained by a currency peg to follow those in the United States—and a pick-up in confidence following the lows of 1989. GDP should expand by 5% during 1993 although a GNP figure, were it available, would perhaps be 2% higher. As Hong Kong's integration with southern China

Simon Ogus: economist with GT Management (Asia) Limited, based in Hong Kong.

increases, it is becoming progressively more difficult to untangle income flows between the two economies.

However, it has been political developments on the mainland that have really boosted the territory's sense of well-being. Deng Xiaoping's push for faster eco-

The cusp of capitalism

1993 figures

GDP growth %

Current account ($bn)

Private consumption growth %

Souce: EIU

nomic reform has forced even the most hardline communist elders to come out in favour of more market-oriented policies. Hong Kong therefore now believes that its economic system will remain virtually intact after 1997, although political freedoms are a different matter.

Problems do still remain. First, inflation is stuck near 10%. Although it appears not to be affecting export competitiveness, it is still uncomfortable for locals. Second, the building of Hong Kong's new airport, with its already huge cost-overrun, and vocal demands for further democracy before 1997, are bound to cause friction with China. Finally, the power struggle in China to succeed Mr Deng will surely intensify in 1993. So expect volatility along with that prosperity—and a hard time for the governor, Chris Patten.

The economy of **Taiwan** has been picking up speed since 1990 and should grow between 7% and 8% during 1993. It remains a well-run and fundamentally sound economy. With a low level of underlying inflation, a current-account surplus of around $10 billion a year, and the highest level of foreign-exchange reserves in the world—over $80 billion—next year's main threat is too much bubble in the economy. The central bank is doing all it can to prevent the stockmarket from taking off again. Interest rates will be kept higher than they need be and as a result the currency will stay strong, forcing exporters to upgrade their products. Next year the government's huge $300 billion six-year development plan will start in earnest. This will boost domestic capital formation as well as improve Taiwan's inadequate infrastructure, by far the worst amongst the dragons.

Political relations with the mainland, which are of vital importance to the island, will improve yet further in 1993. Expect direct flights in the near future. Ever closer economic and political contacts will weaken the position of the pro-independence Democratic Progressive Party. The Kuomintang, which has been in power since the founding of the state, has been gradually extending political freedom and, as in much of the rest of Asia, this seems satisfactory to a people who have prospered under single-party rule.

The presidential election in **South Korea** should reveal that the people of the "Land of the Morning Calm" are also content with a continuation of one-party rule. The economy should grow by around 8% in 1993 but, in contrast to Taiwan, high inflation and a large current-account deficit will persist. The central bank is hampered by an archaic financial system and a powerful, pro-growth Ministry of Finance. The new governor of the Bank of Korea, Cho Soon, will talk tough. He will need to push through further interest-rate deregulation in 1993, and to dismantle the credit-allocation system. This bodes well for a rebound in the stockmarket.

Singapore wins the prize for extreme pessimism. It has probably talked its growth rate down to below 5% during 1992. A combination of declining productivity, weak export performance and the rebound in Hong Kong's fortunes has led to a crisis of confidence. As a result Singaporeans have stopped spending or borrowing, despite lending rates as low as 5%. The national savings rate has also risen towards 50%, helped by a huge public-sector surplus equivalent to 15% of GDP. Export performance will improve in 1993. The government may also decide to reduce its surplus by lowering provident fund contributions.

1993 could be the year when **Thailand** is recognised as the fifth little dragon. The tragic events of May 1992 will turn out to be a watershed for both Thai politics and economics. The military may have been stripped at last of its ability to dominate the political process. Thailand's average growth has been 10% a year for the five years prior to the 1992 hiccough. It might be that again in 1993.

Australia's young men

Paul Kelly

By early next year, with a bitter general election behind it, Australia will be in the mood to break out of its long recession. Once again it will try what it has failed in the past: to open its economy to the world, despite the fact that it is located outside any natural trading block and has little to trade except commodities. Though ambitions will spring anew, troublesome old facts will remain—an accumulated foreign debt of A$150 billion ($107 billion) not least among them.

The federal election will be dominated by the shadow of the recession. The early 1990s has seen a shakeout in finance and banks, the collapse and humiliation of Australia's high-flying entrepreneurs—with America's Cup hero Alan Bond spending a brief period in jail—and a scepticism towards political leaders and the mainstream parties.

But it is political events which will determine the direction in the coming year. In the election, expected around March 1993, Labor will attempt to win its fifth successive election, after being only narrowly re-elected at both the last two polls in 1987 and 1990.

This election will be a deeply personal contest between two young leaders: the prime minister, Paul Keating, 48, a political veteran who was the architect of economic policy during the 1980s, and the liberal leader, John Hewson, 45, an academic economist and political novice who became leader of Australia's main conservative party in 1990.

The backdrop to the election is an unemployment rate that recently topped 11% and will still be above 10% on polling day. The government predicts growth of 3% in the 1992-93 fiscal year and an unemployment rate falling to 10% by mid-1993. But the combination of low commodity prices, corporate strategies of debt retirement, the transition towards low inflation and the collapse in property prices all point to a slow recovery. For Mr Keating the political and economic cycles

Keating has his work cut out

are out of kilter. Mr Hewson, therefore, looks the favourite.

While the two men are ferocious opponents, the overlap in their backgrounds as well as their prescriptions for Australia is significant. Both hail from Sydney's sprawling working-class western suburbs. Both are self-made men, intellectually arrogant, economically sophisticated and politically ruthless.

Mr Keating, a pile driver of a politician, is shaped by Labor politics, the Catholic church and an entrepreneurial instinct. He left school at 15, entered federal parliament at 25, became a minister at 31. He deposed Bob Hawke in a party coup to become prime minister.

Mr Hewson is an outsider from the old Liberal Party establishment, for which he has a contempt. He has spent much of the past 20 years in a frenetic mixture of careers—economics professor, former Liberal-government adviser and merchant banker. He is a product of Australia's financial deregulation—which Mr Keating pioneered in 1983 and which Mr Hewson championed.

Mr Hewson is running for office as a free-market purist influenced by his study of economics and his conviction that the previous Liberal government of Malcolm Fraser failed Australia. He has closed the circle on an economic agenda which turns the Liberals from a party of the status quo into a party of free-market radicalism. He is pledged to lower income tax, less regulation and a massive privatisation programme (including the sale of Telecom, the largest public authority). He would change the charter of the central bank to ensure that monetary policy is conducted with the overriding objective of price stability. There would be major cuts in government spending. Mr Keating will have an uphill task in warning voters that Mr Hewson will wreck the economy when Labor has just presided over the longest downturn for 60 years.

The keys to progress in 1993 lie in ending Australia's century-long commitment to industrial protection. There is bipartisan agreement between Labor and Liberal that protection must be substantially cut during the 1990s.

As long as lower protection remains a bipartisan cause, then the much-heralded change in Australia's industrial relations looks likely to happen. At last an end is in sight for that unique and outdated Australian invention—centralised-wage bargaining. The real story of Australian politics in 1993, which neither side would admit, is the determination of both men to follow an economic philosophy which the public dislikes. It'll do Australia nothing but good.

Paul Kelly: editor-in-chief of the *Australian*.

"More flights. More destinations. Faster transfers."

"So KLM's the choice for choice."

KLM

World timetable

- 997 schedule improvements
- 30% more flights
- faster transfers
- 350 intra European connections
- 7 new destinations

Choice is the keynote of a major rescheduling of KLM's world-wide timetable. Aiming to offer you greater travelling flexibility and more convenience than ever before. Just look at the advantages:

30% More flights plus an increasing number of non-stop flights to major intercontinental destinations.

Faster transfers: within Europe and in connection with our Intercontinental flights.

More convenient arrival and departure times: more early morning and late evening flights between all major European centres and Amsterdam.

More intra-European connections: improved travel efficiency throughout Europe via its best airport. Amsterdam Schiphol.

Seven new destinations: services to Bogotá, Cape Town, Sana'a, Calcutta, Bombay, Kiev and Billund.

Get your copy of our new world-wide timetable from your local KLM office or travel agent today. And discover the choice of the travelling public.

Test us, try us, fly us.

The Reliable Airline

KLM
Royal Dutch Airlines

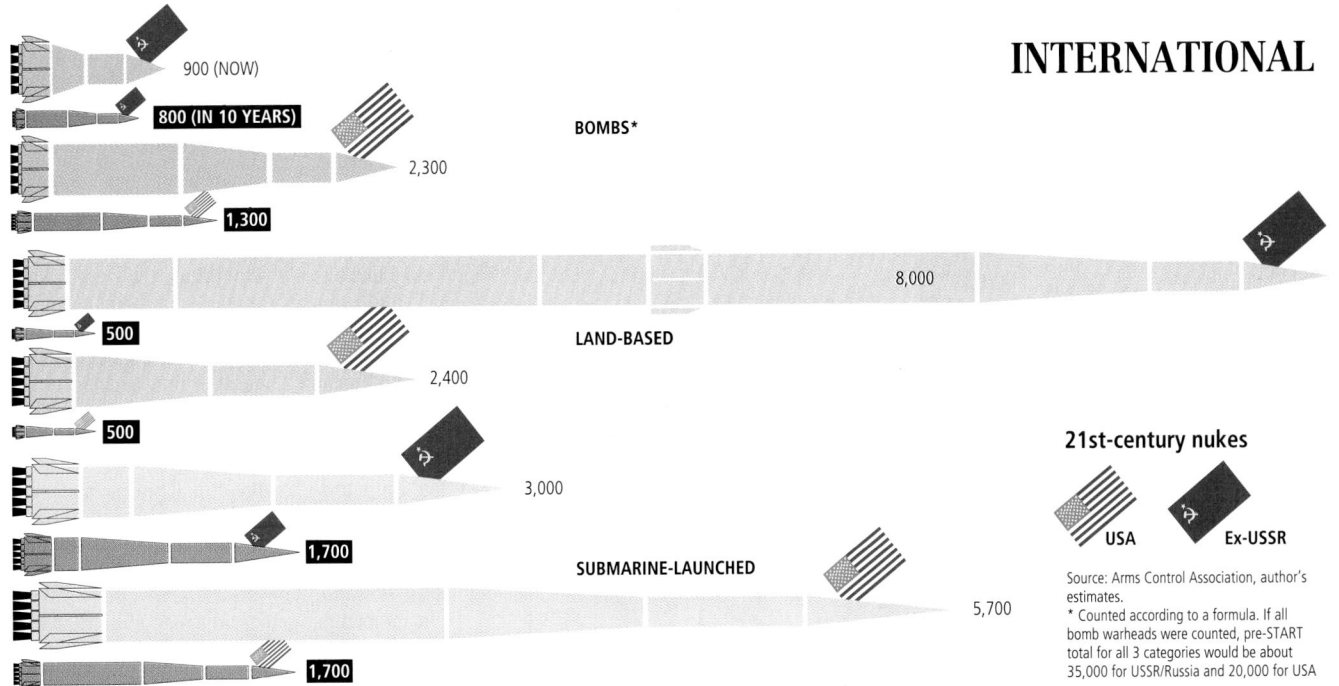

BOMBS*

900 (NOW)

800 (IN 10 YEARS)

2,300

1,300

LAND-BASED

8,000

500

2,400

500

3,000

SUBMARINE-LAUNCHED

1,700

5,700

1,700

21st-century nukes

USA   Ex-USSR

Source: Arms Control Association, author's estimates.
* Counted according to a formula. If all bomb warheads were counted, pre-START total for all 3 categories would be about 35,000 for USSR/Russia and 20,000 for USA

Danger: warheads being dismantled

Frank von Hippel

From next year the United States and the former Soviet Union will begin in earnest to dismantle almost 50,000 nuclear warheads. The programme will last a decade. It will release about 1mkg of uranium and 200,000kg of plutonium. The way in which the warheads are taken apart, and the subsequent storage, safety and use of the material, are all-important to the safety of everyone.

Getting out of the age of nuclear weapons may be as dangerous as getting into it. So massive an operation involving nuclear warheads and materials brings with it many dangers. Most importantly, inadequate international policing may allow the material to fall into the wrong hands. One of the West's most important technical challenges in 1993 is to see that these retired Soviet warheads and their fissile components are held under stringent control.

The nuclear industry itself is, paradoxically, likely to be most immediately hurt by the programme. The uranium released from the disarmed weapons will contain enough U^{235} to fuel the world's power reactors for about three years and will therefore help to keep world prices for natural uranium and uranium-enrichment work at their current all-time lows. And the world's nuclear fuel reprocessing industry, which has already separated

Frank von Hippel: physicist and professor of Public and International Affairs, Center for Energy and Environmental Studies, Princeton University.

more civilian plutonium than the nuclear-power industry is prepared to absorb, will be hastened towards its demise. With so much plutonium around, who needs a reprocessing industry?

Siemens has offered to build a facility in Russia to mix weapons plutonium into reactor fuel. And Japan's Science and Technology Agency has proposed to help the Russians build a fast-neutron plutonium "burner". But both proposals assume large subsidies from the West and Japan—dramatising the fact that, unlike enriched uranium, separated plutonium has a negative economic value.

In 1993 the West will start to supply the equipment to dismantle and store the surplus warheads from the Commonwealth of Independent States. In America, the government is not willing to say that the fissile material taken from American warheads will never be used to make new ones. This weakens the ability of the West as a whole to get international controls on the fissile materials from dismantled ex-Soviet warheads. Russia has, however, offered America "joint control" over fissile materials in an underground storage facility that it hopes to build near Tomsk with American financing.

How it's done

Dismantling starts at the military sites where the warheads are deployed. They have to be disabled on the spot before being packed for transport to central mili-

tary storage sites. There they will stay, perhaps for years, waiting their turn to go to the dismantlement factory. The United States has only one such plant, PANTEX, near Amarillo, Texas, which can take about 2,000 warheads a year. Russia has four such facilities with a combined capacity of 6,000 warheads a year. (Russia has about twice as many warheads to dismantle.)

To dismantle most warheads the fission "primary" explosive must first be separated from the thermonuclear "secondary" explosive. Then, in a special bunker, the high-explosive implosion system is painstakingly removed from around the plutonium-containing "pit".

In the United States, since the Rocky Flats plutonium-processing plant outside Denver has been shut down with safety problems, these " pits" will be accumulated in the bunkers at PANTEX. The thermonuclear "secondaries", which contain most of the highly-enriched uranium, will be sent to Oak Ridge, Tennessee, where the weapons uranium is separated out and put into storage.

In Russia, according to a proposal in June 1992 by the Russian Ministry of Atomic Energy, both fissile materials, uranium and plutonium, are to be reduced to standardised small cylinders of metal containing 4-5kg of plutonium or 10kg of weapons uranium. These will be placed in sealed containers filled with inert argon and then stored all together in

No more excuses

Frank von Hippel

Next year is likely to see the collapse of the nuclear reprocessing industry across the world. And the world will be a safer and cleaner place as a result. The collapse will come, as these things do, just at the moment that some countries will be completing major new reprocessing plants. France and Britain will both finish plants to recover plutonium, and Japan will begin one of its own. The dismantling of tens of thousands of American and ex-Soviet nuclear warheads means that the world will be awash with plutonium. With the attendant collapse of the world's plutonium-breeder reactor programmes, interest in plutonium as a fuel will evaporate almost completely.

For those concerned about non-proliferation, the demise of reprocessing cannot come too soon. Israel's nuclear

weapons are made with plutonium from a reprocessing plant built by a French company. India was helped in building its first plant by American and French companies. After the Indian nuclear test of 1974, only American intervention prevented the French from supplying reprocessing technology to Pakistan, South Korea and Taiwan. The military governments of Brazil and Argentina also sought reprocessing technology.

Intelligence services next year will be watching most closely what happens to the reprocessing plant now being built by North Korea. This plant has been explained away in propaganda as being the foundations of a future commercial nuclear industry. The collapse of the reprocessing industry across the world next year will put this troublesome myth finally to rest.

sia will agree to denature its weapons uranium in this way if the United States does not, remains to be seen.

With plutonium, however, there is an entirely different problem. It cannot be isotopically denatured. (It would be virtually impossible to produce the only effective dilutant isotope Pu^{238} in the quantities that would be required.) A few alternative proposals for getting rid of the plutonium have therefore been put forward. Some of these, such as using fast-neutron reactors to fission the plutonium, or shooting it into the sun, would be expensive and take a long time to develop. Others, such as mixing the plutonium into molten rock produced by underground nuclear explosions would probably be rejected by public opinion. The short-term options that appear most practical are to subsidise the use of plutonium in the fuel of current-generation light-water reactors or to mix the plutonium back into the high-level radioactive waste from which it was originally separated.

In the United States, at the Hanford and Savannah River military reprocessing plants, billion-dollar facilities are being built to turn huge tanks of liquid high-level radioactive waste into radioactive glass. Enough glassified waste is due to be produced to fix all American weapons plutonium (about 90 tonnes) at a concentration of about 0.4% by weight. There is already a waste "vitrification" plant in operation at the Russian reprocessing plant in the Urals near Chelyabinsk.

At the moment, the Russian Ministry of Atomic Energy dismisses as heresy any proposal to treat its weapons plutonium ("a national heritage") as waste. The ministry is still fighting to keep its plutonium breeder reactor programme alive, although even the French finally accepted in 1992 that this reactor will not be economic for decades, if ever. The American nuclear-weapons establishment also considers its stockpile of weapons plutonium as some sort of national heritage.

Though technical, these will become vital matters of public debate in 1993. And in 1995 the 150 countries which forswore nuclear weapons by signing the Non-Proliferation Treaty must renew their pledges. When the United States and the Soviet Union pressed these countries to sign that treaty 25 years ago, they promised in exchange to pursue nuclear disarmament in good faith.

If next year they start to dilute surplus weapons-grade uranium; dispose of surplus weapons plutonium; and accept the same safeguards on civilian nuclear fuel-cycles as countries which do not have the bomb, they will have shown that good faith indeed.

Tomsk. This single storage space would be designed to take all the fissile material in the ex-Soviet nuclear weapons. Altogether it could house 100,000 containers. Assuming the same 5:1 ratios of weapons uranium to plutonium as in the American arsenal, about 140,000kg of plutonium and 700,000kg of weapons uranium could be stored there. This would be consistent with published estimates of the cumulative Soviet production of these materials.

In August 1992 Russia agreed in principal to sell 500,000kg of weapons uranium to the United States over a period of 20 years for use as fuel. The former Soviet republics are hard-pressed for money and could realise about $10 billion from this sale. If the weapons uranium is diluted down to the low-enrichment levels used in power reactors immediately after its recovery, the size and cost of the high-security fissile-material storage facility

proposed for Tomsk could be considerably reduced. Its principal purpose would be to store plutonium.

Despite all the talk in Japan and Western Europe about the importance of using plutonium as a fuel, there is no interest among these countries in Russian plutonium; it is cheaper to fuel reactors with low-enriched uranium. If the nuclear-weapons material is not to be left sitting around indefinitely, other disposal plans will have to be devised.

In principle, the weapons uranium, which contains about 90% U^{235}, can be rendered unusable or "denatured" by diluting it with natural uranium (0.7% U^{235}) down to enrichment levels of only a few per cent. At enrichments below 20%, uranium cannot be used to build a nuclear explosive. Its only use as fuel is for power reactors. If the weapons uranium is to be committed to this purpose, it might as well be diluted early as late. Whether Rus-

Latin America prepares to sprint

Roland Dallas

Latin America's turn towards democracy and free-market economics has been widely and rightly celebrated. What will matter in 1993 is the depth of these reforms: will they be in place to take advantage of the next upswing in world growth? Or have they just been a few sops to get the IMF off Latin backs?

The pattern is now unmistakable. In election after election, free-marketeers win office. Privatisation starts. Ignoring the example of the "Giant of the North", budgets are frequently balanced. Inflation falls to still-imperfect but reasonable levels. Flight capital flies back. Exports flourish. Growth resumes.

The United States and the commercial banks have helped. Debt-reduction agreements between Latin governments and the banks under the "Brady Plan", named after the American secretary of the treasury, Nicholas Brady, have been made with Mexico, Bolivia, Uruguay, Venezuela, Argentina and Costa Rica. (Chile and Colombia do not need them.) It is an impressive achievement that will bear fruit in 1993.

As usual some countries will do better than others. Leading the pack will be **Chile**. President Patricio Aylwin and his talented finance minister, Alejandro Foxley, have followed the sober policies of ex-President Pinochet and his finance minister Hernan Buchi with notable success.

In 1992 GDP was expected to grow by 7% with inflation at 12% and the trade surplus predicted to reach $1 billion. Privatisation is almost complete. Providing Mr Aylwin and Mr Foxley do not veer off on a spending binge, Chile is on course for prosperity.

Mexico too is faring well, although it has weaknesses: the large trade deficit, jobs and inflation. An agreement to extend the American-Canadian North American Free Trade Area to Mexico was signed in 1992 and sent to the three parliaments for ratification.

The agreement seems certain to bring much foreign direct investment to Mexico as a low-wage base

Roland Dallas: editor of *The Economist*'s Foreign Report.

for penetrating the American and Canadian markets—and to provide a more open Mexican market for American and Canadian exports. Capital investment in Mexico is vital not only to create urgently needed jobs but also to cover Mexico's huge and growing trade deficits, caused by tariff cuts in recent years.

The other worry about Mexico is that its inflation of 16% at an annual rate in 1992 was much higher than America's 3%. Mexico steadily devalues the peso against the dollar but not fast enough, and the peso is becoming over-valued. Nonetheless, under President Carlos Salinas de Gortari and his respected finance minister, Pedro Aspe, Mexico's economy will grow stronger next year.

Another good bet, de-

spite a potentially over-valued currency, is **Argentina**, where President Carlos Menem and another exceptional Latin-American finance minister, Domingo Cavallo, have managed a dramatic economic turnaround. Expect high-speed privatisation to continue in 1993. Flight money is returning in large quantities to Buenos Aires from Miami and New York. GDP was growing at about 6% in 1992 and is likely to continue at this level in 1993.

The only trouble in 1992 was that inflation, although extremely low by Argentine standards at about 25%, was well above the American rate even though the peso was pegged to the dollar. Something will have to give.

Expect more rumblings from volatile **Venezuela**, where President Carlos Andres Perez is under fire from a legion of critics amid rumours of more attempted coups. Even in the unlikely chance that he is unseated, his successors will have little alternative to following his macro-economic policies as agreed with the IMF. These have turned round the economy, bringing down inflation from 36% in 1990 to a probable 25% in 1993. Expect steady GDP growth of about 4.5% in 1993.

Mr Perez still has a long way to go in privatising the giant state sector, which guzzles the country's oil revenues. More important, he is not doing enough to improve public services. Hence the discontent and the hot-headed coup talk.

Potentially prosperous **Colombia**, with its recently discovered huge oil reserves, is full of promise. It is developing free trade with Venezuela, with which it is forming a common market with a joint population of 53m. It is also opening up to foreign competition by slashing import tariffs. But inflation remains high at 18%. Drug money and flight capital are pouring back into the country. The trick will be to turn this sea of dollars into job-creating enterprises. The government will need to make peace with the remaining guerrilla movements and to hold on to the many drug-traffickers now in jail; it can afford no more escapes such as that of the drug chief Pablo Escobar, who breezed out of jail in 1992. Once the government does get a grip on the guerrillas and the traffickers, the economy will take off.

Bolivia, one of the first and most dramatic converts to economic reform, is keeping the faith despite many internal pressures. Inflation for the first six months of 1992 was an annual rate of only 10% compared with a brief peak of 23,000% in 1985. Slowly but steadily it is beginning to attract foreign investment and its economy is beginning to grow. **Ecuador**, which drifted under President

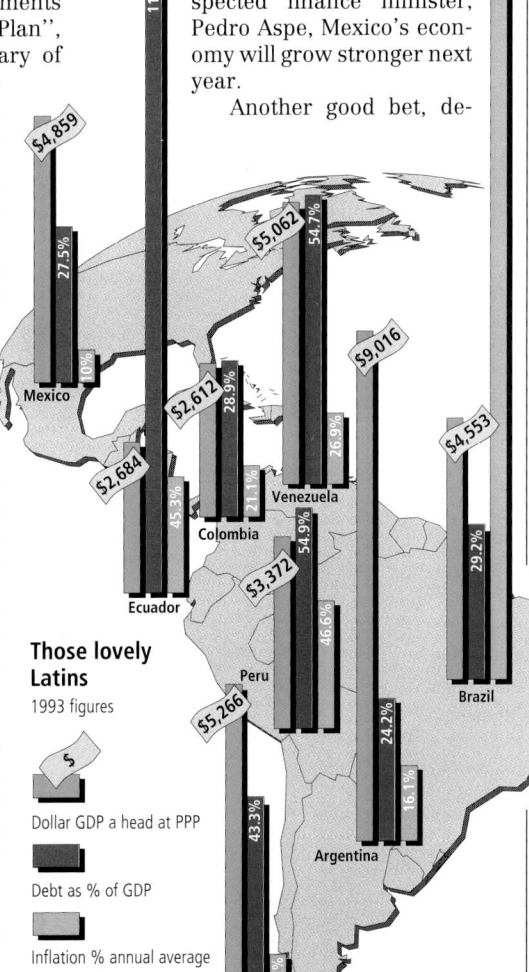

Those lovely Latins

1993 figures

Dollar GDP a head at PPP

Debt as % of GDP

Inflation % annual average

Source: EIU

Rodrigo Borja, will go for reform under President Sixto Duran, elected in 1992.

The most unexpected success story in the region in 1993 will be in Central America. The six countries of the isthmus, **Guatemala, El Salvador, Honduras, Nicaragua, Costa Rica** and **Panama**, are enjoying freedom, democracy, peace and economic growth for the first time since they broke away from Spain at the start of the 19th century. Although they are, with the exception of Costa Rica and Panama, still poor, they may well do better in 1993.

All six countries are applying sound money policies and have brought inflation rates down to manageable levels.

Guatemala and El Salvador are developing a common market which Honduras may join, with a joint population of 20m. The trio's economies may even "converge", EC-style, on inflation, interest rates and fiscal deficits as a proportion of GDP. Their privileged access to the United States' market, through Ronald Reagan's

North Africa's misery comes to Europe

Roland Dallas

North Africa, never quiet, will force itself more and more on the West's attention throughout 1993. Grabbing the emotional headlines will be the ever-growing number of boat people and their inevitable disasters: in the summer of this year at least 20 Moroccans were drowned while sailing across the Strait of Gibraltar to Spain. Nobody knows how many Moroccans reach Spain but the number is substantial and increasing. The Moroccans are not fleeing political oppression; their goal is simply a better life. More Moroccans, and their fellow North Africans from Algeria, Libya, Tunisia and Egypt, will try to make the crossing by boat or by air in 1993—adding to the hundreds of thousands already in Western Europe.

The reason for the exodus is economic. Morocco is undergoing painful reforms prescribed by the International Monetary Fund; Algeria's economy, apart from its oil and gas, is in ruins; Libya is feeling the pain of low world oil prices; Tunisia has never been able to attract enough investment to provide jobs for its people; and over-populated Egypt suffers from a swollen state sector, excessive subsidies and heavy dependence on foreign aid.

In this unhappy world, where the infidel West can be easily blamed for economic woes, Islamic fundamentalists thrive. They were active in 1992. They will be busier in 1993. The extremists who assassinated Algeria's President Mohammed Boudiaf have a list of targets for 1993 including Morocco's King Hassan. The men who killed the anti-Islamist writer Farag Foda in Cairo in 1992 also have the Nobel prize-winning author Naguib Mahfouz on their list. Many Islamist leaders are in jail: in 1993 they will be replaced by younger, tougher men.

In Morocco King Hassan has seen off the Islamists so far by saying he is a descendant of the Prophet Muhammad and describing himself as "Commander of the Faithful". He has built a giant mosque in Casablanca. But the trade unions which for decades co-operated with him no longer do so. If the economy does not improve, expect trouble. While telling Moroccans to

tighten their belts, the king is sensibly renovating his French chateau at Tournan-en-Brie.

Algeria's discredited regime is certain to run into trouble next year. President Boudiaf was ready to crush the Islamic Salvation Front; his successor, Ali Kafi, is not as tough.

In Tunisia the leading Islamists from Ennadha (the awakening) were tried and jailed for crimes against the state in 1992. President Zine bin Abidine Ben Ali says he wants to foster multi-party democracy. But he declines to extend this policy to Ennadha. Ben Ali is in control. But his regime looks vulnerable.

So too does Muammar Qaddafi's in Libya. Libya's isolation over the bombing of a Pan Am plane, which exploded over Scotland, has led to internal debates and public criticism of "The Leader". Mr Qaddafi's hold on power has begun to look weak.

In Egypt, only an assassin's bullet

appears likely to budge President Husni Mubarak from power. But that may be exactly what the country's fundamentalists have in mind, as they did for the late President Anwar Sadat. Their numbers are growing. Those in the south, at Asyut, receive smuggled arms and ammunition, as well as encouragement and possibly training, from Islamist-run Sudan. The Islamists will focus on three targets in 1993: the police; the Coptic Christians (6m out of Egypt's population of 58m); and intellectuals suspected of having doubts about Islam.

The rulers of North Africa have their wits about them and may continue to keep the lid on the Islamists in 1993. But this is far from certain. Islamist turmoil, the population explosion and an accelerated economic decline could be a fatal mixture. In any event expect more North African emigrants knocking on the doors of Western Europe.

Boat people at work

Caribbean Basin Initiative, plus the modest internal market, may well attract foreign investors next year. Nicaragua faces an uncertain future because the country is still dominated in part by the Sandinists. Costa Rica and Panama, which look down their noses at the rest of Central America, will pursue special trade and aid deals direct with the United States.

Basket cases

The outlook is shaky for **Brazil**, Latin America's biggest and most populous country. In mid-1992 inflation was running at roughly 20-25% a month.

Fernando Collor, suspended from office in September 1992 on charges of corruption, faced impeachment. His vice-president, the undynamic Itamar Franco, took over and threw the business community into gloom by picking a tax lawyer for the key job of finance minister. Brazil is, however, a resilient country.

Privatisation is slowly under way. Brazil still manages a tidy trade surplus and to stay on good terms with its creditors. All this will continue, more or less, in 1993. But how much longer the traditionally easy-going Brazilian poor will continue to put up with living under incompetent government in a blatantly unjust society is anybody's guess.

However bad Brazil looks, **Peru** is much worse. Ravaged by poverty, grotesque misgovernment and the savagery of Maoist guerrillas, it seems almost beyond the reach of traditional economic and political remedies. President Alberto Fujimori, having closed down Congress and chosen to rule by himself, claims to be aiming for the impossible: to eradicate corruption, destroy the guerrillas and drug-traffickers, privatise state enterprises and restore business confidence.

It makes sense. "El Chino", as Peruvians call their ethnic-Japanese president, is tough and single-minded. He listens to the advice of Chile's hard-boiled Mr Buchi. Peru has enough oil and minerals to be the basis of a small but sound economy—if they are exploited efficiently. In 1992 the leader of the Shining Path guerrillas, Abimael Guzman, and members of his executive committee were arrested. This was Peru's best news in years.

As always, **Haiti** is the poorest country. Having ousted the elected priest-president, Jean-Bertrand Aristide, because he implied in a speech his approval of the "necklacing" murders of his opponents, the army replaced him with an able ex-World Banker, Marc Bazin, as prime minister. Democrats in the hemisphere voted for sanctions. Attempts to work out a compromise seem doomed to continue to fail. Meanwhile Haiti will get poorer.

The blue hats
United Nations peace-keeping forces
Annual cost

Balkans 14,370 people 12 dead $607m

Cyprus 2,158 soldiers 158 dead $31m

Jerusalem 300 soldiers 28 dead $31m

Lebanon 5,758 soldiers 185 dead $157m

Golan Heights 1,325 soldiers 30 dead $43m

Iraq/Kuwait 500 people $67m

Kashmir 39 soldiers 6 dead $5m

Western Sahara 375 people $59m

Somalia 550 people $23m

Angola 840 people $110m

Cambodia 18,000 people $1,900m

San Salvador 1,149 people $58.9m

Source: UN

When should we intervene?

Roland Dallas

Unpredictable conflicts are likely to erupt in 1993, especially in Eastern Europe, the Middle East and Africa. The world will start to deal with them in new and changing ways.

For decades the world community, working through the United Nations (UN), operated by consent. It has acted as peacekeeper with the consent of two warring parties, sending observers for ceasefires.

But during the cold war the UN rarely got that consent because each country in dispute usually belonged to one cold-war camp or the other. Now the UN will do more. And not only the UN. An ever-increasing number of international agencies are taking it on themselves to intervene in countries whether they are wanted or not.

The Security Council has the power, under Chapter Seven of the UN Charter, to use both force and trade sanctions. It authorised the intervention, unwanted by Saddam Hussein, to remove Iraqi forces from Kuwait. It has imposed sanctions against both Iraq and Libya.

The Council has obliged Iraq, against its wishes, to permit international inspections of its nuclear facilities and to keep clear of the Kurdish areas in the north of the country. It ordered Libya to hand over two men suspected of planting a bomb aboard the Pan Am airliner which blew up over Lockerbie, in Scotland, in 1988, and imposed sanctions. It has imposed sanctions against Serbia.

Getting a taste for this sort of thing, the secretary-general, Boutros Boutros-Ghali, has proposed that a standby force of UN peacemakers should be specially trained to go into countries when they are needed. Since this would cost money, and many UN members are already deep in arrears, the idea is unlikely to fly. But it shows the way to other organisations that are just as ready to intervene, invited or not, in foreign countries. Among them:

The North Atlantic Treaty Organisation (NATO). In mid-1992 American-led NATO was helping to co-ordinate the international intervention to protect food convoys trying to reach Sarajevo, the capital of Bosnia & Hercegovina, and to organise the arrival of western warships off the Bosnian and Serbian coast.

The European Community (EC). The EC is ready to intervene very cautiously. Its intervention in Yugoslavia was for months through mediators, first Lord

Carrington and later Lord Owen, and aid convoys.

The Western European Union (WEU). This ten-member organisation, which France wants to become the military arm of the EC, helped co-ordinate military operations in the Adriatic. The United States and Britain are not keen on the WEU because it would marginalise the Americans.

The Conference on Security and Co-operation in Europe (CSCE). This organisation, including the United States, Russia and most countries in-between, is particularly interested in preventing disputes in Eastern Europe turning to violence. It can be expected to co-ordinate peacemaking or peacekeeping if ethnic trouble erupts, for example, between Hungary and Romania.

Most European peacemaking inter-ventions will be carried out by one or more of these three. But none will be dominant. The result: decisions to intervene militarily will be taken, if they are taken at all, by the Security Council.

Expect other forms of intervention. The UN's **Commission on Human Rights** sends observers to investigate violations of human rights. The commission will become more vigorous in 1993. In 1992 it was (for the first, belated, time) critical of Cuba. In August 1992 it was convened to discuss human-rights violations by the Serbs in Bosnia.

The **High Commissioner for Refugees**, Sadako Ogata of Japan, is strapped for cash and trying to handle too many disasters around the world. But she has a role as an intervener in disputes. She is active, for example, in ex-Yugoslavia.

Western aid donors who meet under the aegis of the **World Bank** as consultative groups for various countries, suspended new aid to Kenya and Malawi in 1992 until their respect for human rights (as well as their handling of foreign aid) improves. Expect more of the same next year. Third-world dictators should start worrying.

The **International Monetary Fund (IMF)** already plays a decisive role in the economies of Eastern Europe, Latin America and Africa. Russia's economic programme in 1993 depends on the IMF. As other independent republics of the ex-Soviet Union evolve their own economic policies, they too will depend on the IMF. The Fund will not intervene. But its insistence on getting its policies in place before handing out loans to them amounts to the same thing. With so many bossy forces for good about, who dares do wrong?

Next year's losers

Will 1993 be the year for Iraq's **President Saddam Hussein** to fall from the absolute power he has held in Baghdad since 1979? United Nations sanctions in 1992 were making life increasingly difficult for Iraqis, although some supplies were arriving from neighbouring Jordan. Slowly, much more so than expected, spare parts are becoming unavailable and production lines and public services are coming to a halt or working below standard.

An attempted military uprising took place in July 1992 but was put down by troops loyal to the Iraqi dictator. As the situation deteriorates, more such attempts are inevitable—and Mr Saddam knows it. Expect displays of brutality and ruthlessness to scare his generals into submission. To a lone gunman with a martyr complex, however, such displays will be a spur to action.

The big question in Cuba, and in Miami, is how long the "old man", **President Fidel Castro**, can last. Mr Castro, who has bossed Cuba without a free election since 1959, has everything going against him—except the security police. His position is dire. Rationing is severe. Food is in short supply. Electricity supplies are cut daily. Buses and trains are few and far between because there is not enough petrol and there are no spare parts. Cuba has no foreign-exchange reserves. Its sugar harvest was poor and could no longer be sold to the Russians at subsidised prices. At the slumping world price of 9 American cents per lb, Cuba swapped its sugar for Chinese bicycles.

Nonetheless Mr Castro has survived. Why? Because the ministry of the interior and its security police strike fear into the population. Dissidents are mostly in jail. Cubans have virtually no experience of democracy. For generations they lived under Spanish colonial rule, then American rule and finally the dictatorships of Batista and Castro. The experience has made them docile.

In Africa, the end is drawing in for **President-for-life Kamuzu Banda** of Malawi. The octogenarian Dr Banda has ruled Malawi with an iron rod since he returned home from a medical practice in Britain in 1956. The election of a one-party puppet parliament in 1992 fooled nobody. Western aid to Malawi is being frozen until the country displays a commitment to multi-party democracy. Exiled opposition leaders who have returned have been jailed, provoking international protests. Expect more demonstrations against Dr Banda in 1993.

Three heads for rolling

We have what it takes. Thousands of trucks, hundreds of planes. And computers to keep track of them all and the parcels they carry.

But we also know that this is not enough. So, wherever your shipment is

After 80 years in the package delivery business, the greatest compliment you can give UPS is to describe us as totally predictable.

going, there is an important, additional benefit to using UPS. Predictability. In other words, it won't simply arrive, it'll arrive when we say it will.

Because we know there's something else that is totally predictable: every improvement in transportation efficiency directly influences your company's profitability.

United Parcel Service
As sure as taking it there yourself.

Arabian squabbles

Paul Barker

The Arabian peninsular states need money in 1993. Their governments alone will be looking for more than $75 billion in revenue. Where will it come from? Not all from the oil market. The world oil price is unlikely to budge much above an average $21 a barrel next year—unless there is another conflict in the region. War noises might put the price of oil up but they would disrupt the stability needed to encourage investment.

There may well be such noises in 1993, most linked to territorial disputes. Take for instance the still unresolved problem of Iraq's claim on Kuwait. This will be aggravated by the decision of the UN special commission to grant Kuwait some of what was previously accepted as Iraqi territory rather than the other way round. The proposed new border will merely perpetuate Iraq's sense of grievance at not having a more assured access to the sea.

Even more pressing for the states of the Gulf Co-operation Council (GCC)—Saudi Arabia, Kuwait, Bahrain, Qatar, the UAE and Oman—are two other border problems, both of which could flare up early in 1993.

• The UAE and Iran both claim possession of the strategic Gulf islands of Abu Musa, and the Greater and Lesser Tumbs. In the summer of 1992 Iran unilaterally tore up a 1971 agreement which allowed both countries to use Abu Musa and shared the revenues from the surrounding oil field between Iran and Sharjah. Quiet diplomacy has done nothing to resolve the dispute.

Next year it may escalate as some gulf states and their western protectors use the issue to halt Iran's new regional assertiveness and military build-up.

• The dispute over the Saudi-Yemeni border has come to a head as the periodic renewal of the 1934 Taif agreement fell due in September 1992. (This agreement ceded the south-western peninsular regions of Najran, Azir and Jizan to Saudi Arabia.)

Paul Barker: principal of the London-based economic and banking consultancy, Paul Barker Associates.

With relations between the two countries already soured by the two Yemens' decision to unite and by the subsequent stance of the unified country on the Gulf war, Saudi Arabia exacerbated tensions in 1992 by holding military manoeuvres along the border. It has also made claims on Yemeni oil concessions.

The gulf states seldom see eye-to-eye on these "common" external disputes. There will be widely differing views on how to respond to the growing power of Iran. And individual states will not agree on how or whether to get back on terms with Iraq and Saddam Hussein. It is by no

Whose border is it anyhow?

means certain that the majority of them would back Saudi Arabia if its dispute with Yemen escalates. And they have their own internal border disputes to resolve as well.

Their greatest difference next year will be over the pace of political reform. Since the Gulf war widespread pressure has built up for democracy in the region. In 1992 the Saudis established a centralised consultative council and a series of regional consultative bodies. They have made it abundantly clear that they do not want to move further or faster towards more open government. So they look askance at other gulf states that are going further towards democracy.

Thus they did not like the October

1992 Kuwaiti parliamentary elections, even though these were almost an American precondition of the restoration of the monarchy in Kuwait after its liberation from Iraq. They did not like the Omani decision to televise meetings of their consultative council, at which ministers had to defend their record. And they hate the idea of Yemeni general elections in which a proclaimed socialist party wins a sizeable portion of the votes and in which women are enfranchised.

On the economic front, expect progress during 1993 towards a formal GCC customs union. Nonetheless, different governments will go it alone in their efforts to create economic growth and jobs. There will be tax holidays, customs exemptions, and duty-free zones. No problem there. But in this rivalry there is the risk of one major mistake: ever-growing subsidies to lure investors. These will distort the market. They will put a strain on expenditure just when spending should be cut. It already threatens to get out of hand in 1993 with:
• Increased military budgets.
• New capital-investment in power and water-capacity. (This is necessary because of population growth. But it will be made far greater by the subsidies that encourage wastage.)
• Expansion of the oil industry.
• An ever-upward trend in civil-service salaries.

With the central reserves of many of the Gulf states now depleted, there will be substantial budget deficits clocked up in 1993. In the case of Saudi Arabia, for instance, this will run at 5% of GDP. This sum will be financed largely by domestic savings. Private lending may be squeezed out and unproductive debt servicing will start to take up too large a share of future government budgets.

Next year will, therefore, see further talk of privatisations, of reducing the social-welfare net and of encouraging foreign borrowing if necessary. All of these would lessen the immediate strains.

In all this, there will be barely a whisper of increased taxes—either direct or indirect, especially on Gulf nationals. The thought of taxing anything other than oil has remained unpalatable. But the gulf states may learn in 1993 to acquire a taste for much that was previously unpalatable.

Western Europe

AUSTRIA

GDP: Sch2.15trn; $190bn
GDP per head: $23,800
Population: 7.7m; % change 0.4
GDP growth: 1992 2.2%; 1993 2.6%
Inflation: 1992 3.8%; 1993 3.2%

• In harmonising legislation with the EC, Franz Vranitzky's coalition will prove itself more European than many of the Europeans. It has already adopted more directives necessary for the single market than some EC countries. Austrian neutrality will be controversial. Austrian bureaucracy will remain among the most bloated in Europe.

• Expect a long-overdue reorganisation of government departments. Transport should get its own ministry and some departments will be abolished.

To watch
Immigration from Eastern Europe will continue to create problems with education and housing. Housing shortages already constrain mobility. Tighter limits on immigration could be imposed.

BELGIUM

GDP: Bfr7.56trn; $225bn
GDP per head: $22,600
Population: 10m; % change 0.2
GDP growth: 1992 1.6%; 1993 2%
Inflation: 1992 2.8%; 1993 3%

• The deficit target of 5.2% of GDP for the 1993 budget is seen as soft. Opposition Liberals will call for tougher austerity measures to bring the deficit closer to the 3% required under the Maastricht treaty. The national debt, a worrying 130% of GDP, will also have to be reduced next year.

• The regional question brought down the last government. It will remain the biggest threat to the present one. The need to improve the fiscal situation of the Walloon regions will anger the Flemish. A law for regional direct elections will need a two-thirds majority but the Liberals will object to anything that makes it look as if Belgium is not a country. Perish the thought.

All figures are 1993 forecasts unless otherwise indicated. 1992 figures are estimates.
Inflation: year-on-year annual average.
Dollar conversion rates: 1993 forecasts.
Source: except where indicated

E·I·U
The Economist
Intelligence Unit
incorporating
BUSINESS INTERNATIONAL

DENMARK

GDP: Dkr910bn; $145bn
GDP per head: $28,200
Population: 5.2m; % change 0.1
GDP growth: 1992 1.8%; 1993 2%
Inflation: 1992 2.6%; 1993 2.6%

• Political scandals and a failure to muster enough support for much of its legislative programme has damaged Poul Schlüter's coalition government. The Maastricht referendum holed it below the waterline. A new government will be in place well before the scheduled December 1994 elections.

• Danish monetary policy has suffered a severe setback with the rejection of EMU. Expect a period of currency instability. International investors will look elsewhere.

• The shift of resources from the public to the private sector will continue. There will be a decline in the accustomed standards of service in areas like transport, health and education.

FINLAND

GDP: Fmk540bn; $105bn
GDP per head: $21,000
Population: 5m; % change 0.3
GDP growth: 1992 -1.5%; 1993 1.5%
Inflation: 1992 3.1%; 1993 4%

• Finnish politicians will look longingly to EC membership as Finland seeks to reorient itself westwards and restore equilibrium to its fragile economy.

• Emergency measures will cut public spending by Fmk10bn in 1993 and reduce borrowing.

• Falling real incomes, unemployment and high interest rates will keep consumer spending growth to a minimum.

Relative labour costs %

FRANCE

GDP: FFr7.46trn; $1.36trn
GDP per head: $23,900
Population: 56.9m; % change 0.4
GDP growth: 1992 1.8%; 1993 1.9%
Inflation: 1992 2.9%; 1993 2.8%

• The Socialists face defeat in the legislative elections in March. Unemployment and dislike of the 11-year status quo will count against them. The centre right should win the legislature. The right's hopes for the presidency in 1995 will be complicated by the squabbling of old foes Jacques Chirac and Valéry Giscard d'Estaing. Where will the new faces come from?

• France is exceptionally well placed to fulfil the convergence criteria of the Maastricht treaty with inflation below 3%. But it will be difficult to keep the budget deficit within FFr165bn, which is the government's target for 1993. This figure is based on an over-optimistic estimate of 2.6% growth in 1993.

• Partial privatisation will be stepped up, but the state will keep at least 51% of all state-owned companies until after the election. Expect more privatisation if the centre right UPF alliance wins.

GERMANY

GDP: DM3.16trn; $1.95trn
GDP per head: $24,120
Population: 80.9m; % change 0.3
GDP growth: 1992 1.2%; 1993 1.8%
Inflation: 1992 4.6%; 1993 4%

• There are no elections in 1993 and Helmut Kohl will take the opportunity to get painful policies out of the way.

• Bonn will not want to cut spending in the east, as this would send the chancellor's popularity down yet another rung and mean more migration westwards. Employment prospects could brighten a little in the east in 1993 in a modest investment-led recovery. Wage increases ahead of productivity improvements in eastern Germany will put more pressure on Bonn to increase capital spending.

• The Treuhand will finish its work of privatising eastern Germany's industries.

• In the face of government reluctance to attack the budget deficit, the burden will remain on the Bundesbank to set monetary policy to counter the inflationary effects of this.

GREECE

GDP: Dr17.12trn; $80bn
GDP per head: $7,600
Population: 10.4m; % change 0.6
GDP growth: 1992 1.7%; 1993 2.1%
Inflation: 1992 16%; 1993 10.5%

• Austerity policies as part of the Maastricht convergence programme will be a part of growing government unpopularity. It will have to work hard to keep the privatisation programme on track.

• EC cash for the Greek infrastructure will stimulate a modest pick-up in growth.

• Greeks will not want to compromise on the Macedonian question. This, together with Greece's objections to EC aid to Turkey and the insistence on keeping in with Belgrade, will bring more reprimands from fellow EC countries.

REPUBLIC OF IRELAND

GDP: IR£31bn; $50bn
GDP per head: $14,700
Population: 3.5m; % change -0.2
GDP growth: 1992 2.2%; 1993 2.7%
Inflation: 1992 4%; 1993 4%

• Arguments between the coalition partners could mean an election before the scheduled date of June 1994. Economic policy will remain on much the same track.

• There will be problems for the public finances in 1993. A deal to defer public-sector pay rises until 1993 is storing up difficulties. VAT revenue will fall thanks to single market abolition of collection at the point of entry; commitments to tax cuts will mean more painful spending decisions in 1993 and 1994.

• The Irish recovery will gather strength in 1993. Having one of the highest unemployment rates in the EC will remain the main economic worry of the government.

• A slow realignment of Irish politics will continue. Pressure on the role of Fine Gael as the main opposition party will continue as the prominence of both the Labour Party and the Democratic Left continues to rise. These parties will be prepared to address old taboos like abortion and other social reforms with new urgency.

ITALY

GDP: L1,610trn; $1.17trn
GDP per head: $20,200
Population: 60m; % change 0.2
GDP growth: 1992 1.5%; 1993 1%
Inflation: 1992 5.5%; 1993 6%

• The continuing misfortunes of the lira and the risk of higher interest rates, together with the weakness of the domestic economy and the budget nightmare, will keep the Amato government focused on reform. Budget savings of up to L100trn will be needed in 1993.

• Privatisation in Italy would be the largest state sell-off in the EC. The state companies have assets of L70trn, 15% of non-agricultural jobs, 25% of fixed investment and two-thirds of the banking system.

• Referendum-backed changes in the pipeline include: reform of government intervention in the south; single-member constituencies in the senate; majority system for local elections; removal of political control over savings-bank appointments; transfer of central control over industry, tourism, health and agriculture to the regions.

Current-account balance $bn

-12.7	1990
-15.9	1991
-15	1992
-12.8	1993

NETHERLANDS

GDP: Fl600bn; $330bn
GDP per head: $21,400
Population: 15.2m; % change 0.4
GDP growth: 1992 1.2%; 1993 2.2%
Inflation: 1992 3.6%; 1993 3.8%

• Prime minister and Christian Democrat leader Ruud Lubbers will probably stand down after the Dutch go to the polls in September 1993. Support for the coalition is slipping, especially for the Labour Party. The all-important issue for next year is the overhaul of the welfare state.

• More Dutch companies will face hostile takeover bids from both inside and outside the Netherlands as the chill wind of Brussels (fanned by domestic shareholders) blows away Dutch protection practices. Competition commissars will also have price-fixing Dutch cartels in their sights.

NORWAY

GDP: Nkr770bn; $120bn
GDP per head: $28,200
Population: 4.3m; % change 0.4
GDP growth: 1992 2.2%; 1993 2.8%
Inflation: 1992 2.5%; 1993 3.4%

• Doubts about the EC will increase divisions over the issue in Norway, the most sceptical of the non-EC Nordic countries. Timing of the application to join will depend largely on the nature of the deal which the EC stitches up with the Danes. Interest rates will be kept high by the pegging of the krone to the ecu.

• General elections in September. Gro Harlem Brundtland's Labour Party should stay in power despite reduced support. Lost votes will go to small anti-EC parties rather than to the main opposition parties.

• Unions and employers will oppose attempts to loosen up the labour market.

To watch
Green clashes between government and industry. Penalties for all types of emission, corporate and consumer, will go up. Prime targets like aluminium and paper makers threaten to leave Norway for dirtier climes.

PORTUGAL

GDP: Esc12.24trn; $80bn
GDP per head: $7,600
Population: 10.5m; % change 0.3
GDP growth: 1992 2.5%; 1993 2.9%
Inflation: 1992 9%; 1993 7.8%

• Unpopular anti-inflationary measures will mean a swing away from the governing Social Democrats in the local government elections in 1993.

• Portugal is trying to maintain low unemployment while reducing inflation, controlling the balance of payments and maintaining growth. Unemployment will be the one to give next year.

SPAIN

GDP: Pt60trn; $540bn
GDP per head: $13,600
Population: 40m; % change 0.1
GDP growth: 1992 1.6%; 1993 1.3%
Inflation: 1992 6.4%; 1993 5.5%

• Elections are due by October 1993. The governing Socialists could bring them forward before spending cutbacks and EMU convergence policies dent their popularity further. Corruption scandals involving all the major parties will mean a low turn-out.

• To sell itself, Spain will spend more on training an under-qualified workforce. It will overhaul employment practices which lead to excessive turnover of temporary staff.

• A new pact with the regional governments will help control their spending which amounts to a sizeable part of the deficit.

GDP real % change

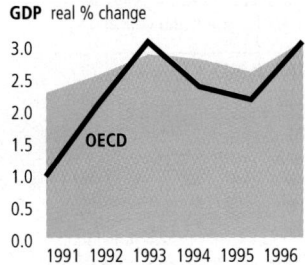

SWEDEN

GDP: SKr1,520trn; $260bn
GDP per head: $29,600
Population: 8.7m; % change 0.4
GDP growth: 1992 -1.0%; 1993 -0.3%
Inflation: 1992 2.4%; 1993 1.8%

• Prime minister Carl Bildt hopes that negotiations with the EC on the timing of Swedish entry will be over by the end of 1993. A referendum is pencilled in for early 1994.

• The cat's cradle of Sweden's wealth taxes will begin to be unravelled to encourage the growth of small businesses; sacred cows such as the collective wage-bargaining system are also set for the chop. Privatisation gets going, albeit slowly and with stringent controls over transfer of ownership.

To watch
Sweden will strengthen its commitment to the ten-country Council of Baltic States, which it will promote to its own people as a counterweight to Brussels.

SWITZERLAND

GDP: SFr360bn; $240bn
GDP per head: $35,500
Population: 6.8m; % change: -0.4
GDP growth: 1992 0.5%; 1993 2%
Inflation: 1992 4%; 1993 3.4%

• The Federal Council is likely to apply for full membership of the EC before the March referendum on membership of the free trade European Economic Area. Swiss ways which will suffer include light central government (the Council will want to be fully empowered to deal with Brussels); direct democracy (more decisions would be made by the EC and the Federal Council without reference to the citizens); and Swiss farming.

• Switzerland will move out of recession in 1993. Consumer spending and investment will increase but overall growth will pick up only slowly.

TURKEY

GDP: TL130trn; $130bn
GDP per head: $2,170
Population: 59.9m; % change 1.8
GDP growth: 1992 5.3%; 1993 5%
Inflation: 1992 70%; 1993 58%

• With wars and insurrections on or near all of its borders, Turkey will walk the diplomatic tightrope in 1993. It will build influence in former Soviet Central Asia and make capital out of the economic treaty it has signed with fellow Black Sea countries.

• The reform programme will remain hamstrung until the feud between President Ozal and Prime Minister Demirel ends. Mr Demirel could call an early election and insist on a trial of strength with the president.

To watch
Privatisation, going at a crawl up to now, will gather pace, especially in the food sector. The government will not tackle eagerly the biggest state loss-makers like the Hard Coal Corporation.

North America

UNITED KINGDOM

GDP: £640bn; $1trn
GDP per head: $17,300
Population: 57.9m; % change 0.3
GDP growth: 1992 -0.8%; 1993 1.3%
Inflation: 1992 4%; 1993 4.8%

• John Major's right-of-centre government will find its economic policy still heavily influenced by the Bundesbank. Any attempt to bring interest rates far below those of Germany would risk a further collapse in the value of sterling. If sterling stabilises at a competitive rate, a bashful return to the ERM is likely in 1993.

• Spending will be rigidly controlled. The budget deficit will be worryingly high but overall debt is sustainable.

• Expect another outcry as the council tax replaces the poll tax. Higher bills for the middle classes.

• The trade gap will widen throughout next year. There will be monthly horror stories in the press about it, but at least the recession will be over.

• Public services will remain the main field in which the government is criticised. The acceptance of free market thinking will grow.

Industrial production % annual change

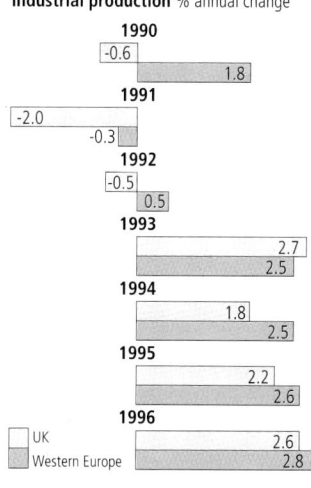

1990	
-0.6	1.8
1991	
-2.0	-0.3
1992	
-0.5	0.5
1993	
	2.7
	2.5
1994	
1.8	2.5
1995	
2.2	2.6
1996	
2.6	2.8

UK
Western Europe

CANADA

GDP: US$588bn
GDP per head: US$21,710
Population: 27m; % change 1.5
GDP growth: 1992 1.5%; 1993 3%
Inflation: 1992 1.6%; 1993 3%

• A federal election will probably take place in the summer. If the Liberals are to gain, they will be under pressure to become more pro-business by making more positive noises about free trade with the United States and Mexico, and recognising the need for tight controls on spending.

• The future of Canada's catch-all health service will be a major political issue as medical costs spiral and spending is squeezed. Expect all the provincial governments to watch health spending carefully in 1993.

• Canada will pull all its 7,000-odd troops out of Europe by the middle of the 1990s, further weakening defence ties between North America and Europe.

USA

GDP: $5.67trn
GDP per head: $22,520
Population: 251.8m; % change 0.6
GDP growth: 1992 1.7%; 1993 2.8%
Inflation: 1992 2.9%; 1993 3.5%

• The January intake in the House of Representatives will include up to 130 new members. They will on the whole be of better calibre than their predecessors. Expect more budget rumpus between Capitol Hill and the White House.

• Major corporations will lobby energetically for strong government intervention in healthcare to reduce their insurance costs. The administration and Congress will dither.

• New rules on how cross-border taxation is treated will benefit domestic companies and penalisè foreign ones.

Eastern Europe

THE BALTIC STATES

Estonia*
GDP:Rb29bn ; $968m
GDP per head: $613
Population: 1.58m
GDP growth: 1992 -20%; 1993 -5%
Inflation: 1992 500%; 1993 100%

Latvia*
GDP: Rb22.3bn; $744m
GDP per head: $279
Population: 2.66m
GDP growth: 1992 -25%; 1993 -10%
Inflation: 1992 900%; 1993 200%

Lithuania*
GDP: Rb29.9bn; $996m
GDP per head: $265
Population: 3.76m
GDP growth: 1992 -15%; 1993 -5%
Inflation: 1992 900%; 1993 100%

• Expect moves to ease second-class citizenship for Russians living in the Baltics (such as deprivation of the franchise) in return for withdrawal of the troops that the Russians claim are guaranteeing the safety of their people. There could be border tiffs around Pskov and St Petersburg.

• The state of the Baltic economies will remain dire. Output will be hurt by raw material and energy shortages, and will fall sharply, especially in Latvia. Trade with the EC will be hampered by a lack of hard currency and a lack of anything the EC wants to buy. There will be some invisibles earnings from transit trade through the Baltic ports eastwards.

• Total borrowing will reach $1.7bn over the 18 months to the end of 1993, most of it on very favourable terms from Nordic countries. Thanks to this, debt servicing should remain manageable.

Gross industrial product % change

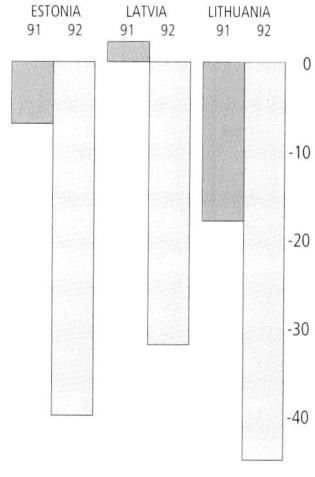

	ESTONIA	LATVIA	LITHUANIA	
	91 92	91 92	91 92	10
				0
				-10
				-20
				-30
				-40

BULGARIA

GDP: Lv285bn; $8.8bn
GDP per head: $1,021
Population: 8.6m; % change 0
GDP growth: 1992 -10%; 1993 -3.5%
Inflation: 1992 110%; 1993 70%

• 1993 will see a struggle for political and economic stabilisation. Destabilising political influences will include Turkish Bulgarians; two very influential trade unions which will want strikes; and aspiring King Simeon II.

• The privatisation programme will get under way: foreign bids willingly accepted. The target of completion by 1997 is over-optimistic. Liberalisation of trade will be hampered by the disastrous state of the domestic economy, which will mean import controls in the short term.

To watch
Strife in neighbouring Macedonia and Kosovo could embroil Bulgaria.

CZECH AND SLOVAK REPUBLICS

Czech republic
GDP: Kcs743bn; $26.6bn
GDP per head: $2,562
Population: 10.4m; % change 0
GDP growth: 1992 -3.7%; 1993 0.9%
Inflation: 1992 11%; 1993 14.3%

Slovakia
GDP: $10bn estimate
Population: 5.3m; % change 0.5
GDP growth: 1992 -5.8%; 1993 -4%
Inflation: 1992 11%; 1993 25%

• Slovakia will suffer more from the divorce between the two countries which is granted on January 1st. Its economy is far less diversified than that of the Czech republic and it will lose subsidies from Prague.

• In the Czech republic, the tax system will be overhauled at the beginning of the year to prop up falling revenues. At the same time, the second round of voucher privatisation will get under way. The much-abused voucher scheme will be supplemented by more traditional methods.

• The Czech republic will see more foreign capital and western technology and management skills. This, together with some easing of monetary policy, will bring a modest economic upturn which should speed up in 1994. Slovakia will get far less investment and will remain in the doldrums.

Asia Pacific

HUNGARY

GDP: Ft3.17trn; $40.2bn
GDP per head: $3,896
Population: 10.3m; % change -1
GDP growth: 1992 -2.2%; 1993 1.2%
Inflation: 1992 26%; 1993 15%

• Joseph Antall's government will soldier on through its full term into 1994, cushioned from its unpopularity by a constitution that makes it almost unassailable.

• Hungary will face the common problem of East European countries, balancing the need to appease the IMF with a tight stabilisation programme and the threat of mass unrest. Expediency will probably win the day.

• Privatisation (especially in the financial sector) will speed up, but will not reach the government's target of 50% by the end of 1993.

POLAND

GDP: Zl1.21trn; $63.7bn
GDP per head: $1,660
Population: 38.4m; % change 0.2
GDP growth: 1992 -1.5%; 1993 2.4%
Inflation: 1992 74.3%; 1993 39.1%

• President Lech Walesa has given strong backing to the new Suchochka government. Chances for political stability look high and Poland should be the first former communist country to return to growth (albeit with high inflation).

• Someone forgot to provide a stop-button in the Polish electoral system. There are 29 parties in the Sejm. A new electoral law will be passed before the next elections, likely in 1994.

• A deal will be reached with commercial creditors early next year which will ease the heavy invisibles deficit. After 1993, the current-account position should improve.

• Expect better telephones and motorways thanks to loans from the EBRD, IMF and World Bank.

ROMANIA

GDP: Lei6,858bn; $15.8bn
GDP per head: $680
Population: 23.2m; % change 0
GDP growth: 1992 -7%; 1993 -1.2%
Inflation: 1992 145%; 1993 80%

• Expect a year of political fragmentation and unstable government following Ion Iliescu's victory in the October 1992 election.

• The economy will begin to bottom out in 1993 as structural reforms make themselves felt and the rise in private-sector output counterbalances the fall in the state sector. Agriculture should recover slightly after a dreadful 1992.

• Nationalist pressure and public support will grow for closer ties and eventual unification with Moldova. This will not mean intervention in Moldova's war with its Russian minority.

RUSSIA

GDP: Rb48trn; $137.8bn
GDP per head: $929
Population: 149m; % change 0.7
GDP growth: 1992 -16.5%; 1993 -8%
Inflation: 1992 2,000%; 1993 750%

• Boris Yeltsin will face growing opposition from the Civic Union, headed by communist apparatchik Arkady Volsky and Russian nationalist Alexander Rutskoi. The Union's call for slower reform will become more popular as economic chaos continues throughout next year.

• Mr Yeltsin will need to reassure the West that reform is on track. Expect demands for quicker western assistance, up to now politically invisible in terms of its use in countering Mr Yeltsin's critics.

• If nationalists gain the upper hand in Moscow, expect intervention in disputes between Russians and local nationalities both in Russia itself and in other parts of the old USSR.

• Western companies will maintain their wait-and-see attitude towards investment. Political uncertainty, economic confusion and a legislative morass will hold them back for most of 1993. Oil and gas will be an exception.

UKRAINE*

GDP: Rb291.6bn; $9.7bn
GDP per head: $188
Population: 51.8m; % change
GDP growth: 1992 -23%; 1993 -15%
Inflation: 1992 2,000%; 1993 1,000%

• Relations with Russia will dominate every aspect of Ukrainian policy. The Crimea will be the main bone they will fight over. Division of the Black Sea Fleet has been postponed until 1994.

• President Leonid Kravchuk will be very popular as the strongman against Russia. This will distract from his difficulties in implementing economic reform through a hierarchy which is dominated by obstructive ex-communists.

• Ukraine will be busy building political and economic links with countries outside the old USSR. To the West, relations with Poland will be pursued; Ukraine will approach Iran to try to diversify its oil and gas supplies.

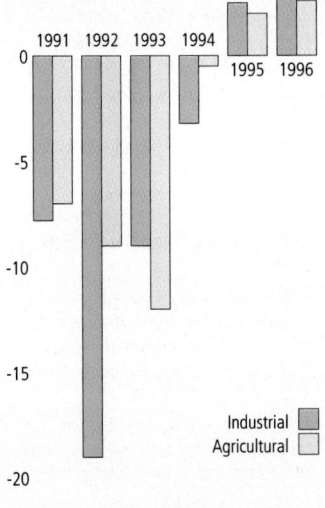

Economic Growth of former USSR
% change

| Industrial |
| Agricultural |

*GDP and GDP-per-head figures for marked countries are estimates based on proportions of 1991 GDP of the USSR, and on a rate of Rb1=$30.

AUSTRALIA

GDP: A$422bn; $308.7bn
GDP per head: $17,320
Population: 17.3m; % change 1.6
GDP growth: 1992 2%; 1993 3.4%
Inflation: 1992 2.4%; 1993 3.7%

• Arguments in the 1993 election campaign will be about the speed of reform. It should be close. Despite an emerging recovery, unemployment will not fall much before the election. To balance this, voters may see the aggressively reformist Liberal Party as being too business-centred.

• Short-term measures to kick-start the economy will include investment in infrastructure projects, but economic and investment recovery is unlikely to be swift and could fall back after 1993. An ever-fattening external debt and widening deficit will mean demand having to be held back.

CHINA

GDP: Rmb2.87trn; $475.9bn
GDP per head: $399
Population: 1.19bn; % change 1.4
GDP growth: 1992 13%; 1993 7%
Inflation: 1992 6.5%; 1993 10%

• Following the 14th Party Congress a consensus will emerge for reform which will show through in the appointment of a new batch of senior apparatchiks in March and April next year. The new standing committee of the Politbureau will resist further devolution. Old age and death will continue to deplete the ranks of the hardliners.

• The economy will start to overheat bringing associated raw materials shortages, transport and electricity problems and bottlenecks in the supply chain. Policies to slow growth will be seen from the middle of the year.

To watch
A baby boom will mean more demand for toys and baby food and opportunities for foreign firms to make up a big shortfall in Chinese production.

HONG KONG

GDP: HK$866bn; $111bn
GDP per head: $18,800
Population: 5.9m; % change 0.6
GDP growth: 1992 6%; 1993 5.3%
Inflation: 1992 10%; 1993 11%

• Although new governor Chris Patten will enjoy more prestige with the Chinese than his predecessor, he will be faced by similar difficulties. The British will have little strength in bargaining with China. If Mr Patten says he will introduce democracy, the Chinese will remove it.

• Confidence will be maintained by spending on social and infrastructure projects. A strong stockmarket will help. Expect growth of over 5% in 1993, mainly stimulated by strong expansion on the mainland.

• Wrangles will continue next year over financing the airport project. The Chinese do not want to inherit a big public debt in 1997.

INDIA

GDP: Rs7.5trn; $236bn
GDP per head: $269
Population: 878m; % change 1.9
GDP growth: 1992 3%; 1993 6%
Inflation: 1992 10%; 1993 8.5%

• Narasimha Rao's government should last out the full five years of its term.

• Economic reform will continue apace. It is tacitly supported by the main opposition, and helped by finance minister Manmohan Singh's consensual approach. Red tape and scandals will cause delays in implementation. But Indian Thatcherism will get irresistibly under way in 1993. The restructuring of the public-sector textiles industry will be one of the toughest challenges: 75,000 jobs could go.

• Congress (I) will start trying for a political solution in Jammu and Kashmir. India may revoke the special constitutional status of the province.

To watch
The beginnings of a solution to the border dispute with China, following overtures from Beijing.

INDONESIA

GDP: Rp296trn; $140bn
GDP per head: $740
Population: 189m; % change 1.8
GDP growth: 1992 6.3%; 1993 7.2%
Inflation: 1992 8.3%; 1993 6.8%

• President Suharto will duly be elected for a sixth consecutive term until 1998. Don't expect much argument about who governs before then. Criticism of the government, such as it is, will centre on the presidential family's business interests.

• Supply-side reforms will stimulate further growth in the economy. There will be more liberalisation of foreign investment rules—foreigners can now own 49% of Indonesian banks.

• Mr Suharto will keep a firm grip on the madder dogs in the military. Further high-profile outrages could result in the interruption of aid and investment flows.

JAPAN

GDP: ¥503trn; $4trn
GDP per head: $32,018
Population: 125m; % change 0.4
GDP growth: 1992 1.9%; 1993 3.4%
Inflation: 1992 2.1%; 1993 2.2%

• Japan's economic slowdown, not western complaints, will be the main determinant of how the Miyazawa government approaches the trade surplus. If company investment and consumer spending do not fall too far, then there will be room to cut the surplus. If not, the government will go for an export-led recovery to appease a disaffected public, less than half of whom bothered to turn up for the 1992 elections.

• Some of the centrist opposition parties, along with sections of the Social Democratic Party and even one or two of the LDP could group together to form a moderate opposition. The trade union movement would support this.

• Despite their reputation being hit by scandals, bureaucrats will continue to grip the levers of power, "descending from heaven" into top industrial jobs and determining many policies.

KAZAKHSTAN*

GDP: Rb77.4bn; $2.6bn
GDP per head: $155
Population: 16.7m

• Fears of a fundamentalist Islamic state will prove unfounded. Kazakhstan will opt for a western-facing secular Islamic state, Turkish-style. Fundamentalism will make inroads into some poorer parts of Central Asia.

• President Nursultan Nazarbaev is an enthusiastic capitalist. Expect privatisation and encouragement of foreign investment. Oil companies will be most welcome. 1993 will see a joint venture with Chevron getting under way in the 25bn barrel Tengiz oil field.

To watch
Outside countries vying for influence in Central Asia will include Turkey, Iran and China. Mr Nazarbaev will be keen to maintain close ties with Russia to counterbalance this.

MALAYSIA

GDP: M$166bn; $66bn
GDP per head: $3,468
Population: 18.17m; % change 2.4
GDP growth: 1992 8.7%; 1993 8.3%
Inflation: 1992 4.8%; 1993 4.6%

• Malaysia will try to tackle its invisibles deficit with incentives for service companies to locate there rather than in Singapore. But reliance on Singapore will keep the deficit wide.

• There will be strong domestic criticism of the government's policy of gradually removing the laws that favour ethnic Malays. Prime minister Mahathir Mohamad will deflect much of the criticism towards the alleged excesses of the nine sultans and their families.

• Labour supply and cost will be the potential brake on development. Foreign labour will not be a solution. What the government has given by allowing it in it has taken away by slapping on a levy.

• The importance of agriculture, the original driver of economic growth, will continue to diminish. Subsidies will fall. Concentration will be on export of manufactured goods.

NEW ZEALAND

GDP: NZ$77bn; $43bn
GDP per head: $12,300
Population: 3.5m; % change 0.8
GDP growth: 1992 3.2%; 1993 3.2%
Inflation: 1992 1.8%; 1993 2.5%

• Election time again. Jim Bolger's government should scrape back. The country is less depressed about itself than for many years.

• New Zealand had the world's first comprehensive welfare system, but it won't be preserved for its architectural interest. A stubborn budgetary problem will have finance minister Ruth Richardson hacking at spending on health and benefits.

• Assets worth up to NZ$700m will be privatised.

Leading export markets % of total

Market	%
Australia	18.5
Japan	16.4
USA	13.0
UK	6.5

PAKISTAN

GDP: PRs1.4trn; $53bn
GDP per head: $430
Population: 122.8m; % change 3.1
GDP growth: 1992 7.8%; 1993 5.5%
Inflation: 1992 10%; 1993 8.5%

• Nawaz Sharif's IDA coalition will keep a strong hold on government through the support of provincial governors. The opposition will regroup, strengthened by defections from the government.

• Privatisation and liberalisation of the economy will go ahead slowly. More time will be taken up dealing with violence in the provinces and the perpetual stand-off with India. Pakistan will also be busy playing the Great Game to the north. Pakistan's strong influence in Afghanistan will be weakened by cuts in American aid.

• Politics will take precedence over economics, denying Pakistan the changes being experienced in India and China.

Main exports $m

Export	$m
Cotton yarn	1,192
Clothes	834
Cotton fabrics	679
Raw cotton	427
Rice	351

Latin America

PHILIPPINES

GDP: P1.66trn; $54bn
GDP per head: $823
Population: 61.9m; % change 2
GDP growth: 1992 1.5%; 1993 4.2%
Inflation: 1992 13%; 1993 11%

• President Fidel Ramos will carry on with liberalisation of the domestic and trading economy. A good flow of foreign investment, the end of foreign-exchange restrictions, big international reserves and remitted wages from Filipinos working abroad will provide much needed help.

• Patching up relations with the United States, having sent home the American military, will be a priority. So will replacing the hard currency which the bases supplied.

• Reform policies are one thing, but putting them into practice is something else. Parliament won't be happy to toe the line of a president with only 23% of the vote. Government in the Philippines largely rests with local feudal bosses (not known as reforming zealots). There will be plenty of lost opportunities in 1993.

SINGAPORE

GDP: S$83bn; $52bn
GDP per head: $18,143
Population: 2.8m; % change 1.8
GDP growth: 1992 5.6%; 1993 6.8%
Inflation: 1992 2.4%; 1993 3.5%

• Opposition to Goh Chok Tong's PAP government is unenthusiastic and will grow only slowly. The opposition parties will have a higher profile in 1993 by-elections, but there will be no major shocks.

• Labour shortages and rising costs will prompt the government to invest in training, computerisation and promotion of high-tech industries to keep the loyalties of foreign investors.

To watch
Singapore Telecom has been restructured for privatisation, likely next year. The Public Utilities Board and the Mass Rapid Transportation Corporation could follow.

SOUTH KOREA

GDP: W274trn; $354bn
GDP per head: $8,040
Population: 44.1m; % change 1
GDP growth: 1992 7.1%; 1993 7.8%
Inflation: 1992 7.8%; 1993 7%

• Fear of inflation will mean growth being kept under 8%, curbing construction projects and reining in demand. The government's attempt to keep wage rises down to half the level of inflation will fail.

• Lower inflation and interest rates will help with the liberalisation of the antiquated financial system.

• The Stalinist fossil of North Korea could disintegrate at any time now that Beijing has ditched it, as well as Moscow. Some South Koreans, looking at Germany's experience, would prefer a gradual move to unification. Easier said than done.

TAIWAN

GDP: NT$5.99trn; $241bn
GDP per head: $11,500
Population: 21m; % change 1.1
GDP growth: 1992 7.6%; 1993 6.9%
Inflation: 1992 5%; 1993 5%

• Pressure will continue to grow for direct presidential elections as the new elected National Assembly gets into its stride. The constitution will not be amended in 1993.

• Relations with China will get warmer. There will be a relaxing of rules on trade. Taiwanese businessmen have been getting round them for years.

• A liberalised banking system and massive demand for funds will put strains on the financial system. The underground financial system (which the new private banks are supposed to eliminate) is about 30% of total banking (more than $60bn). New banks will take a share of this unregulated business.

THAILAND

GDP: Bt2.98trn; $117bn
GDP per head: $1,605
Population: 59m; % change 1.4
GDP growth: 1992 7.6%; 1993 7.8%
Inflation: 1992 4.7%; 1993 4.8%

• The new government will have to make sure the military does not feel elbowed out, for fear of direct intervention by the army. Immature democratic institutions and a fragmented parliament will mean more of the same: bureaucracy and corruption, and strong economic growth.

• The United States complains that Bangkok is not doing enough to protect intellectual property rights. Sanctions might mean $500m lost in exports.

• Big public transport projects in Bangkok and two oil refineries, which were delayed by the troubles of 1992, will get going in late 1993.

To watch
Thailand will need to upgrade its technology more quickly if it is to keep pace with neighbouring Malaysia and avoid being left with low value-added textiles and agricultural commodities, while Malaysia grows rich on electronics.

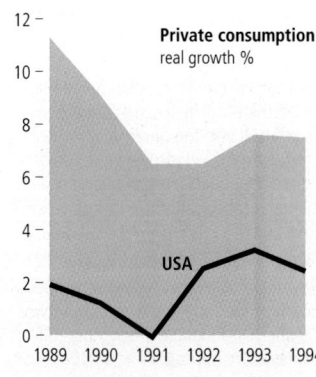

Private consumption
real growth %

USA

ARGENTINA

GDP: P261bn; $273bn
GDP per head: $8,142
Population: 33.5m; % change 1.2
GDP growth: 1992 5.5%; 1993 5.5%
Inflation: 1992 25.3%; 1993 16.1%

• If he can muster enough support in Congress and the economy stays healthy, president Carlos Menem could have another go at changing the law to allow him to stand again for president in 1995.

• Conquest of hyperinflation has revived growth. But the present round of privatisations will wind down in 1993 and it may prove hard to sustain the momentum of reform.

• An overvalued peso will be a problem. This will worry Argentinian industry. A "crawling peg" against the dollar similar to the Mexican system will probably come in during 1993.

• The opposition UCR will spend 1993 trying to work towards economic liberalism.

BRAZIL

GDP: Cr$22,572trn; $393bn
GDP per head: $2,466
Population: 159.2m; % change 1.9
GDP growth: 1992 1%; 1993 1.7%
Inflation: 1992 984%; 1993 1,045%

• The inexperienced new government of Itamar Franco will not inspire confidence. It has promised no shock plans or price freezes to combat inflation, but will rely on making deals with industry to pre-fix prices and wages. Structural reform remains a distant light.

• The constitutional referendum in April might support a change to a parliamentary system, but the Brazilian public is seldom predictable.

• The bitter fiscal measures needed to firm up the foundations of Brazil's stumbling economy will prove hard to pass.

• Export growth will be the one bright spot as domestic demand is held back by the long fight against inflation.

Africa

CHILE

GDP: P16.27trn; $43bn
GDP per head: $3,074
Population: 13.8m; % change 1.5
GDP growth: 1992 7.5%; 1993 7%
Inflation: 1992 15.3%; 1993 12.1%

• Congressional and presidential elections will be held in December 1993. There seems little to challenge the invincibility of the Christian Democrats. Their party president, Eduardo Frei, should get the top job. Weaker parties will fall into line with the Christian Democrats, and the centre-left coalition looks set for some time.

• The current-account deficit will worsen to 2.7% of GDP. This can be sustained. Chile has large foreign reserves, strong inward investment and good access to international credit.

• Mr Frei's business background will mean a continuation of open-door, non-interventionist policies. Privatisation should speed up.

To watch
Chile will make a strong bid to be the next member of the North American Free Trade club. But geography is not on its side.

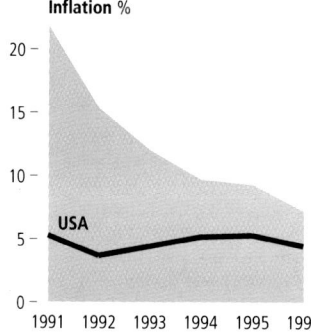

Inflation %

MEXICO

GDP: P1,170trn; $382bn
GDP per head: $4,186
Population: 91.3; % change 2
GDP growth: 1992 3%; 1993 4%
Inflation: 1992 16.4%; 1993 10.2%

• In the wake of the North American Free Trade agreement, expect increased pressure from both north and south of the Rio Grande for President Carlos Salinas to open up Mexico's political process. There will be secretive jostling in 1993 for Mr Salinas' successor.

• The need for more flexible working practices will challenge the government's cautious labour strategy. There will be unwelcome clashes with the powerful and hitherto supportive trade union movement.

• Privatisation and agrarian reforms are well on the way to completion. Stubborn problems still to be overcome will include inflation and the current-account deficit.

To watch
Tourists. They are second only to oil as a source of foreign currency, bringing in $2bn a year. Mr Salinas wants 20% more of them. To this end, expect strong private and public-sector investment in tourism–deregulation of air travel, more highways and 50,000 extra hotel rooms.

VENEZUELA

GDP: B5.34trn; $66bn
GDP per head: $3,110
Population: 21.2m; % change 2.4
GDP growth: 1992 4.2%; 1993 4.3%
Inflation: 1992 30.6%; 1993 26.9%

• Popular pressure, worries about another possible coup attempt, and elections in December will lend urgency to the government's hitherto sluggish efforts at reforming Venezuela's unloved national institutions. Eduardo Fernandez of the Christian Democratic opposition is likely to become president on a ticket of accelerated economic and constitutional reform.

• Falling oil revenues will keep the government deficit high. Social-spending programmes will help appease a disillusioned population.

KENYA

GDP: K£17bn; US$8.1bn
GDP per head: $320
Population: 25.3m; % change 3.3
GDP growth: 1992 1.5%; 1993 2.8%
Inflation: 1992 23%; 1993 19%

• President Daniel arap Moi's Kanu government will hang on until the last possible moment (multi-party elections in March 1993) and lose to the Forum for the Restoration of Democracy (FORD), if the main opposition group can stop itself splitting along tribal lines.

• International aid will not be restored until free and fair elections have been held. The public-sector bureaucracy remains bloated. This, together with inadequate rainfall, will make for weak growth in 1993.

• Electioneering will become increasingly violent as it combines with existing ethnic hatreds. Expect anti-democratic hardliners within Kanu to incite as much disruption as possible during the polls.

NIGERIA

GDP: N555bn; US$27.8bn
GDP per head: $301
Population: 92.2m; % change 2.1
GDP growth: 1992 2.5%; 1993 5.8%
Inflation: 1992 35%; 1993 20%

• Ibrahim Babangida's military government will hand over to civilians in January 1993, barring upsets. But many upsets are possible: trouble from the army; religious and ethnic fighting; and the absence of credible potential civilian leaders or of an embryonic political structure. It will be largely stage-managed anyway.

• The dire state of the economy will imperil the transition. The government has already made itself unpopular by floating the naira. The new civilian government will have to do far more to win a badly needed rescheduling of its debt next year.

• Servicing of debts remains way above budget, contributing to a balance-of-payments deficit amounting to some 11% of GDP.

SOUTH AFRICA

GDP: R389bn; US$123.3bn
GDP per head: $3,312
Population: 37.2m; % change 2.7
GDP growth: 1992 -0.5%; 1993 3.5%
Inflation: 1992 13%; 1993 13%

• Next year should see the first universal adult suffrage elections following on from the appointment of a multiracial interim government. Violence is a certainty. In the run-up to the elections, expect the political realignment in South Africa to continue. As the ANC leadership moves towards the centre, it will find itself under pressure not to compromise socialist principles, however out of date they may be. The National Party will try to attract black voters.

• Expect a rash of business and diplomatic agreements with African countries. The interim government should be admitted to the Organisation of African Unity.

• South Africa has been in a protracted recession. Drought, political uncertainty, world recession and a weak gold price keep prospects dim. Diamond prices will remain catastrophically low. It will not be possible to return to 1981 living standards before the next century. This will mean an interim government pushing for faster growth (and redistribution of wealth) and ignoring IMF pleas.

Gold mining share prices 1985=100

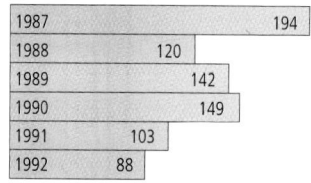

Source: IMF

Middle East

ZIMBABWE

GDP: Z$29.3trn; $4.1bn
GDP per head: $412
Population: 9.9m; % change 2.7
GDP growth: 1992 -8.5%; 1993 4%
Inflation: 1992 35%; 1993 20%

• The ruling Zanu-PF will get even more thoroughly unpopular as unemployment gets worse. But it will stay in power for 1993 thanks to disorganisation among opposition parties.

• President Robert Mugabe's increasing retreat from active policy determination could presage stepping down.

• The drought overshadows the country in the short term. But Zimbabwe will have the full support of international financiers for a structural adjustment programme. The World Bank has faith that Zimbabwe, with its diversified economy and the relative success of earlier economic policies, will be its much-needed African success story.

$m	Imports	Exports
Machinery and transport equipment	693	Tobacco 341
Petroleum products & electricity	288	Gold 239
Manufactures	306	Ferro-alloys 239
Chemicals	287	Nickel 101

ALGERIA

GDP: AD1.2trn; $47.2bn
GDP per head: $1,696
Population: 27.8m; % change 3.3
GDP growth: 1992 3.6%; 1993 5%
Inflation: 1992 35%; 1993 30%

• With thousands of Islamic supporters and leaders imprisoned for ten years, the immediate threat from the Islamic movement has been crushed for the crucial 1992-93 period. But support remains strong in the mosques and universities. Even the military/security establishment will find it hard to winkle it out. Repression will continue. There will be no elections until early 1994 at the earliest.

• The return of the military to centre stage makes civil war a real possibility. The harsh regime could polarise society. If sympathy for the fundamentalists inside the army is more widespread than thought, it could split.

• Algeria will not become a market economy for many years. Its troubles will be felt ever more keenly in southern Europe.

EGYPT

GDP: E£149bn; $42.7bn
GDP per head: $751
Population: 56.9m; % change 2
GDP growth: 1992 2.8%; 1993 4%
Inflation: 1992 17%; 1993 12%

• Egypt's and Hosni Mubarak's international standing will stay high. Egyptians head both the Arab League and the UN. In the peace-talking Middle East, Egypt will seek to lead a more cohesive Arab world into better relations with the West.

• There will be more trouble from Islamic militants in the south founded in economic discontent. Christians could be driven out of some areas. The government will use tough anti-terrorist laws.

• Reform will remain slow and cautious in the interests of internal stability. Both privatisation and foreign investment will continue to be lengthy and bureaucratic procedures.

To watch
Increasing Egyptian influence in Libya. Most people living in the east of Libya are already Egyptian. One day the whole country might be an Egyptian province. Why not?

IRAN

GDP: IR75.4trn; $60.3bn
GDP per head: $957
Population: 63m; % change 3.4
GDP growth: 1992 6.1%; 1993 6.1%
Inflation: 1992 35%; 1993 35%

• Conservative/radical factions will remain in retreat, as was confirmed by president Ali Akbar Hashemi Rafsanjani's comfortable election victory. But they have not gone away.

• Equally problematic for the Rafsanjani government will be the introduction of further economic reforms, particularly the reduction of high consumer subsidies. Rising inflation, growing disparities in wealth and other negative effects of reform increase the possibility of demonstrations.

• The Rial's multiple exchange rates will be unified. The government will want to set a high new rate.

• Other economic reform issues to be tackled include: restructuring the public-sector oil industry (although not to allow much private-sector involvement); reduction of state control over the economy; and rooting out corruption.

IRAQ

GDP: ID146bn; $20.8bn
GDP per head: $1,000
Population: 20.8m; % change 3
GDP growth: 1992 23.3%; 1993 31.4%
Inflation: 1992 200%; 1993 50%

• Proper reconstruction of the economy will begin only when UN sanctions are relaxed. Potential exports of 2m barrels a day could induce Mr Hussein to adhere to strict UN conditions to being allowed to trade his oil. Then all the UN has to do is make sure he keeps his side of the bargain.

• The United States will want Iraqis to be fed using cash from frozen Iraqi assets rather than Western charity.

To watch
Massoud Barzani and Jalal Talabani will be struggling for leadership of Iraqi Kurdistan. Mr Barzani will be in favour of talking to Baghdad. Mr Talabani will take the populist attitude of no talks. Their feuding will hamper attempts to set up a political system as a basis for autonomy.

ISRAEL

GDP: NIS185bn; $71bn
GDP per head: $12,241
Population: 5.8m; % change 4.4
GDP growth: 1992 6%; 1993 7%
Inflation: 1992 11%; 1993 9%

• Any autonomy for Palestinians would exclude defence and administration of the Jewish settlements. More progress in talks with the Palestinians necessitates an end to clashes between them and the Israeli army. The upshot could be lots more blue helmets in the Middle East to allow the army to withdraw while keeping the Palestinians in order and local Israelis safe.

• Investment in the infrastructure to accommodate the continuing stream of immigrants from the former USSR will be shifted from the West Bank into Israel proper. The Israeli government will still be struggling with its old problem of how to get sustained growth. Reform is in the air. Social spending cuts, privatisation, lower taxes, open trade and foreign-exchange liberalisation are all being mooted. But the immigrants will keep unemployment high (it is already at a record 11.5%).

SAUDI ARABIA

GDP: SR458bn; $122.4bn
GDP per head: $7,463
Population: 16.4m; % change 3.1
GDP growth: 1992 4.5%; 1993 5%
Inflation: 1992 2.5%; 1993 2.5%

• The Consultative Council which the king has appointed will not be the beginning of an end to absolute monarchy. King Fahd has said enough is enough. Further concessions, if they are made, are likely to be to Islamic rather than liberal points of view.

• Making friends of their neighbours will not be a priority for the Saudis. Expect them to throw their weight around OPEC with growing assurance as oil capacity expands to 10m barrels a day by the middle of the decade.

• Saudi Arabia will want to make sure that the present Iraqi regime is replaced by one amenable to its wishes. It will seek to counterbalance the growing influence of Tehran.

• Expect some structural investment in the economy to extract more benefit from the private, non-oil economy and provide work for the increasing numbers of younger, educated Saudis.

General trends

• Partnership will be the theme for 1993 as companies look for ways of surviving capacity reduction. Computer makers, car makers, plane makers and airlines will all be looking for joint-venture partners and friends for cross-shareholding arrangements. Rumours of new partnerships will be as common as rumours of acquisitions used to be. Some of this will be a cheap way of imitating the 1980s lust for acquisitions and quick access to new markets. But many industries will also be forced into new relationships with their competitors by the escalating costs of R&D and of keeping up with the growing mountain of regulations which national governments and international agreements impose.

• There will be polarisation between the very big international firms and the small specialists, with the players in the middle suffering. The airline business is a good example where only mega-players and small regional carriers will be there by the end of the century. This process is already well on the way to completion among aerospace companies.

• The United States will be highly competitive as it comes out of recession. The weak dollar, low interest rates, five years of slimming, and steady wages will all make American goods desirable.

Industries

AEROSPACE

Worldwide stockmarket performance (aerospace and defence technology September 1992)

% change from previous year: -12.9
% change from 1.1.92: -14.7
% change from high: -23.3
Price/earnings ratio: 10.4

• The three main aircraft manufacturers (Boeing, McDonnell Douglas, and Airbus) will all scale back production in 1993 as orders fall off and options are left unfulfilled.

• McDonnell Douglas is undergoing the most far-reaching cost cutting of the big three manufacturers. There are doubts about its commercial aircraft business which looks like losing market share to the other two.

• California, home of high technology, will suffer very badly from the defence cuts. At least 30,000 jobs will go in defence by the end of 1994. With related sectors like civil aircraft and space in trouble as well, there could be some highly-skilled grape-pickers around.

To watch
The launch of Airbus's first four-engine long-haul jet.

AGRICULTURE

• 1993 will be the first full year of common agricultural policy (CAP) reforms at work in Europe. The idea is that subsidies will gradually be replaced by income support for poorer farmers. This, the reformers hope, will mean that the money goes to poor peasant farmers rather than north European agro-industrialists.

• GATT: the Europeans will try to persuade the Americans that CAP reforms really do mean big production cuts. The Americans won't believe them and will bring in tariffs on selected European items.

• More wonderful ways will be found to keep European farmers busy. After golf courses, rows of willow trees could be grown in the fields of Westphalia, not to meet a sudden enthusiasm for cricket in Germany but rather to be incinerated for electricity.

CHEMICALS

World ethylene capacity, demand & utilisation

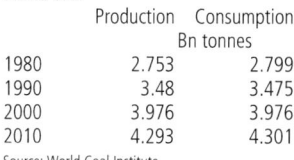

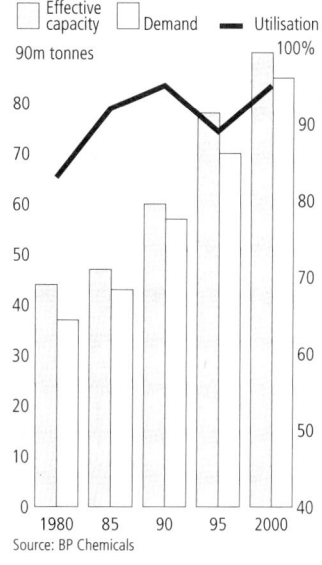

Source: BP Chemicals

Worldwide stockmarket performance (September 1992)

% change from previous year: 0.8
% change from 1.1.92: -1
% change from high: -11.4
Price/earnings ratio: 18.3

• Overcapacity rather than recession will be the main problem facing the world chemicals industry. Petrochemicals capacity in Asia brought on stream between 1988 and 1995 will be equivalent to more than half European production.

• Capacity in Europe will continue to grow at about the same rate as demand (1–5%) at least until 1995. Companies will continue to restructure (not all as radically as Britain's ICI). But costs will remain high and, if there is a recovery in demand, American imports will flood in. Export to Asia will become a thing of the past.

• Speciality chemicals makers, whose products are directed at specific users such as the car and construction industries, will be better placed for recovery. They have done a much better job at reorganising than the bulk chemicals business, but the odds are that Asian competitors will land the same blows on European manufacturers as their shipbuilders and fibre manufacturers already have.

COAL

World coal

	Production	Consumption
	Bn tonnes	
1980	2.753	2.799
1990	3.48	3.475
2000	3.976	3.976
2010	4.293	4.301

Source: World Coal Institute

• More power stations in Japan will push its coal imports up to 15m tonnes by 1995. South Korea will increase rapidly as well.

• The future for EC coal will depend on political factors. Will the commission's no-subsidy policy or some national governments' security of supply policy win? Without government mollycoddling, less than one-third of EC production (led by the remnants of British Coal) will be competitive by the middle of the decade because of high extraction and labour costs.

• Asia (especially China), together with South Africa and Australia, accounted for some 95% of the increase in production in the 1980s. Asian exports will increase still further thanks to skilled and cheap labour, a high level of investment, proximity to export markets and economical open-cast techniques. Latin America will be the next major importing region. Exports from the former USSR will halve by 2010. Poland will import coal by 2010.

World coal trade balance m tonnes

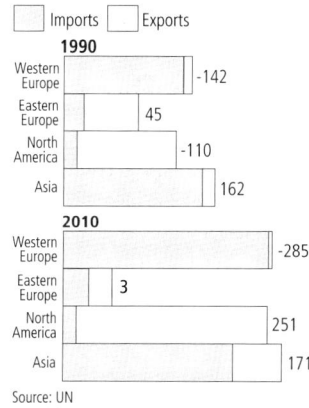

Source: UN

Sources: Stockmarket performance figures: Morgan Stanley Capital International.
Beddows & Company; James Capel; EIU; PA Consulting; Saatchi & Saatchi; UBS Phillips & Drew; S G Warburg; World Coal Institute

COMPUTERS

Worldwide stockmarket performance (September 1992)

% change from previous year: -21.3
% change from 1.1.92: -11.6
% change from high: -53.7
Price/earnings ratio: loss

• Collapsing margins in the personal computer industry, as low-cost producers in Asia churn out clones (copies) of IBM models and sell them very cheap, will make some of the leaders think of getting out of PC-making altogether. IBM is demerging its PC division because it can't compete on cost. Clone suppliers are taking market share, and this, combined with weak demand, will hit the established names hardest.

• Europe will be hurt worst. High-cost producers like France's Bull, who only continue thanks to the largesse of governments, might not pull through. Survival will be thanks only to alliance with Japanese or American producers (Fujitsu's ICL in Britain will continue to do rather well).

• Customers will want to be moving to flexible open systems (Unix) rather than the proprietary networks traditionally offered. Only about 20% of systems are like this, and, again, European producers are badly placed.

• The big players will continue their move into higher value-added services such as facilities management. As the muscle of IBM and Digital starts to make itself felt in these fields, previous providers will be squeezed.

Worldwide markets $m

1990	$314,480
1991	$327,457
1992	$345,506

Source: International Data Corporation

CONSTRUCTION

Worldwide stockmarket performance (Construction and housing, September 1992)

% change from previous year: -23.9
% change from 1.1.92: -23.5
% change from high: -49
Price/earnings ratio: 21.4

• Eastern Europe's enormous potential demand will be unlocked only in cheap projects and hard-currency earners like oil and gas pipelines.

• Survival will be the only thing on the minds of British building companies. They have attacked costs and become used to tight margins. Many of them have done all the slimming they can, and are now lean service companies who farm out work to subcontractors. With domestic housing construction still stagnant and commercial construction nonexistent, there will simply be very little for British builders to do.

• Projects: Hong Kong will remain the world's biggest building site; a long-discussed link between Denmark and Sweden could get under way; Prague needs a new sewage system; and "wider and deeper" refers not just to Eurojargon but to plans for the Suez Canal; the Channel Tunnel will be finished.

ELECTRICAL COMPONENTS

Worldwide stockmarket performance (September 1992)

% change from previous year: 7.3
% change from 1.1.92: 4.4
% change from high: -18.1
Price/earnings ratio: 20.7

• Future developments in chips will be international. As R&D becomes ever more expensive and fears increase that the computer market will not grow quickly enough to finance innovation, R&D will become concentrated in joint ventures among the biggest companies.

• In the United States: isolationists will complain that technology is flowing out of the country and that publicly funded technological research is being purloined by the Japanese. The manufacturers will say they have to use Japanese manufacturing capability which is not available in America and that no one company has the necessary resources to research and bring a product to market.

ELECTRICAL CONSUMER GOODS

Worldwide stockmarket performance (September 1992)

% change from previous year: -17.3
% change from 1.1.92: -13.6
% change from high: -36.1
Price/earnings ratio: 18.9

• Few current goods with high added-value and consumers increasingly wary of minor tinkerings with existing technology will add to the stagnation in demand. The more capitalist bits of China will be the much-needed bright spot for 1993.

• Philips will put a lot of faith in the digital compact cassette. But it will be some time before innovations like this become cheap enough to be mass successes. Digitalisation in all fields will be the thing.

• Expect continuing pressure on manufacturers from the EC to reduce price differentials across Europe. Philips and its competitors will defend to the death their right to charge the Italians twice as much as they charge the Germans for the same television.

ELECTRICITY

Worldwide stockmarket performance (Utilities, September 1992)

% change from previous year: 1.1
% change from 1.1.92: -5
% change from high: -10
Price/earnings ratio: 16.7

• Asia will account for 29% of capacity additions up to the end of the century. Japan and South Korea will be the key countries.

• Britain's generators will be negotiating new contracts at the end of March. Interested parties are: generators (want long and fat contracts); distributors (want to get electricity for a reasonable price); government (wants windfall from selling off remainder of the generating companies); regulators (want to intervene as little as possible); British Coal (the meat in the sandwich).

• Mixed privatisation possibilities in Europe: supply in Ireland might be sold off; the Spanish government may offer more Endesa shares; the finances of Italy's Enel preclude anything; France will agonise over nuclear exports; German companies will move beyond eastern Germany to carve up the Czech and Slovak markets between them.

FOOD

Worldwide stockmarket performance (Food and household products, September 1992)

% change from previous year: 10.7
% change from 1.1.92: -0.6
% change from high: -0.9
Price/earnings ratio: 17.3

• The Euro-sausage will come into being, not from Brussels regulation, but from sleek cross-border marketing and the clout of international food companies.

• Variable spending on commodities will come down as agricultural reforms bring down prices of raw materials. The consumer will only see the difference in fresh food prices.

• Money spent on marketing will increase as companies develop international premium brands. A downside will be an increasing reliance on suppliers as packaging assumes greater importance.

• The lead enjoyed by the number one in each food sector will grow as market leaders capitalise on their economies of scale in cross-border marketing and R&D.

MECHANICAL ENGINEERING

Worldwide stockmarket performance (September 1992)

% change from previous year: -12.7
% change from 1.1.92: -11.4
% change from high: -31.5
Price/earnings ratio: 26.7

• A new-found competitiveness makes British engineering firms well placed for an upturn and they will be pitching energetically for international business.

• Recovery for Japanese machine-tool makers will depend on the fortunes of small and medium-sized firms, which account for some 70% of their business. But these are the firms who are going to find capital for investment in plant hard to come by.

• Makers of electricity generators are better rationalised than many engineering sectors. Expect the biggest companies (such as ABB, GE, Mitsubishi Heavy Industries, Westinghouse and Siemens), together with clutches of regional partners, to draw clear of the rest of the field.

MOTOR VEHICLES

Worldwide stockmarket performance
(September 1992)

% change from previous year: -5.7
% change from 1.1.92: -4.3
% change from high: -31.2
Price/earnings ratio: 41.4

• Expect manufacturers to be thinking up every kind of new device to get you to buy their cars and keep buying them. This will not just be a response to dreadful sales (and will have little effect on that) but to longer-term pressures such as environmental and safety legislation which make it more and more difficult to tell one car from another.

• 1993 will show whether the slight revival of the Big Three American car makers can be sustained or if it is a result of short-term "buy American" campaigns. Europe will remain the biggest market for cars. It passed the North American total in 1991 and 1992 and, with demand growing more quickly (current level about 13m a year), the continent's dominance will continue to grow next year.

• 1993 will be the first full year of production for the three big Japanese producers who have set up shop in Britain. Mazda, the only big Japanese company not to have declared its hand in Europe, will do so in 1993. Logic should take it to Britain (which recently displaced Spain as the cheapest place in Europe to build cars); it may decide it does not want to follow the crowd and go elsewhere.

• Perpetually troubled British Aerospace will be allowed to get rid of Rover after April 1993. If it can, it will.

• Concentration in the European truck-making industry will continue throughout the 1990s. The Japanese will be happy to see competition becoming rather less fierce before making their move.

To watch
Commercially viable electric cars from Fiat and GM; wing mirrors from Japan that have heaters to keep off the ice, wipers to keep off the rain and little memories that automatically set them to the angle you want.

OIL AND GAS

Total world reserves of natural gas
124 trillion m^3

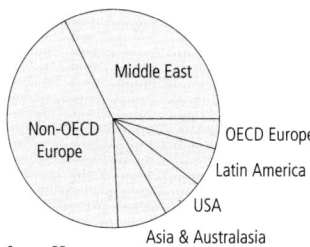

Source: BP

Worldwide stockmarket performance
(Energy sources, September 1992)

% change from previous year: -5.4
% change from 1.1.92: -2.5
% change from high: -10.6
Price/earnings ratio: 22.9

• OPEC countries want to increase capacity—Saudi Arabia, Iran, Venezuela, Mexico, UAE, Nigeria and Libya could add 20m barrels a day to capacity by the middle of the decade. That's without allowing for Kuwaiti and Iraqi production to return to pre-war levels. Non-OPEC production will remain stable. Production from former Soviet states will decline, but some of these countries, like Kazakhstan, are getting their houses in order.

• Improved exploration technology will get at new reserves in fields which were previously thought to have been exhausted. Slimmer drilling holes, unmanned rigs and improved deep-water drilling techniques will reduce production costs.

• Gas will continue to expand its uses at the expense of coal. It keeps environmentalists happier than either coal or oil and new technology can make it into very cheap electricity. It is no longer seen as a scarce resource and four times more is discovered than consumed each year. Expect demand to grow by up to 50% over the next 20 years. A problem will be whether gas production technology, in fields often far away from the main markets, can keep pace with this demand.

PAPER AND PACKAGING

Worldwide stockmarket performance
(September 1992)

% change from previous year: -9
% change from 1.1.92: -9.6
% change from high: -23.2
Price/earnings ratio: 55

• Any economic recovery in industrialised countries would lead to swift recovery in demand for paper in main uses like advertising, printing, offices and packaging. The industry will be ready to meet a surge in demand. Expansion of capacity in Europe is planned until at least 1994; there are ample supplies of raw materials; and there is aggressive competition from the major producers.

• In the self-contained and slow-growing American market, there could be further anti-dumping actions against European imports.

• Canada's virgin pulp industry will suffer from environmental legislation which is being put into action more rapidly than elsewhere in the world. There could be an opportunity to divert exports to Europe where there will be a deficit in forest products. This will not be enough to prevent a long-term contraction in the Canadian industry.

Increase in capacity
1990-94 m tonnes

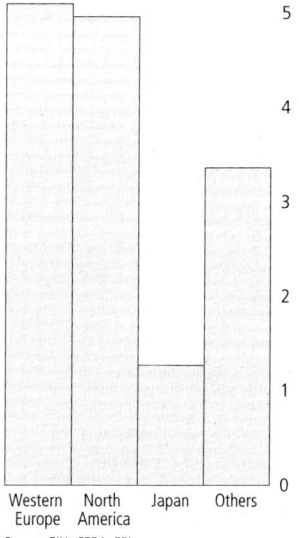

Source: EIU; CPPA; EPI

STEEL

Worldwide stockmarket performance
(September 1992)

% change from previous year: -28
% change from 1.1.92: -19.7
% change from high: -63.9
Price/earnings ratio: 139.7

• Decline in production will be most marked in Japan and Eastern Europe. Output in developing countries will continue to increase.

• Prices for steel continue to decline almost everywhere, and export prices are down to the depressed levels of the early 1980s. Production in the western world will not show signs of real recovery before 1994.

• Krupp Steel's acquisition of Hoesch will be followed by other big mergers as painful rationalisation in Europe and the United States goes on in the face of intense competition.

• Dumping rows between American and European producers could mean more protectionism.

To watch
Big Steel's last redoubt against the unstoppable mini-mills, flat roll steel, has now been cracked by Nucor of the United States. Watch mini-mills roll up market share everywhere.

TEXTILES AND CLOTHING

Worldwide stockmarket performance
(September1992)

% change from previous year: -11
% change from 1.1.92: -10.7
% change from high: -26
Price/earnings ratio: 20.6

• China will be the big export success story of 1993. Expect the People's Republic to invest $1.2bn in replacing out-of-date equipment by 1995. China's ability to swamp developed markets will overshadow trade talks.

• "Nearby sourcing" and "distant sourcing" will be industry buzzwords for next year. "Nearby" means getting upmarket materials and quick response fashion stuff from your own region; "distant" means cheap, standardised materials with long production runs which are not required immediately and can be bought from low-cost producers, often in Asia.

Services

ADVERTISING

Advertising revenue as a % of GDP 1991:

USA 1.4; Japan 1; France 0.7; Germany 0.9; Italy 0.7; Spain 1.51; UK 1.33; Australia 1.23

• The threat of a total ban on tobacco advertising has receded. The EC in particular now favours a phasing out. Other contentious areas (alcohol and pharmaceuticals) should get away with self-regulation.

• Recession retains its grip on key markets in America, Britain, Germany, Australia, even previously high-flying Spain. Asia is the bright spot.

• Major advertisers will appoint media specialists, independent of creative agencies, to handle media buying and, in some cases, planning. As the media world grows in sophistication and complexity this will increase.

• Advertising will enter a new period of accountability. Payment by results and a focus on how advertising affects sales will be wanted rather than abstruse references to image and awareness. Advertisers will spend time and money advertising advertising.

Media revenue
% change from previous year in $ terms

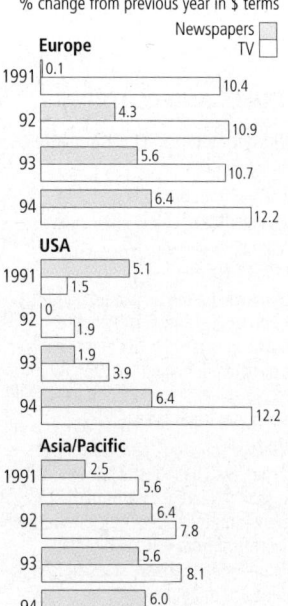

Source: Zenith Media Worldwide

AIR TRANSPORT

Worldwide stockmarket performance (September 1992)

% change from previous year: -16.2
% change from 1.1.92: -17.8
% change from high: -36.8
Price/earnings ratio: loss

• Against a background of massive financial losses, changes are in train which, by 2000, will result in there being about a dozen giant international carriers, based on existing American, European and Asian groups. The high entry barriers to becoming international and the marketing and financial muscle of these giants will stop anyone else from breaking out of countries or regions.

• Of the three American airlines currently protected under chapter 11 of the bankruptcy laws, America West and perhaps TWA could be out of business by the end of the year. Continental should pull through. But unless demand recovers well, others could go into chapter 11. North West does not look happy at the moment. America West and TWA going under would go some way towards tackling the overcapacity problem and pricing discipline should stick. If they survive, the price wars will go on.

• Progress towards open skies will remain slow. On the North Atlantic routes, bilateral negotiations will be favoured. Holland and Britain will be in the lead. France and Germany will grumble at being left out. There will also be strong pressure to reduce capacity restrictions in Europe.

• There will be strong opposition in the United States to any moves to allow full foreign ownership of American airlines.

• Recovery for some of the biggest airlines will be threatened by a fall in cargo rates. Freight is worth about $20bn a year to carriers. Overcapacity in this market will lead to joint ventures.

To watch
Asia will be where airlines will make money next year. Garuda, Korean, Malaysian and Taiwan's China Airlines will be among the stars. There will be strong growth in air travel in the People's Republic. Asian markets will stay heavily regulated and labour costs low.

INSURANCE

Worldwide stockmarket performance (September 1992)

% change from previous year: 4
% change from 1.1.92: -4.2
% change from high: -13
Price/earnings ratio: 22.5

• A New Jersey court will decide in 1993 whether insurers can be held liable for cleaning up toxic-waste sites. New Jersey contains some 10% of the American total. 37,000 have been identified across the country for inspection and possible clean-up. At a conservative $50m a site to clean, liability on only a small percentage of those 37,000 would be enough to ruin the American insurance market, which has a capital base of under $200bn. That's before you consider third-party claims, litigation costs, etc.

• British insurers will find policies for domestic mortgage indemnity a continuing headache as mortgage arrears pile up and the housing market stays depressed.

• The "get ready for the single market" acquisition fever that gripped European insurers in the late 1980s has been purged. Many buyers overpaid for acquisitions which underperformed. Alliances will replace expansion, profits will replace the scramble for market share, and focus on known strengths will replace the finger in every pie.

• German and Swiss insurers, in heavily protected markets, will be vulnerable as things loosen up.

ROAD AND RAIL TRANSPORT

Worldwide stockmarket performance (September 1992)

% change from previous year: -4.4
% change from 1.1.92: -9.9
% change from high: -38.7
Price/earnings ratio: 46.4

• The EC wants to develop a Europe-wide "combined transport system", linking up sea, road and rail. The idea is to take the pressure off the roads and speed up distribution. Expect rows over who pays for the scheme before it is shelved.

• In America fortunes for truckers depend on the timing of recovery. Fortunes for railroaders depend on how much grain goes to Russia and how quickly American coal exports pick up.

SHIPPING

Worldwide stockmarket performance (September 1992)

% change from previous year: -21.2
% change from 1.1.92: -18.2
% change from high: -43
Price/earnings ratio: 27.6

• Shipping rates will remain low and owners will often find it more economical to lay their vessels up and defer essential repairs.

• Yards will switch their attention to repairs and refits but this will not be enough to counterbalance the continuing lack of ship orders.

• Latin American governments will start to sell off ports, ships and shipyards.

To watch
Foreign shipowners will flee the United States as new environmental liability laws push up their costs. The pending Gibbons legislation, a protectionist measure with draconian provisions, could make it impossible for many ships which have been built with subsidy to operate in United States waters.

TOURISM

Worldwide stockmarket performance (September 1992)

% change from previous year: 3.9
% change from 1.1.92: 1.3
% change from high: -15.1
Price/earnings ratio: 21.9

• The biggest factor for the industry next year will be whether the dollar stays weak. America will no longer be seen as a long-haul destination for European travellers.

• There will be an increasing polarisation. Only the biggest operators will be able to offer the high volume/low margin packages which made the words Mediterranean and concrete synonymous. At the other end, a large number of operators will offer high-margin specialist holidays.

• Spain will continue its decline as a holiday destination as prices go up. The Spanish will start going to the Costas in larger numbers.

To watch
Lots of moaning Minnies (and Mickeys) in Eurodisney. Why pay £250 for a long weekend in soggy Northern Europe, when £600 will get you two weeks in Florida?

CS FIRST BOSTON GROUP

ITS EUROPEAN ORGANISATION CONTINUES TO LEAD THE WAY IN THE 1990s

1990

Equity House of the Year

1990

Best Eurobond Lead Management House

1990

Swap House of the Year

1991

Best Eurobond Lead Management House

1991

International Options House of the Year

1991

Users' Favourite Derivatives House

1992

Best Bank for International Capital Raising

1992

Best Eurobond Lead Management House

1992

Award for Excellence in Derivatives

Sources: International Financial Review, Euromoney

NEXT YEAR'S WORLD

European exporters will thrive next year with the opening-up of the wealthiest free trade area in the world. Watch their exports per head soar. Trade among neighbours will grow quickly everywhere. Air travel will more than double by 2010. Join the rush to invest in Spanish-speaking countries. America will have a high murder rate and also a fat surplus on its other commercial services. Kuwait will bask in the glow of youth while Sweden's cohorts of pensioners will keep its deficit high.

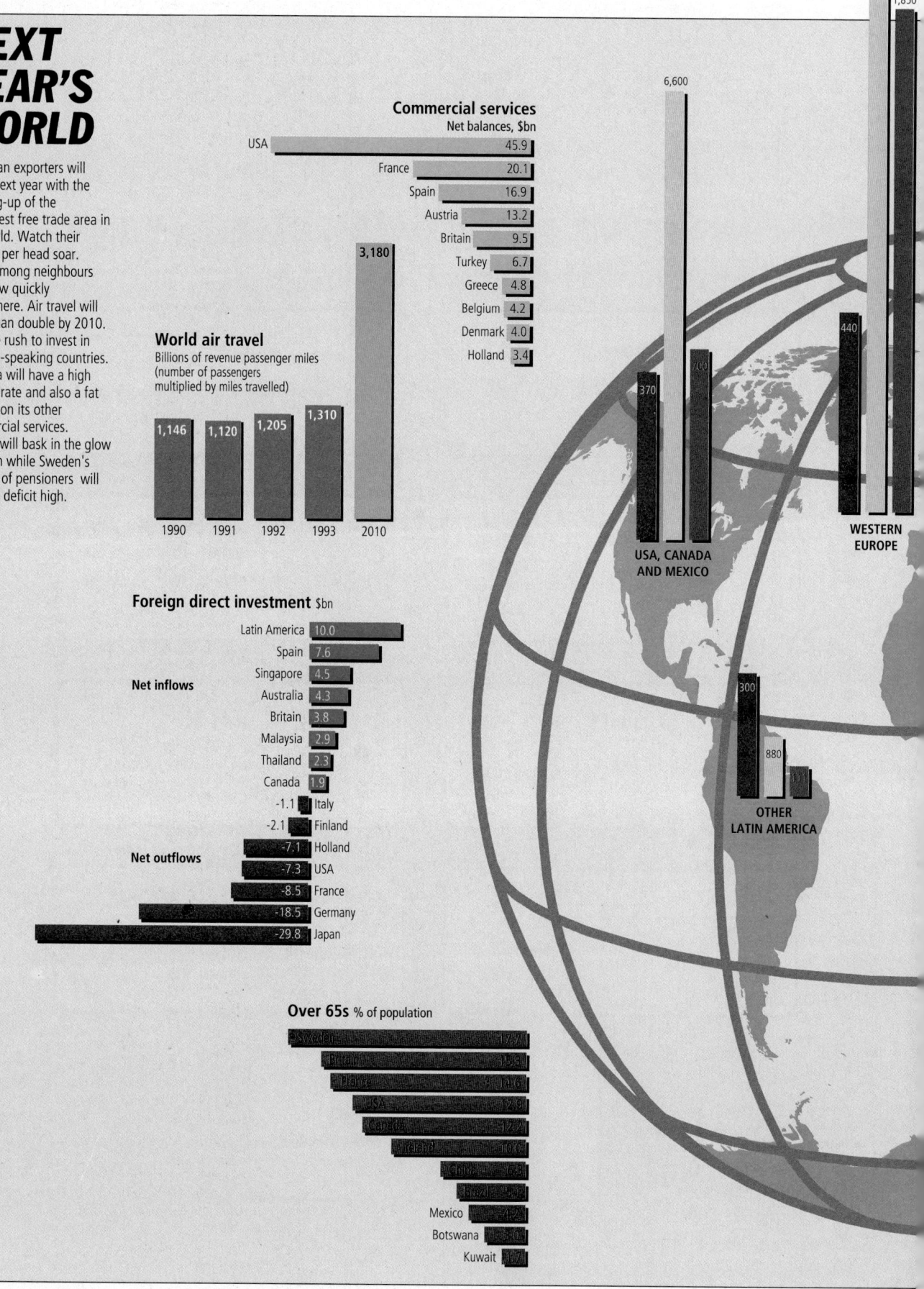

Commercial services
Net balances, $bn

USA	45.9
France	20.1
Spain	16.9
Austria	13.2
Britain	9.5
Turkey	6.7
Greece	4.8
Belgium	4.2
Denmark	4.0
Holland	3.4

World air travel
Billions of revenue passenger miles (number of passengers multiplied by miles travelled)

1990	1991	1992	1993	2010
1,146	1,120	1,205	1,310	3,180

Foreign direct investment $bn

Net inflows

Latin America	10.0
Spain	7.6
Singapore	4.5
Australia	4.3
Britain	3.8
Malaysia	2.9
Thailand	2.3
Canada	1.9

Net outflows

Italy	-1.1
Finland	-2.1
Holland	-7.1
USA	-7.3
France	-8.5
Germany	-18.5
Japan	-29.8

Over 65s % of population

Sweden · Britain · France · USA · Canada · Ireland · China · Brazil · Mexico · Botswana · Kuwait

Globe labels: USA, CANADA AND MEXICO; WESTERN EUROPE; OTHER LATIN AMERICA — 8,000 · 1,850 · 6,600 · 440 · 370 · 700 · 300 · 880

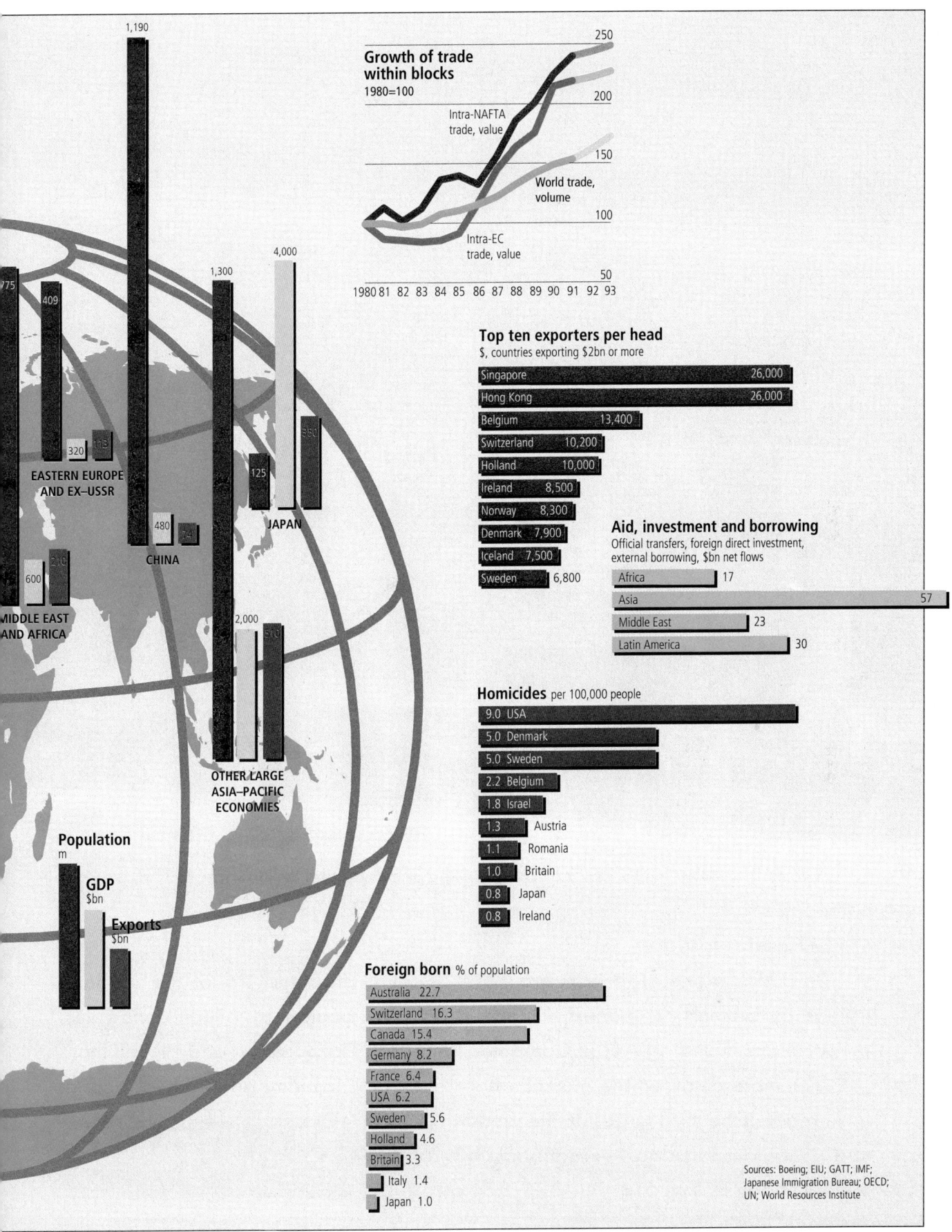

Growth of trade within blocks
1980=100

Intra-NAFTA trade, value

World trade, volume

Intra-EC trade, value

250
200
150
100
50

1980 81 82 83 84 85 86 87 88 89 90 91 92 93

1,190

675

409

320 113

EASTERN EUROPE AND EX–USSR

480 74

CHINA

4,000

550

125

JAPAN

600

210

MIDDLE EAST AND AFRICA

1,300

2,000

510

OTHER LARGE ASIA–PACIFIC ECONOMIES

Population
m

GDP
$bn

Exports
$bn

Top ten exporters per head
$, countries exporting $2bn or more

Singapore	26,000
Hong Kong	26,000
Belgium	13,400
Switzerland	10,200
Holland	10,000
Ireland	8,500
Norway	8,300
Denmark	7,900
Iceland	7,500
Sweden	6,800

Aid, investment and borrowing
Official transfers, foreign direct investment, external borrowing, $bn net flows

Africa	17
Asia	57
Middle East	23
Latin America	30

Homicides per 100,000 people

9.0	USA
5.0	Denmark
5.0	Sweden
2.2	Belgium
1.8	Israel
1.3	Austria
1.1	Romania
1.0	Britain
0.8	Japan
0.8	Ireland

Foreign born % of population

Australia	22.7
Switzerland	16.3
Canada	15.4
Germany	8.2
France	6.4
USA	6.2
Sweden	5.6
Holland	4.6
Britain	3.3
Italy	1.4
Japan	1.0

Sources: Boeing; EIU; GATT; IMF; Japanese Immigration Bureau; OECD; UN; World Resources Institute

N°1 IN NEW FIELDS

Question: which US stock market is the most fertile environment for growth companies?

Answer: Nasdaq.

In 1991 alone, The Nasdaq Stock Market attracted 26 of the 27 new listings by biotech companies – following a path beaten by billion-dollar-plus corporations including Apple Computer, Microsoft Corporation and Novell Inc.

For more detail on the market whose efficiency, liquidity and ease of access have made it the third-largest in the world in just 21 years, contact Nasdaq International, 43 London Wall, London EC2M 5TB. Tel: 071-374 6969.

NASDAQ
INTERNATIONAL

THE STOCK MARKET FOR THE NEXT 100 YEARS

Poor little big boy

David Manasian

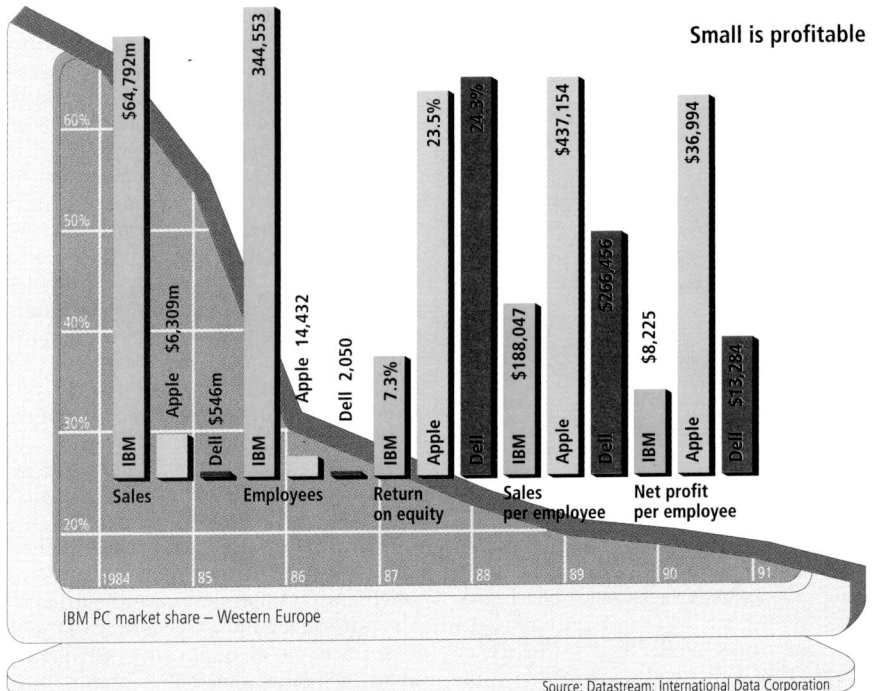

Small is profitable

Sales: IBM $64,792m, Apple $6,309m, Dell $546m
Employees: IBM 344,553, Apple 14,432, Dell 2,050
Return on equity: IBM 7.3%, Apple 23.5%, Dell 24.3%
Sales per employee: IBM $188,047, Apple $437,154, Dell $265,456
Net profit per employee: IBM $8,225, Apple $36,994, Dell $13,284

IBM PC market share – Western Europe

Source: Datastream; International Data Corporation

David Manasian: business editor of The Economist.

For the past four decades, most companies have chased the "economies of scale". The race is over. If there is a world economic recovery in 1993, even a gentle one, it will reveal that the coming decades will be dominated by a stampede in the opposite direction: to avoid the increasing "diseconomies of scale". Once growth returns, big companies will no longer have the excuse of recession to explain away their poor performance. And yet in almost every industry they will continue to perform poorly compared with smaller, more nimble competitors. As the 1990s roll by, corporate giants will struggle to cope with the attacks of these gnats, and fail. "Big" will become a synonym for costly or inefficient.

It was not supposed to be this way. When "globalisation" became a buzzword ten years ago, most businessmen assumed that big firms would benefit most from the reduction in trade barriers and the homogenisation of consumer tastes. Global markets were supposed to demand global brands from global companies managed globally. Companies, no matter what their size, rushed to get bigger; and everywhere companies rushed to get into each other's markets.

Pundits confidently predicted consolidation in a wide range of industries, from car making to banking to entertainment. Eventually, they said, a group of huge, stateless multinationals would bestride the world of business.

In the EC a local version of the globalisation mania was especially virulent. The biggest firms pushed hard for a dismantling of internal trade barriers and the creation of a single European market. They argued that a huge home market would help them to grow to a size where they could compete head-to-head with Japanese and American rivals.

Computers and electronics were also going to launch an automation revolution on the factory floor, making mass production even more efficient. Companies big enough to spend heavily on computeris-ing offices and factories would gain the most. In 1982 General Motors, the world's largest manufacturer, plunged into an $80-billion drive to re-equip its factories. IBM and hundreds of other big companies also spent lavishly on factory automation, convinced that this would make them unassailable as the "lowest-cost" producers in their industries.

In fact, all of these trends—falling trade barriers, computerisation, automation and the globalisation of consumer tastes—are tilting the advantage in world markets not to big companies, but to small and medium-sized ones.

It has long been recognised that expanding a business incurs extra costs, both managerial and financial. Firms become more bureaucratic and less flexible as they become bigger. They also become more wasteful because employees, feeling themselves mere cogs, are less accountable and more difficult to motivate in large organisations. Though enormous, such diseconomies have always been grossly underestimated, and the economies offered by greater size always grossly overestimated. Making either mistake in the future will threaten any firm's survival.

Far from presenting big companies with new opportunities, falling trade barriers are opening them to attack. The myriad difficulties of running a business or selling products in dozens of different countries may have annoyed multinationals in the past, but they were the only companies with the ability to surmount such hurdles. Smaller firms often could not afford to tailor products to the standards of foreign markets, employ people overseas or cope with the legal and tax complexities of international business. The dismantling of trade barriers and opening of markets are removing many of these obstacles and making it easier for once-parochial companies to sell their products all over the world.

Computers, against all expectations, have turned out to be the ally of small firms, the bane of big ones. Large companies have discovered that collecting vast

1993 INDICATORS

Japan will not give up its crown next year as the most competitive country but Germany will be closing in. The openness of countries like Denmark and Ireland puts them high up the league. America, despite new-found price competitiveness, slips up on poor standards in education and workers' skills, as well as its managers' lack of international experience. Greece will limp further behind. Gross-operating surplus (the difference between value-added and wage bills) is the measure used for return on capital. Spain will stay the star if rising labour costs do not eat into its lead.

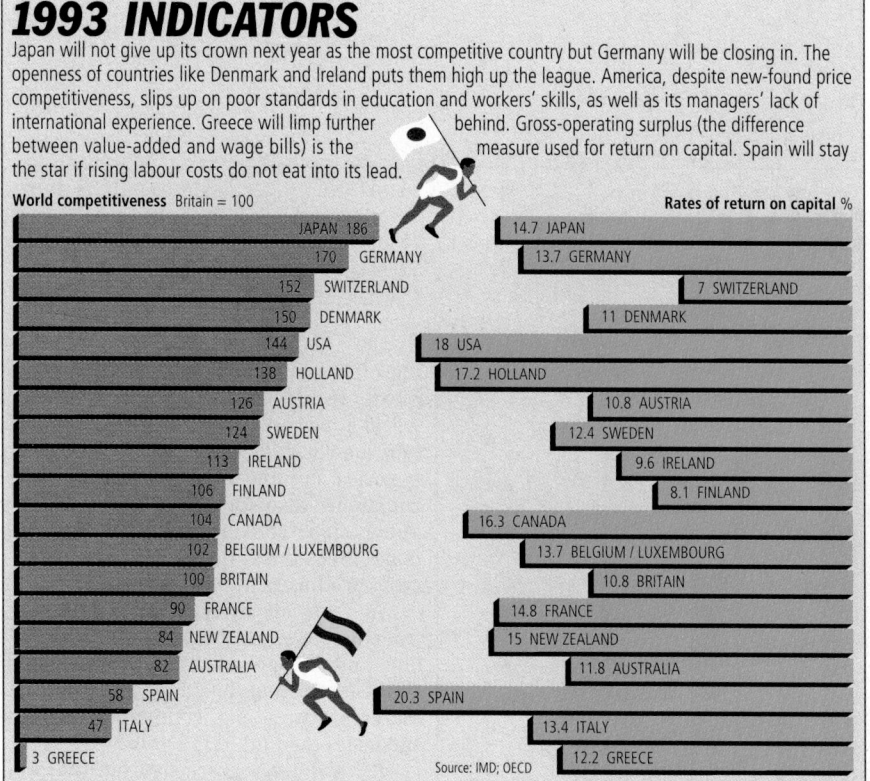

World competitiveness Britain = 100	Rates of return on capital %
JAPAN 186	14.7 JAPAN
170 GERMANY	13.7 GERMANY
152 SWITZERLAND	7 SWITZERLAND
150 DENMARK	11 DENMARK
144 USA	18 USA
138 HOLLAND	17.2 HOLLAND
126 AUSTRIA	10.8 AUSTRIA
124 SWEDEN	12.4 SWEDEN
113 IRELAND	9.6 IRELAND
106 FINLAND	8.1 FINLAND
104 CANADA	16.3 CANADA
102 BELGIUM / LUXEMBOURG	13.7 BELGIUM / LUXEMBOURG
100 BRITAIN	10.8 BRITAIN
90 FRANCE	14.8 FRANCE
84 NEW ZEALAND	15 NEW ZEALAND
82 AUSTRALIA	11.8 AUSTRALIA
58 SPAIN	20.3 SPAIN
47 ITALY	13.4 ITALY
3 GREECE	12.2 GREECE

Source: IMD; OECD

amounts of information about their businesses in computer databases is not only extremely expensive, but not worth doing unless large numbers of employees, not just the top managers, have access to it. The flow of data has become a flood, threatening to drown big-company chiefs in a sea of numbers. The people who can make real use of the information are those much lower down the ladder, who need to make day-to-day decisions on spending, pricing, staffing and responding to the tactics of competitors. But employees with information are also employees with power. They want to act on their own. They question their superiors. Multiplied by tens of thousands, they are incredibly difficult to boss around.

On the factory floor computerisation is reducing even more dramatically the advantages of being big. Instead of increasing the economies of mass production, automation is making it possible to manufacture products just as cheaply in much smaller volumes. Beyond a certain number, the gains from increasing manufacturing volumes run up against the rule of diminishing returns. Computers have done less to breach this barrier than to make factories more flexible, and so more economic at lower volumes. As a result small, flexible manufacturers will be able to compete with much bigger companies.

Another blow to big companies is the growing efficiency and globalisation of world capital markets. One of the most durable barriers to entry for many industries has been the need for any interloper to find large amounts of money to challenge the industry's established companies. In the past, big firms have often been the only ones which could raise such sums. This is no longer true. Some of the world's most capital-intensive industries are being transformed by small firms.

Drug companies, once considered almost immune from new competitors because of the large amounts of money needed to develop new drugs and then get them approved, are now anxiously courting hundreds of small biotechnology firms which they expect to discover the industry's most lucrative new treatments. When America's airline industry was deregulated in 1978, scores of new airlines had no trouble borrowing the hundreds of millions of dollars needed to get started. After a period of industry-wide losses and consolidation, small regional airlines are again making a comeback in America.

Finally, two other trends will accelerate the move away from corporate behemoths: the erosion of loyalty among both employees and consumers. In the 1980s great swathes of middle managers and professionals, the people who hold big companies together, lost their jobs in both America and Europe. Such cuts may have been necessary. But they shattered the allegiance of many white-collar workers, including those who were not sacked.

Big companies traditionally held on to their best employees—the kind with the skills or confidence to start their own company or to join a smaller rival—with good pay, lavish perks and, most of all, job security. These often compensated talented people for the stifling atmosphere of big firms. But such ties are gone. Even in Japan, the land of "lifetime" employment, they are beginning to fray as baby boomers move into their 40s and suddenly find themselves being shunted aside or prematurely ushered out the door. Working for a big firm is no longer a sure ticket to prosperity or prestige, so many employees are more willing to try the excitement and satisfaction of working for a smaller company.

The loyalty which consumers feel to established brands, one of the biggest advantages enjoyed by big firms such as Procter & Gamble, Unilever or Coca-Cola, is evaporating just as quickly. Partly this is a rational response: the universal application of new quality-control techniques pioneered in Japan means that there is little variation in the quality of most goods, so consumers assume less of a risk when switching from a familiar brand.

But it is also irrational: barraged by advertising messages from all directions, consumers are increasingly indifferent—and fickle. More and more frequently they opt for the newest or the cheapest item whether or not they have ever heard of it. The advertising industry views this trend with alarm, but does not know what to do about it. Many established brands may survive on store shelves because of the clout which their producers enjoy with distributors—one of the few advantages a large size may continue to confer. But their profit margin, the true test of a brand's strength, will not be much higher than those of newer items making their way forward. Many of these new brands will come from smaller companies.

Of course, big companies will not disappear overnight. Many will try to cope with the increasing pressures on them by continually reorganising to reduce the liabilities of size. Others will grow larger simply because successful businessmen, like successful politicians, are natural empire builders. And there will be a limit to how small, as well as how big, a company can be in any particular industry and still compete over the long term. But the optimum size for companies in most industries is dropping fast. This will turn the "small is beautiful" romanticism of E.F. Schumacher on its head. Small firms will thrive not because they will be more humane than large ones, but because they will be more ruthlessly competitive.

Of board stiffs and pet rocks

Tim Hindle

The company boardroom will be at the top of the corporate agenda in 1993. The driving force (certainly in Anglo-Saxon countries) is a concern about "corporate governance", about how companies are governed and to whom they are accountable. There is a feeling that the boardroom, the place where the ultimate responsibility for corporate governance lies, badly let industrial society down in the 1980s.

This feeling is not new. In 1985, Carl Icahn, an American corporate raider who saw inside more than one boardroom, said, "What goes on in there is a travesty. The chairman doesn't want someone under him who is a threat, so he picks someone a little less capable: it's the survival of the unfittest, and it's getting worse."

A year later, in 1986, before he was ousted from the board of General Motors for being too critical of its management, Ross Perot described his fellow non-executive directors on the GM board as "pet rocks". Accounts of board behaviour in the decade's many takeovers suggest that directors all too rarely raised their eyes above the parapet of self-interest.

The cries for action became irresistible when this self-interest turned into skulduggery. Blatant cases like that of Robert Maxwell, a chairman of a public company who was able to dip into the company's pension funds for his own private benefit, have left few satisfied with apologists who argue that it is impossible to design a system to be proof against the determined crook.

One attempt to do something to improve matters was the setting up of a committee in Britain to look into "the financial aspects of corporate governance". Under the chairmanship of Sir Adrian Cadbury, its draft recommendations were published in May 1992. Its final report will be out in 1993.

Sir Adrian recommended that large British companies should have what large companies in the United States already have: namely, an audit sub-committee to appoint the auditors and vouch for their objectivity; and a remuneration sub-committee to fix the pay of those who fix the pay of everybody else.

This fragmentation of boards has disturbed those who believe in the merit of the unitary board, of the force and vitality of a group of like-minded people set on an inspiring common course. One of them— Sir Owen Green, chairman of the conglomerate BTR—accused Sir Adrian of cowardice for not going the whole hog and recommending the introduction of a two-tier board structure, as in Germany. Large German companies have a management board (executive) and a supervisory board (non-executive).

The debate about boards has exposed a deep divide between Anglo-Saxon and continental European forms of corporate governance—a divide that threatens to look wider as other differences between companies in the EC diminish. It is not just a question of unitary or two-tier boards. It is also a question of which of the company's "constituencies" are represented on the board, and how. German supervisory boards are usually split 50-50 between worker representatives and shareholder representatives; Anglo-Saxon boards find the idea of worker directors second in horror only to a communist takeover.

Those bent on building better unitary boards are compelled to focus more closely on the number and nature of their non-executive directors. Sir Adrian wants their appointment to be more formalised—and thus to be extended well beyond the circle of the chairman's chums. Some fear that if the circle is extended too far the board will become just a diffuse collection of characters, about as effective as a meeting of Commonwealth heads of state.

Different countries favour different groups for their non-executive directors. Germans go in for their bankers; Americans for other companies' bosses. Britons choose ex-politicians and the French ex-

The global board

Tim Hindle

This comes in five distinct varieties:
• **The token slot**. Here there is one foreigner among a bunch of locals. Such companies tend to go in for tokenism, so if the foreigner can be a woman at the same time, so much the better. Needless to say, nobody pays any attention to her.
• **The tower of babel**. Here interpreters have to be present at board meetings— not only to translate the languages but also to translate the cultures. At CMB, an initially disastrous merger of Britain's Metal Box and France's Carnaud, the merger's authoritarian chairman, Jean-Marie Descarpentries, was openly referred to as Des Carpenter by his English fellow directors. He was forced to resign after every board meeting became an Agincourt.
• **The frightfully fair**. Often the result of a friendly merger where neither side wants to be unfriendly by suggesting that the other shed some of its directors. When Sweden's Asea merged with the Swiss Brown Boveri to form ABB, its chairman was Swiss one year, Swedish the next. Any linguistic unfairness was eliminated by choosing English as the language of the boardroom—fortunately a language which most directors could understand.
• **The avant-garde**. These are boards that embrace all the latest fashions. Sometimes ICI looks a bit like one: it had a Japanese director long before anybody else in Europe had decided that this was not such a good idea; and more recently it appointed a European director: she is a German banker.
• **The old guard**. A small number of very large companies have been successfully multinational for so long that they no longer think of themselves as having a nationality. Such companies include Philips and Nestlé, and the Anglo-Dutch pair, Shell and Unilever. Their boards are an international mix that has developed organically over time. It may have helped that they are all closely connected to two very small outward-looking nations, the Netherlands and Switzerland.

Tim Hindle: freelance journalist and author of "The Sultan of Berkeley Square", an account of the life and times of Asil Nadir.

civil servants. Occasionally, fashions sweep in and out of the boardroom: hottest at the moment is the exhortation to think "foreign". The global product is giving birth to the global board, particularly among European multinationals.

There is little sign yet of foreigners infiltrating the boardrooms of German or Japanese companies. It will come. But wise companies will not appoint foreign directors primarily because they are foreign. They will appoint them because they can help the company to understand new foreign markets, or to gain access to new sources of funds.

Likewise, wise companies will appoint more and better women directors. Too many women are on boards for public relations reasons. They are too often non-executives. The corporate world has been good at giving women important jobs in the past decade, bad at promoting those who do them to the board. That will start to change in 1993.

The IT factor

Other changes will have an influence on the future structure of company boards. First there is change itself: increasingly rapid change in society and in markets will demand a wider point of view. This will increase the demand for more flexible and far-sighted boards than any company can expect to find in one small group of individuals, however powerfully and entrepreneurially they work together as a team.

As this demand arises so will the technological means to supply it. Perhaps the most stimulating single idea in management for a decade is that of the "informated" company. Most closely associated with Harvard's Shoshana Zuboff, it is about the power of information technology (IT)—computers and telecommunications—to change the way we think about technology itself and about organisational structure. In the past, technology meant automation and a diminution of human effort. IT is the first technology to do exactly the opposite, and to require an increase in human effort. By enabling virtually anybody within a corporation to have access to any information, it enhances and diffuses the nature of work.

What might be the impact of this on company boards? Well, in an IT world, boards can be formed almost ad hoc from those stakeholders in the company who are most suited to consider the point in question. Informatics has the power to create a board the size of a whole company, or indeed to create a "phantom" non-existent board where all decisions are delegated to relevant sub-committees.

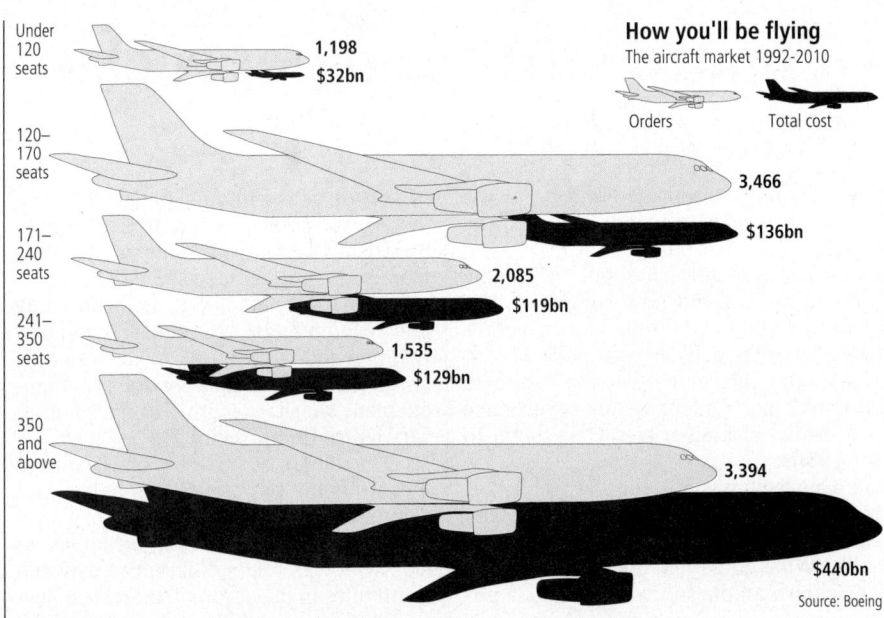

How you'll be flying
The aircraft market 1992-2010

Orders   Total cost

Under 120 seats — 1,198 $32bn

120–170 seats — 3,466 $136bn

171–240 seats — 2,085 $119bn

241–350 seats — 1,535 $129bn

350 and above — 3,394 $440bn

Source: Boeing

Flying foreign

Harvey Elliott

Many of the aircraft in which you will be flying for the rest of your life will be decided upon next year. Boeing, for example, is pressing ahead with its 777 twinjet, which it hopes will dominate the medium-sized aircraft market well into the next century. Assembly will start in 1993 from parts that are now being delivered to the main Boeing plant in Seattle from more than a dozen countries—underlining just how extraordinarily international this huge industry is becoming.

About 20% of the 777 will be built in Japan by Mitsubishi, Kawasaki and Fuji Heavy Industries. Its engines will be supplied by the three main manufacturers—Rolls-Royce, Pratt and Whitney, and General Electrics. Alenia of Italy is making the outboard wing flaps. Embraer of Brazil is responsible for the fin and most of the wingtip assembly. Korean Air makes part of the wingtip. Nose-gear doors are being made by Shorts of Northern Ireland and Singapore Aerospace. The rudder is made in Australia. Hundreds of other companies are involved.

Boeing's next big decision is whether to build a 750-seat long-range aircraft. If a completely new aircraft is shown to be in demand, Boeing is planning a "triple bubble" with passengers seated on three decks, one above the other.

Then there is a successor for Concorde to be considered. The hope is to have an aircraft certified for commercial

service in 2005. It would carry 300 passengers over 5,800 miles at two-and-a-half times the speed of sound, with a delta wing design. If such an aircraft were built, it would almost certainly be multinational, with Britain, France, Germany, Italy, Russia and Japan all working together with America to produce the first truly global airliner.

Airbus, the European consortium which pioneered international collaboration, believes that demand for new aircraft will resume in 1993 and grow strongly in 1994, leading to orders for 12,050 new aircraft over the next 20 years from all manufacturers. Of these, they believe, 7,050 will represent replacements; the remainder will be needed to cope with passenger growth.

Airbus, which is now repaying its original loans at the rate of at least $1 billion a year, is an undoubted success; it has taken orders for 1,300 aircraft over the past six years and is now making a healthy profit. To extend its family of aircraft still further, Airbus is pressing ahead with the stretched A321: its first flight should be in March 1993.

The Germans are rapidly emerging as a major force in the European aerospace industry. Deutsche Airbus successfully persuaded the other partners in the consortium to allow final assembly of both the A321 and the A319 to take place in Hamburg, rather than Toulouse. Deutsche Aerospace has taken a controlling interest in Holland's Fokker and is eyeing addi-

Harvey Elliott: air correspondent for *The Times*.

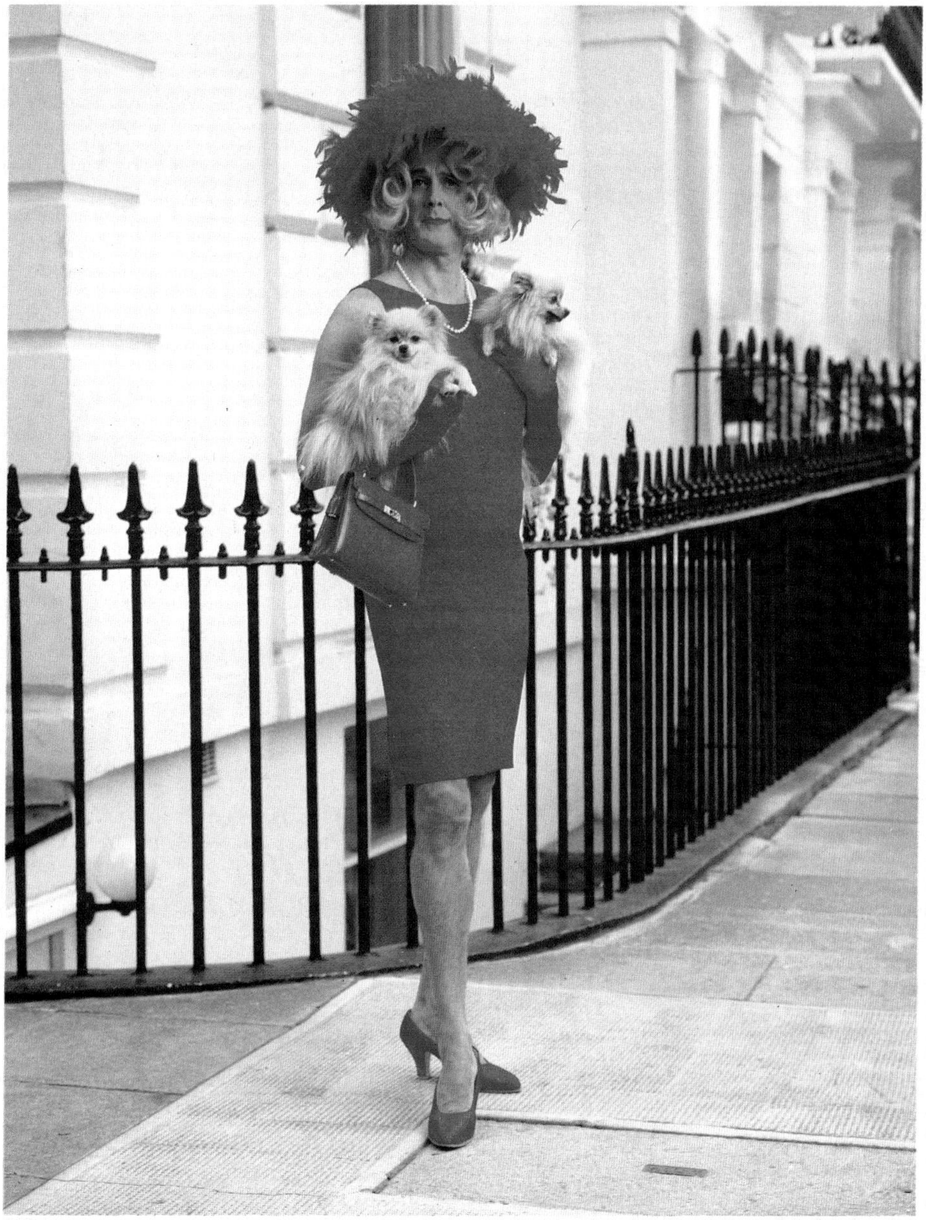

John Cleese. Cardmember since 1971.

Membership Has Its Privileges.®

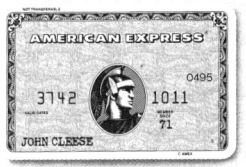

Stuck in the mud

Richard Branson

Passenger transport is among the most important of industries. World commerce depends upon it. For hundreds of millions of people it makes their annual holiday the high point of each year. Passenger transport feeds the world's largest employer: the tourist industry. It fosters trade and prosperity. It overcomes the barriers of time and distance. It adds to human enjoyment and the quality of life.

How well it will meet these important needs in 1993 and beyond depends on three groups of people: technologists, operators and rule-makers.

One hundred and seventy years after passenger services began, railways are being transformed by technology. Trains are speeding up, using unprecedented power from new motors, computer signalling and sometimes new tracks. The next generation of rail travel will be highly competitive.

For the airlines, the technologists are making important contributions of a different kind. Lower costs and greater reliability are the result of improved engines, better aerodynamics and air-traffic control systems.

However, the way that the operators of most of the world's railways and airlines go about their business has been shaped by at least half a century's government protection, ownership and control.

Almost to its sad end, Pan Am sometimes seemed to think it was an arm of the State Department. And one only has to listen to a British Rail train guard addressing his "customers" to actually hear the quotation marks which signal his distaste for them.

Taking pride in service quality and passenger satisfaction is a prerequisite of taking action. And when the British government allowed more competition at Heathrow airport, British Airways revealed its pained surprise by cancelling its contribution to the Conservative Party. Lack of competition means that airline costs and air fares are commonly 30% higher than necessary.

Blame the rule-makers. They will determine the future of the transport industries and the satisfaction of its customers. They are more important,

---

Richard Branson: chairman and founder of the Virgin Group of Companies.

---

but less progressive, than the technologists or even the operators.

The market-economy stream has never been seen more clearly as mankind's main channel of progress, even though recession has weakened its flow. The alternative command-economy channel has been revealed as a shallow silting backwater. Only the most compelling arguments could justify running an industry as important as transport as a command economy.

Yet that is exactly where it starts in 1993. Transport is a command-economy mudbank in the middle of the market-economy stream, choking its flow, a hazard to the navigation of free enterprise.

On the rails it is early days yet; much hard thinking and talking has to be done, but at least the process has started in Britain. In the air, some British and EC rule-makers sincerely believe that they

> *"Transport is a command-economy mudbank in the middle of the market-economy stream"*

have made another in a series of breakthroughs and that the benefits of effective competition are about to flow. Reality, alas, persistently fails to catch up with them. In 1993 four determined actions are needed if airline competition is really going to work.

1. Adopt pro-competition rules.
The many anti-competitive limitations on market entry, product quality, output and price need stripping away. But that is not enough. Little is achieved by decanting old-established airlines into a supposedly open marketplace and then sitting back for competition to happen. It will be a long wait. These oversized duopoly-bred operators know little of competition and care for it less.

Airlines must be exposed now to the full weight of pro-competitive regulation. That means controlling mergers, monopoly practices, subsidies and predatory behaviour. There is absolutely no reason to exempt air transport any longer from the full

application of the competition articles of the Treaty of Rome.

2. Remove all barriers.
During decades of protected oligopoly, old-established airlines accumulated layer upon layer of barriers to consumer choice and competition. So long as a single one remains it will block progress. All of them must go.

The EC's latest breakthrough is said to liberalise air services from the first day of the single market in 1993. That is true only up to a point. Yes, it should open abundant opportunities for efficient airlines to offer better service and enhanced value-for-money on Europe's trunk routes. Mediocre service standards and high costs among the established airlines leave much scope.

But no entrepreneur in his right mind will venture into this market. Why? Because this supposed breakthrough leaves intact a number of obstacles which ensure that competition and new airlines alike are firmly excluded.

3. Let consumers choose.
The essence of competition lies with the consumer. Competition exists when the consumer can choose from a wide range of clearly-stated options and if there is nothing to stop new suppliers entering the market on the same terms as old-established operators. This is not the case with air travel in Europe, nor will be after 1993.

4. Obliterate "rights".
Aviation's most common competition-killer is historical precedence. The rule-makers ensure their own failure by continuing to tolerate the allocation of scarce resources on the basis of who had them first. That guarantees that nothing can change.

Aviation cannot operate without some scarce resources. Runways, for example, come in quite useful. No airline can make a go of it without a competitive schedule, using a runway at the right airport at the right time. To deny access to airports, or to distribute take-off and landing slots on the basis of first-come first-served ossifies the market.

Only if these four changes are made in air transport, and if the early ideas for rail competition can be carried through, is 1993 going to be a year to remember for all the users of transport, the year in which it was finally retrieved from the mud to rejoin the mainstream of economic progress.

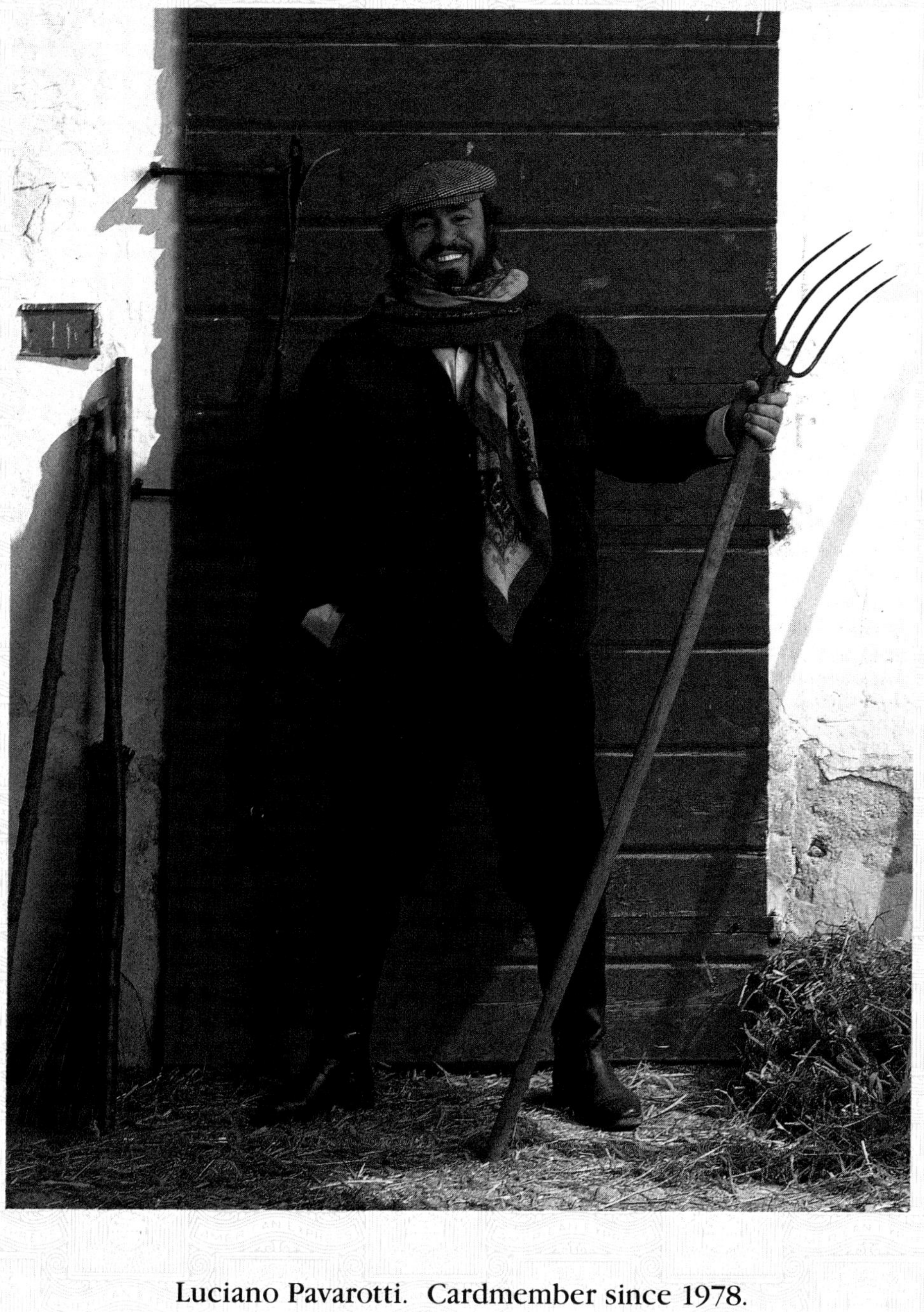

Luciano Pavarotti. Cardmember since 1978.

Membership Has Its Privileges.®

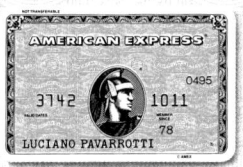

Russia takes wing

Harvey Elliott

Russia, the sleeping giant of world aerospace, is about to wake up. This is one Russian industry that works. Several Russian aircraft will obtain their western certification in 1993. They will then be sold on the world market at very much lower prices than their European or American rivals.

In 1993 Russia will rise in importance both as a supplier of its own aircraft and as a provider of parts to the West. With wages incomparably lower than those in Europe and America, western-equipped aircraft built in Russia will be extremely attractive. Rolls-Royce has formed an alliance with the Tupolev design bureau, and modified Tu-204s with RB211-535 engines will soon be on sale. Pratt and Whitney has teamed up with Ilyushin to

Russia's great white hope

power the Il-96 widebody jet. Yakolev has linked with Garrett and Textron Lycoming as well as with Dowty and Smiths Industries. The helicopter manufacturers, Kamov, are working with Israel on an export version of their proven helicopter.

Watch out, too, for the emergence of Shorts of Belfast as a major player in the aerospace world. Since the company—state-owned and neglected for 40 years—was sold to Canadian-based Bombardier in 1989, the factory has been completely modernised at a cost of £200m ($320m) to make it one of the best equipped and most cost effective in the world. The company is now both making money and hungrily seeking the chance to expand.

tional partners such as Alenia and France's Aerospatiale. It is almost certain to forge much closer links with both Boeing and the Japanese, confusing still further the once clear-cut country-by-country divisions which used to exist.

McDonnell Douglas is still mulling over its plans to launch the MD-95 twinjet, a 105-seater which would be a direct competitor of the A319 and which could be built in China. British Aerospace, too, has formed a joint venture with Taiwan Aerospace to produce regional jets.

No single country, let alone company, can afford to develop and build an entire aircraft; each nation must now concentrate on the few areas of production which it does best.

Get that monopoly off the line

Jim Chalmers

Telecoms will be a growth industry in 1993 everywhere in the world. And that growth will come despite long-overdue reductions in prices to customers who want to call their office-mates across the oceans: calling auntie next door will get more expensive. The pace will not be set by technological change, though there will be plenty of it. The greater change is the accelerating globalisation of the business. Changes in ownership, increased competition and a blurring of the sovereign responsibility for national telecoms will provide ample controversy.

Next year will decide which companies lead the race to become truly global networks. There have been a number of false starts. Some national operators seem to think that a fancy new name and a press release does the job: BT's "Syncordia", France Telecom and Deutsche Telekom's "Eunetcom", and the "Unisource" company, formed by Sweden's Televerket and PTT Telecom Nether-

Jim Chalmers: editor of the monthly *Public Network Europe* magazine.

lands, have yet to prove that they are anything more than marketing creations. They have so far failed to win customers beyond the national markets of their owners.

Much more depends on those major carriers which have yet to declare their global ambitions. Giants such as AT&T, MCI and Sprint of the United States, or Japan's KDD and NTT, have still to choose whether to join one of the existing groupings, go it alone, or form their own, perhaps looser, affiliations with telephone companies from around the world. As these companies get their global networks up and running, the ordinary user sitting at home will see little benefit. It is the world's top multinationals which are the targets. Global carriers prefer to concentrate on the most traffic-intensive routes.

Many of the most advanced services which are available today will remain, therefore, the exclusive preserve of major corporate customers for the immediate future. State-of-the-art technology—such as videophones and machines which har-

ness the increasing sophistication of personal computers over the telephone network—will be ever more in use among the Fortune 500 companies during 1993. Joe Bloggs will have to wait a year or so.

Business calls between two developed countries outnumber private calls by a 3:1 ratio. In addition, some 70% of that business traffic is "intra-corporate". So a single carrier which wins an exclusive contract to handle the telecoms for a Ford, a Citibank or a Heinz hits paydirt.

In 1993 the combination of tough competition for the largest accounts and American-led regulatory pressure (also backed by the EC) to combat over-pricing of international calls should drive tariffs down. This is more bad news for the ordinary telephone user. Charges for residential line rentals and local calls, where telephone companies retain *de facto* monopolies, are likely to rise in most countries next year.

In less developed parts of the world, the major companies of Europe, North America and Asia will continue the process of telecoms "colonisation", whether through forming joint ventures in Eastern Europe or buying out government shares in the state-run monopolies of Latin America. This is the "second front" in the global expansion war. The process may in some cases end in tears. The new *conquistadors*—European companies which have bought into telecoms operating in countries such as Argentina or Mexico—face a difficult task. Having assumed responsibility, they must attempt to raise charges, cut staffing levels and ramp up investment to improve dilapidated networks. A failure to strike the right balance will provoke political resentment. Expect

RANK XEROX

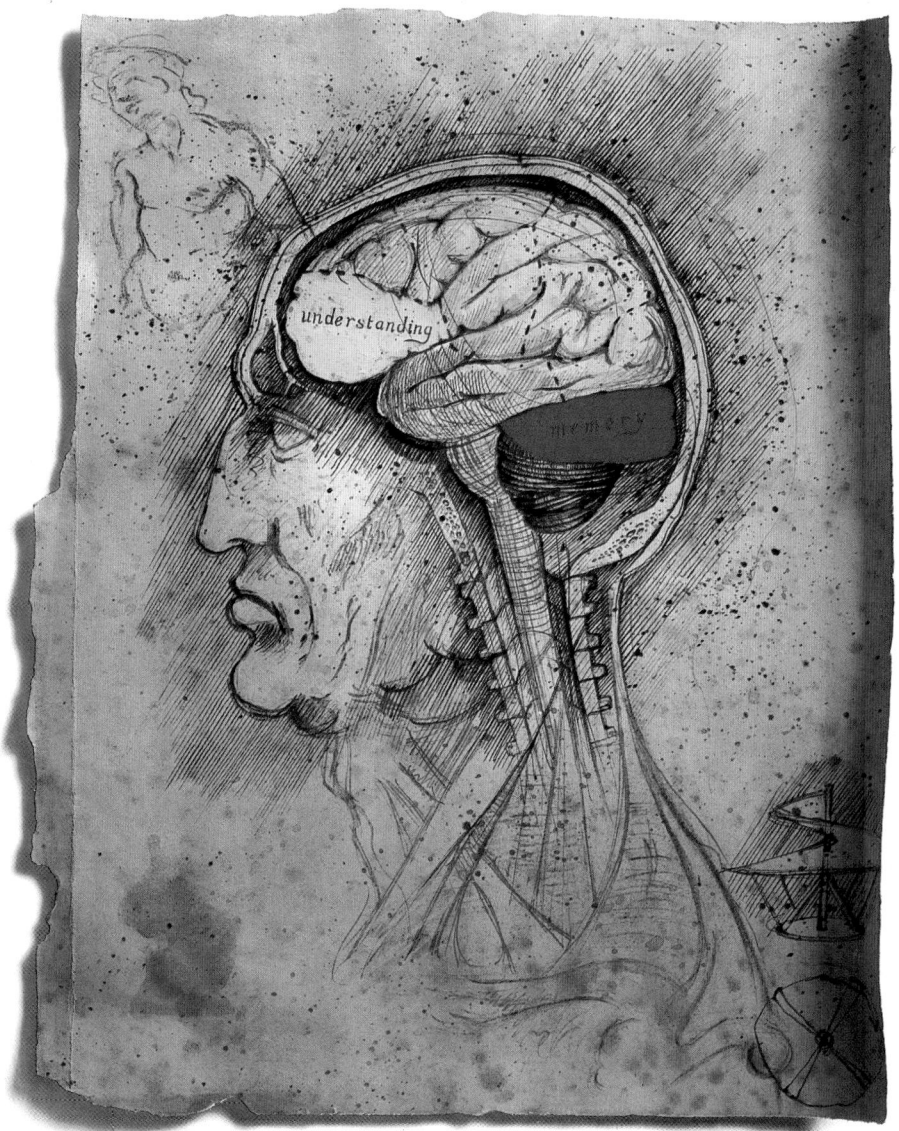

Xerox colour in documents stimulates the grey matter.

Get your head round this. Produce your documents in colour and 52%* more people will read them and remember them.

Colour motivates too. Add red to an invoice and you'll see the colour of people's money 50%† faster.

And for colour technology no one in the world outranks Rank Xerox.

 For the drawing office, data centre, print room or general office, whether you need full or highlight colour, Rank Xerox has the machine. All of which come with a three year guarantee when you take out a full service agreement.

When you want really graphic graphics and punchy print, Xerox colour really gets the grey matter ticking. *Daniel Starch Organisation. †What's Working in Direct Marketing, Sept. 24, 1990.

For more information, please send to Rank Xerox (UK) Ltd, FREEPOST 2, Uxbridge, Middlesex UB8 3BR.

TITLE: (MR/MRS/MISS)   INITIALS

SURNAME

COMPANY NAME

ADDRESS

POSTCODE   TEL NO.

3226

Rank Xerox
The Document Company
Call us free on 0800 010 766

Axe that telephone pole

Jim Chalmers

Who needs a copper wire to connect their home to a phone? And who needs to put up with the muffled uncertainties of cellular, portable telephones? In 1993 both will start to look old hat.

The concept of personal communication networks (PCNS) is based on ending the reliance on copper wires to connect ordinary subscribers to the network. Out goes the copper, in comes a highly sophisticated radio-link. (So sophisticated that you would never in fact realise that it was a radio-link at all.) PCNS represent an expansion of today's commonplace cellular networks beyond the executive market to the everyday mass market.

Any government wishing to provide full competition to an established national operator will licence a radio-based competitor to connect subscribers to the network. That is the best way of getting new companies to bring telephone services to the homes of millions.

The key to the future of such systems lies with the price of the user handsets. This in turn is linked to the size of the market as perceived by manufacturers. Volume production of miniature personal phones collapses the cost. So watch Japanese manufacturers such as Sony, Sharp and Matsushita. Next year they will start producing stylish, high-performance radio terminals at low cost for the mass market. Once they do, and if your government is wise enough to open up the market, you can tell your telephone company what to do with its bit of wire—and its bill.

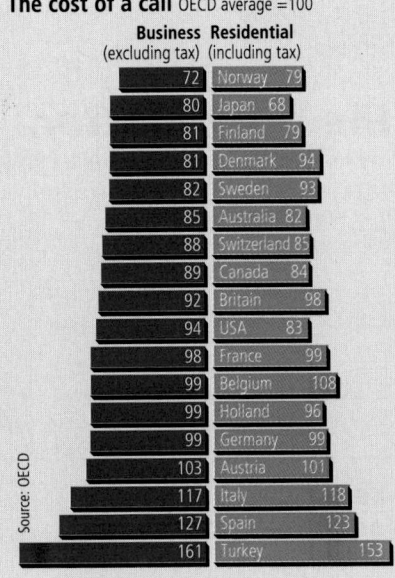

The cost of a call OECD average =100

Business (excluding tax)		Residential (including tax)
72	Norway	79
80	Japan	68
81	Finland	79
81	Denmark	94
82	Sweden	93
85	Australia	82
88	Switzerland	85
89	Canada	84
92	Britain	98
94	USA	83
98	France	99
99	Belgium	108
99	Holland	96
99	Germany	99
103	Austria	101
117	Italy	118
127	Spain	123
161	Turkey	153

Source: OECD

to see at least one major crisis in Latin America during 1993, perhaps even leading to renationalisation.

Led by the example of the privatisation of Deutsche Telekom of Germany next year, European governments should all be looking to take telephone companies out of the state sector. Around half a dozen should announce plans to do so in 1993. Some, such as the French, will most certainly not.

The more ambitious governments should take the opportunity to draw a line between the national operator's competitive businesses and its remaining monopoly activities. In particular, this means spinning off lucrative mobile cellular operations separately from the main monopoly core. As well as making the distinct elements of a former state company more manageable, such a step would create greater flexibility in the competitive businesses. And it would force the remaining monopoly—deprived of cross-subsidy from more profitable businesses—to become more efficient.

Even so, the monopolies in Europe—particularly the basic telephone service—may not survive 1993. EC regulation may yet force change: more likely, the ease and economy with which the latest technology can now circumvent traditional monopolies will do the job, while the politicians dither.

1993's gizmos

Tim Jackson

This summer, huge posters all over Tokyo asked a blunt question of Japanese consumers. "Your summer bonus—what will you do with it?" And underneath, as an answer, appeared nothing but a giant photograph of a *nasu* (eggplant or aubergine), a vegetable that is a Japanese symbol of penny-pinching.

The advertisement, from Fuji Bank, had a clear moral. After years of blowing their spare money on expensive toys and gadgets, the Japanese are becoming more sensible. Tokyo's commonest 1993 men's suit, for instance, will be polyester: not for any intrinsic merits it may have, but because the days are over when the average office worker would be willing to lay out $1,000 on an imported double-breasted lightweight wool pinstripe from Paul Smith.

Companies that come up with gimmicks for the coming year will want to make them seem useful. One is a new feature on a domestic cordless telephone, intended to deal with the troublesome problem of what to do when someone calls while the television is on. A hidden **infrared remote control** inside the phone, compatible with most makes of TV, automatically turns down the sound; when the user hangs up, it will restore the volume to its original level. Already available in Japan, this should make its way to Europe next year.

Tim Jackson: author of *Turning Japanese*, to be published by HarperCollins on January 4th 1993.

Another is a device on a domestic Toyota car that may now be offered as an option abroad. Next to the switch that controls the placing of the driver's door-mirror is a special button. Press it, and the mirror will wiggle gently back and forth, shaking off droplets of rain that have collected while the car was parked. As well as being amusing to watch, this **wiggling mechanism** clears the mirror quicker and with less electricity than some of today's more elaborate heating elements.

A third brainwave is a **platform-washing robot** built by Fuji Heavy Industries for East Japan Railways. Thanks to a gyroscope and an ultrasonic sensor, the computer-controlled machine can glide up and down platforms on its own, washing them down with water and brushes for hours after a human cleaner would have gone home. How long before British Rail gets one?

But the downturn in most industrial economies will have little effect on the research programmes that have been at work for years. Semiconductor companies like Intel and Toshiba are likely to bring out further refinements of the **flash memories** that they are betting will eventually replace rotating magnetic disk drives. Flash memories, which are like standard dynamic random-access memory (DRAM) chips but retain their charge and hence the information that has been stored on them even after the electric current is switched off, promise to make portable computers lighter and able to run for twice as long as at present. In 1993 this new memory medium is likely to fall in price by half; expect it to pop up in computers towards the end of the year.

Again on notebook computers, **colour screens** will become the norm as electronics and computer makers bring their prices down. The technology leader remains Sharp; but a joint venture between IBM and Toshiba in the Japanese castle town of Himeji may well be producing the new active-matrix colour screens more cheaply. A colour notebook computer will probably sell for around $3,000 at the end of 1993.

But the year will be dominated by two new products of epic proportions. One is the **replacement to the cassette**: a gadget that can record music in its pristine digital form, doing to the old cassette what the CD did to the vinyl record. By the end of 1992, two versions of the new product were trickling into the market: Philips's **digital compact cassette**, which plays old-fashioned analogue cassettes as well as the new digital ones; and Sony's **Mini-Disc**, a shrunken, recordable CD. It will be years before the winner emerges: the war between them is likely to make the old video wars (remember VHS versus Betamax?) look like a garden-party. Sony's idea is the more daring, for it forces buyers to junk all their old cassettes; whether it is the eventual victor, however, will depend on how swiftly the Japanese company can get a wide range of pre-recorded titles on to the market.

The other dramatic new product will be Apple's **keyboardless computer**. To look up an address, to check an appointment, or to add a column of figures, the user will simply write letters or numbers with an electronic pen on the notebook-sized screen. To do more complex things, the pen can be used to point at Macintosh-style "icons", each one conveying the meaning of what a given command will do. The wraps are not yet off the product, which is billed as the Newton; but as Apple's symbolic re-entry into consumer products, it may mark the beginning of an American revival in this lucrative business.

Go kick a drug company

Moira Dower

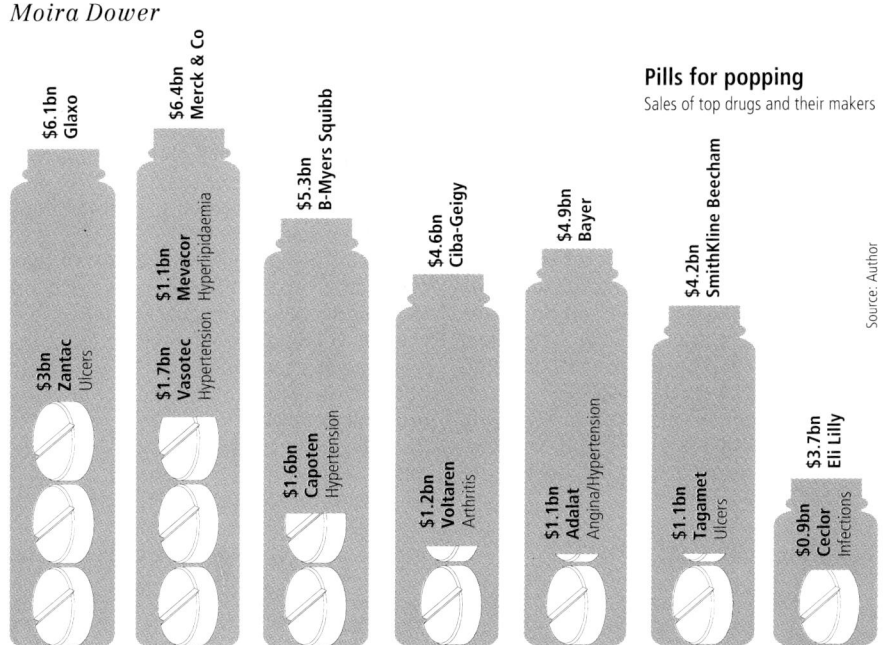

Pills for popping
Sales of top drugs and their makers

Source: Author

What companies do you love to hate? Ten years ago it was the oil companies; then it was the banks; next year's pet hates will be the pharmaceutical giants. Profitable, multinational and with products charged with emotion, the world's drug companies will have a rough 1993, sniped at from all sides.

First complaint: prices are too high. The largest of the free markets in Europe—Germany—succumbed to strict government controls three years ago. There are some cunning methods of price-control about, such as removing products from automatic state reimbursement (if the patient has to pay, he thinks twice about whether he wants the medicine); imposing price freezes; or exerting more control over what, and how much, doctors prescribe.

Even in the United States, now seen as the last bastion of free pricing for pharmaceuticals, political pressure is increasingly forcing companies into "voluntary" curbs on price rises, keeping them to the rate of inflation. The world's largest pharmaceutical firm, Merck, has accepted this line and others are following suit. Drug firms are also being forced to discount heavily to large buying groups, which could account for 60% of the American market by 1995.

The result? Glaxo, SmithKline Beecham and others say that price rises now account for no more than two percentage points of their overall annual revenue growth; only a few years ago price increases accounted for more than 5%.

Next complaint: new products. It is only by coming up with a steady flow of innovative medicines that companies can hope to keep ahead of the competition; new products can also demand higher prices. But new products run into a lot of flak. Either the public wants them now, cheap, and the drug companies get blamed for withholding them. Or the companies are accused of sharp pricing practices in their greed for profits.

This can be galling when the amount of investment is so huge. The estimated cost of developing a new chemical entity is about £125m ($200m). Glaxo spent £130m on its anti-migraine product, Imigran, and is having difficulty in some European markets getting the pan-European price it wants.

The average new product does not break even on its development costs until 21 years after it is patented. (It is said that it takes 12 years, on average, from patenting to marketing.) Only one product in five will become a blockbuster (with sales over $100m), and four in five will not recoup their investment cost.

R&D expenditure by the worldwide pharmaceutical industry is estimated to be about £24 billion next year. Over the past few years R&D as a percentage of sales has been increasing rapidly—10% used to be the norm but the major companies are now spending upwards of 15% of their

Moira Dower: editor, *Scrip World Pharmaceutical News.*

revenues. This will inevitably accelerate as advances are made in the fields of cancer and diseases of the central nervous system, such as Alzheimer's, where the clinical trials are longer, regulatory demands are tougher, and costs are therefore higher.

Group therapy

Next year will see more co-operative R&D agreements, rather than mergers. Pharmaceutical companies have largely abandoned the "not invented here" mentality and are actively seeking co-operation with others in specific therapeutic areas (for example, Organon and Roche for serotonin, Upjohn and Solvay for central nervous system products, Glaxo and Yamanouchi in osteoporosis).

Multinationals are also increasingly quick to pick up on, and exploit, early research by the ever-growing number of start-up companies in the United States (sometimes called research boutiques). The days of going it alone in R&D are gone.

Two developments will boost the financial returns on good research. First, moves have been made worldwide to restore the patent life lost when a drug undergoes testing before marketing. In the EC a new directive becomes effective in January 1993, which awards pharmaceuticals "supplementary protection certificates" of 15 years after they reach their first EC market.

Also, the Uruguay round of GATT has intellectual property protection high on its agenda—whether the GATT talks succeed or fail, they have forced many countries, such as Canada, China and New Zealand, to tighten their intellectual property laws anyway.

The second development that the industry will want to keep in mind, as it gets kicked in the shins in 1993, is the move towards harmonising regulatory requirements for drug registration across the world. This would put an end to duplication of effort in the various animal and human studies needed to gain marketing approval. The prize is the saving of millions of R&D dollars. (It has been estimated that, if 12-month toxicology studies on dogs, for example, were to be abandoned, the savings to the industry would be £39m a year—not to mention the positive gain for animal rights.)

Don't cry too much for the drug companies. Their market grows by the day. For example, the very elderly (those over 75) are prescribed an average of 24 items a year, according to one British estimate. By 2025 there will be 2m people in Britain aged over 80, and 7.6m in the United States.

There is little sign so far of any erosion in the bottom line of an industry that is still highly profitable. In the first half of 1992, leading American pharmaceutical companies were reporting profit growth of 18%. The drug companies can take those kicks and still smile.

Prize diseases

Moira Dower

Here are five diseases for which new drug compounds may become available in 1993, with huge impacts on the profits of the winning drug companies.
• **Alzheimer's disease**. Two new drugs from the same chemical class—Warner-Lambert's tacrine (brand name Cognex) and Hoechst's velnacrine (Mentane)—have been shown to have beneficial effects on memory, language and motor skills, which are impaired in patients with Alzheimer's.
• **Cancer**. Taxol, a novel substance synthesised from the bark of the Pacific Yew tree, has been shown to shrink ovarian cancer tumours by at least 50% in 20-30% of patients. The manufacturer, Bristol-Myers Squibb, is evaluating taxol in other types of cancer.
• **Schizophrenia**. About 1% of the world's population suffers from schizophrenia, and the current market for drugs in this field is about $1 billion. Risperidone (Risperdal), a new antipsychotic drug from a Johnson & Johnson subsidiary, Janssen, is being hailed as an advance on older drugs because it has fewer side effects.
• **Arthritis**. Pfizer's new drug for arthritis, tenidap, has been described as the first anti-rheumatic to have a disease-modifying effect, as well as being able to relieve the pain and symptoms of rheumatoid- and osteo-arthritis.
• **Obesity**. Lilly's fluoxetine (Prozac), which is already on the market for depression, is awaiting approval for the treatment of obesity. It will be marketed under the trade name Lovan and will slim you while fattening Lilly's profits.

The coming competition

Tim Jackson

Over the past decade, one thing in the world's fast-changing computer industry has remained remarkably constant. When a customer in Europe buys a PC, he has to expect to pay the same price in pounds that a customer in America would pay in dollars.

That may now no longer be true. When Compaq launched a new series of cut-price notebook machines in the summer of 1992, the American computer maker decided to ask the same price on both sides of the Atlantic.

That change of policy is a sign of a wider trend: the EC is at last beginning to become a truly competitive market. This is only partly because of the single market, in which hundreds of national restrictions were due to be swept away and new Europe-wide standards put in place overnight on December 31st 1992. It is also the result of five years of increasingly aggressive enforcement of anti-trust law by the competition tsars at the European Commission, Leon Brittan and his predecessor Peter Sutherland.

Good for consumers though it may be, tougher competition in the midst of a recession is a daunting prospect for businesses that have become used to thinking of the fragmented markets of Europe as cosy niches from which to subsidise their American sales. But it is not just a challenge for the EC's big guns. Since much of the pressure is coming from Japan, it will be both European and American companies in the EC market that suffer.

Although the hue and cry from protectionists such as Peugeot's Jacques Calvet may suggest otherwise, the Japanese have so far hardly arrived in the EC. They sell plenty of PCs, but have been largely excluded from selling the big mainframe computers that governments and companies tend to buy. They are hobbled by anti-dumping duties on photocopiers and almost a dozen other industrial products. They sell only one car in nine in Europe, compared with one in three in the United States.

At first sight, Japanese firms seem less threatening in the European market than they did three or four years ago. The pace of growth of their foreign investments has slackened off, and although more than 600 Japanese companies are already inside the Community in time for the single market, their numbers are no longer rising by half every year.

The collapse of the Tokyo stockmarket, and the consequent problems of Japan's banks, gave rise to a hope in Brussels that the god may have clay feet after all. The slowdown in Japan's own economy meant that the formidable cashflow behind Japanese businesses' expansion tailed off.

But despite these short-term outward

Trans*ACTION*

The multinational speciality chemicals company Laporte plc urgently needed to centralise the diverse UK locations of three of its member companies, Gramos Chemicals, Remtox and Oakite.

It had the pick of central UK development sites - and selected one alongside the M5, marketed by the Black Country Development Corporation.

Laporte chose the 4.2 acre site because, in the words of International Estates Manager Donald Andrews, "it places us close to existing customers and suppliers, and... provides excellent access to the national distribution network". Wouldn't your business benefit from a transaction like that?

B L A C K   C O U N T R Y
D E V E L O P M E N T   C O R P O R A T I O N
TELEPHONE: 021-511 2000. FAX: 021-544 5710 / 021-552 0490

Call that a car?

Haig Simonian

Did you see that? 323 centimetres of car zipped into your parking place driven by a giggling trendy. The new Fiat 500 (Cinquecento) mini-car goes on sale in London, Paris, and assorted capitals early next year. The stubby little vehicle, able to seat five, has been named after Fiat's classic budget car of the 1950s, which featured in dozens of Italian movies and took its place alongside other popular classics like VW's Beetle, Citroen's 2CV and the Austin Mini. Keenly priced and easy to drive, the new Cinquecento promises to repeat that performance. It is produced in Poland.

signs, Japanese competition in Europe will be greater in 1993 than ever before. Having indulged in a splurge of spending on new plants in the 1980s, firms from Japan now have the world's most up-to-date factories and machinery. Those are formidable weapons in a decade when high quality and the ability to switch rap-idly from making one product to another will be more important than ever.

The new Japanese investments in Europe can claim similar advantages, but more broadly. Having had the chance to start from scratch in the 1980s, Japanese factories in Britain or France have inherited few of the labour problems that have continued to plague their competitors as they try to make working practices more efficient.

And just as the American businesses that crossed the Atlantic in the 1960s were more able to see Europe-wide opportunities than firms from the Old World, so likewise the later Japanese arrivals have been able to plan their entire operations around the prospect of a single market of 350m consumers in the 1990s.

If this sounds worrying for European business, it is positively frightening for Americans. Many of the United States' leading firms, including such names as Compaq and General Motors, used profits from Europe to keep their North American operations afloat during 1991.

Weaker European firms are rushing to ensure their survival by signing up joint ventures with Japanese and American rivals. Both Siemens and Bull have struck accords with IBM, one to develop next-generation memory chips, the other to get into the profitable market for reduced instruction-set computing (RISC). Olivetti and Philips have signed up with DEC. Daimler-Benz is hoping that its strategic alliance with the Mitsubishi Group will help it to build Mercedes cars more cheaply. That's the way to survive in 1993.

Gates holds the future in his hands

Who'll be computer king?

John Browning

In 1993 all eyes in the computer industry will be on Bill Gates. Perhaps for better but probably for worse, many in the industry believe that Mr Gates, the nerd's dauphin, just might succeed to the throne recently vacated by his former mentor, IBM. At stake is more than whether the personal fortune of Mr Gates, now worth about $7 billion, will overtake that of the Sultan of Brunei, the world's richest man, worth $40 billion or so. The real prize is technological leadership of the computer revolution. Should Mr Gates and Microsoft win 1993's competitive battles, they will have vast power to shape the whole of information technology. To see why, understand the trends that will shape computing in the 1990s.

The first trend stems from the sheer growth in the power of hardware. Today's $2,000 desktop computer has all the computing muscle of the mainframe of a decade ago. By the mid-1990s, desktop machines will have the power of today's mainframes thanks to new RISC processors being developed by DEC, Sun, Intel, IBM and others. Companies are increasingly replacing big, expensive mainframes with smaller, cheaper machines— which wreaks havoc with the profits of companies like DEC and IBM which have prospered by selling big, expensive machines and all the service and support needed to keep them running.

In order to get all the data needed to take advantage of the power of today's desktop computers, the machines need to be linked into networks. Networks are indeed growing at a breathtaking clip.

That growth, in turn, relies on new software that can make manageable the mind-boggling complexity of global networks carrying not only data and text but also video, graphics, digitised sound and all the other components of all-singing, all-dancing "multimedia" computers. Such software creates virtual machines which hide the complexity of the underlying circuitry from those who would use it. In so doing, the software also increasingly makes hardware a commodity.

A single product sits at the crux of all these changes: the unappealingly named "multi-tasking operating system". Though its actual technology is the very stuff that makes most people's eyes glaze over at computer science, the basic idea of multi-tasking operating systems is simplicity itself.

In a conventional personal computer, only one program runs at a time, so that program can treat the machine as its private bailiwick, doing whatever it wants, whenever it wants. On a networked computer, by contrast, lots of programs typically work at once—as they must simultaneously, say, type a letter and handle data arriving unexpectedly from some far-flung network. It is the job of the multi-tasking operating system to choreograph this bustle of activity.

Such virtual machines transform the balance of power in the computer industry. Real hardware, hidden behind the virtual machine, becomes a commodity product, providing only raw computing power. The virtual machine, rather than real circuits, defines the detailed capabilities that distinguish one computer from another. With this generation of technology, software takes charge.

Three contestants have mounted a claim to this key role in computing:
• Microsoft. Microsoft's (not multi-

Everything you need to know and more

John Browning

One of the wonders of the past decade has been the spectacular, but largely unnoticed, growth of computer networks. One of the biggest, called the Internet, links academics, researchers, and others around the world. Over 1m computers are linked into the Internet— though nobody knows exactly how many there are because there is no central administration. The Internet is organised as a network of networks, linked by common technology, and it grows as fast as its components—which for the past several years has been about 20% a quarter.

People want to join the Internet because the resources available on it grow at least as fast as the membership. In addition to providing electronic mail services, the Internet has become a vast repository of information, most of it free. There is a lot of free software and information about computer science.

But there is also an agricultural database called "Not Just Cows", a database of Indian classical music, archives from America's Library of Congress on recent Soviet history, the CIA world map, a children's section called Kidsnet and a catalogue for the library of America's Environmental Protection Agency. Volunteers from Project Gutenberg are putting on-line the complete text of, among others, Peter Pan, Paradise Lost, The Book of Mormon and Shakespeare. There is also a collection of Monty Python sketches.

Though access to the Internet has hitherto been largely restricted to computer-savvy academics, commercial services are fast making access available to anyone with a personal computer and a recently published book by Ed Krol, "The Whole Internet User's Guide and Catalog", provides a useful introduction for the neophyte.

John Browning: writer and consultant on technology, based in London.

tasking) DOS operating system comes with about 90% of the 25m or so personal computers sold each year. In addition, it is selling about 1m copies a month of an extension to DOS called Windows, which makes DOS almost as easy to use as Apple's Macintosh and provides it with many, but not all, of the capabilities of a multi-tasking operating system. Sometime in 1993, Microsoft will launch Windows NT, a true multi-tasking operating system. Should Windows NT eventually become as ubiquitous as DOS, Bill Gates will effectively be king of the computer industry.

• Unix. Originally developed at AT&T's Bell Labs in the early 1970s, Unix is the intellectual inspiration for all of today's operating systems. Unlike its rivals, it is available from a number of companies—and this quality-enhancing competition is one of Unix's strongest selling points. But Unix has never found mass-market commercial success. Though its greatest commercial champion, Sun Microsystems, has grown in a decade to sales of well over $3 billion a year, in volume terms less than 1m copies of Unix are sold each year—mostly for applications that require complicated networking.

• IBM. Big Blue's entry into the crucial operating-systems market is called OS/2. Developed at a cost of nearly $2 billion, OS/2 was originally conceived as part of a vast scheme called Systems Applications Architecture which promised to bring all of a company's computers under a single technological umbrella (with IBM's logo on it). But this proved too complex an undertaking even for IBM. With no grand plan behind it, OS/2 now suffers from the same confusion which bedevils the whole of IBM. It is not clear what market OS/2 is aimed at or what its promised advantages might be.

On technical grounds, Unix is clearly the best. Extensions added to Unix's virtual machine in the early 1980s by researchers at the University of California at Berkeley (many of whom went on to help found Sun) greatly simplify the task of getting programs to run over a network—and are largely responsible for fuelling today's network explosion. Microsoft, by contrast, has been consistently weak in networking. But technical superiority alone will not decide the competitive battle.

Another key factor is volume. Users do not buy operating systems per se, but the word processors, spreadsheets and other software which they run. Creators of such software face what Bill Gates casually refers to as "an order of magnitude thing". They can either develop for Windows and Windows NT, similar technol-

Fully aware of your allowances?

Nicholas Colchester

European tipplers should raise a special glass on new year's eve, for 1993 will be a wonderful year for drinkers, one of consternation for the drinks trade, and one that will drive the collectors of excise duties to drink. In short, this prospect is too good to last.

From January 1st, EC citizens will be able to bring 10 litres of spirits and 90 litres of wine with them across frontiers. In practice they will be able to bring as much as they want, for checks at frontiers within the EC are going to be a rarity, and travellers can disregard even these limits if they can plausibly claim that the bootful of booze is for their own consumption rather than for resale.

These imports will have been bought tax-paid wherever they were acquired. But excise taxes vary so widely across Europe that it will be an odd traveller who does not take advantage of this new freedom. The Briton who pays almost £20 ($32) in taxes per litre of pure alcohol, or £1.26 tax on a litre of still wine, will pay only £9 on the alcohol in a Calais supermarket and virtually nothing on the wine. Should he fly in from Greece he will have paid about £1.50 tax on a litre of pure alcohol.

Meanwhile the strange business of duty-free shopping will become stranger still. At the insistence largely of the British Conservative government, which was lobbied temptingly by the Scotch whisky trade, the European single market will feature tax-free watering holes within it until 1999. How access to these watering holes will be controlled

---

Nicholas Colchester: deputy editor of *The Economist*.

remains a mystery, for tax-free shopping is a creation of customs barriers that will no longer be there.

Duty-free goods arose because goods hoping to compete in export markets could not be taxed before they were exported. In the days of sea travel that meant that drink bought on board was tax-free "for export". Customs men were willing to turn a blind eye to limited quantities of this contraband; and duty-free was born. Remove the customs officers and who controls how much people buy on ships or in the tax-free emporiums?

Most travellers are already aware that these shops allow them to buy far more than their duty-free allowance without batting an eyelid. What is more, from 1993 onwards, travellers will be able to buy those large amounts of tax-paid goods before setting off home. Who is to know, when they arrive at their port of entry, what they have bought tax-free, and what tax-paid somewhere else?

The reluctant Brussels Commission, which would have far preferred to dump the whole system, suggests that the duty-free industry, as it is laughably called, should police itself. It wants the shops to mark on travellers' boarding cards how much of their duty-free allowances they have bought.

Take the two tax dodges together and it is clear that amateur smuggling in excise-bearing goods is going to boom to the point where normal trade in them in a high-tax country like Britain is going to suffer, and where the Treasury will be whimpering. Something will give. Will it be those high duties? Or will it be the frontier-free single market? Guess.

---

ogies which sell over 10m copies a year. Or they can develop for Apple's Macintosh, which sells a couple of million each year. Or they can develop for Unix, which sells a few hundred thousand a year. Given that the costs of developing for each are roughly similar, the greater volume of the Windows platform draws software developers like bears to honey—creating a virtuous circle in which better Windows software sells more Windows, which in turn attracts yet more developers, and so on. Only time will tell whether Unix, OS/2, Apple or anything or anybody else can withstand the mass-market momentum of Windows.

As Microsoft's power grows, trustbusters have begun to hover around it with the same litigious interest as they used to view IBM. America's Federal Trade Commission spent much of 1992

investigating whether Microsoft had abused its power as Windows' creator unfairly to boost its share of the market for spreadsheets, software or word processors which run on Windows.

Industry pundits have begun ruminating about whether consumers and technology developers will have sufficient freedom and choice in Microsoft's world. Which is precisely why 1993 will be such a fascinating year for the computer industry. It is a year in which consumers and technologists alike will be deluged by choices in both software and hardware. But they also have a choice to make about choice itself: 1993 could be the year in which the world decides whether they would like to make technological choices for themselves—or pass the decision-making buck on to Mr Gates, just as they used to pass the buck to IBM.

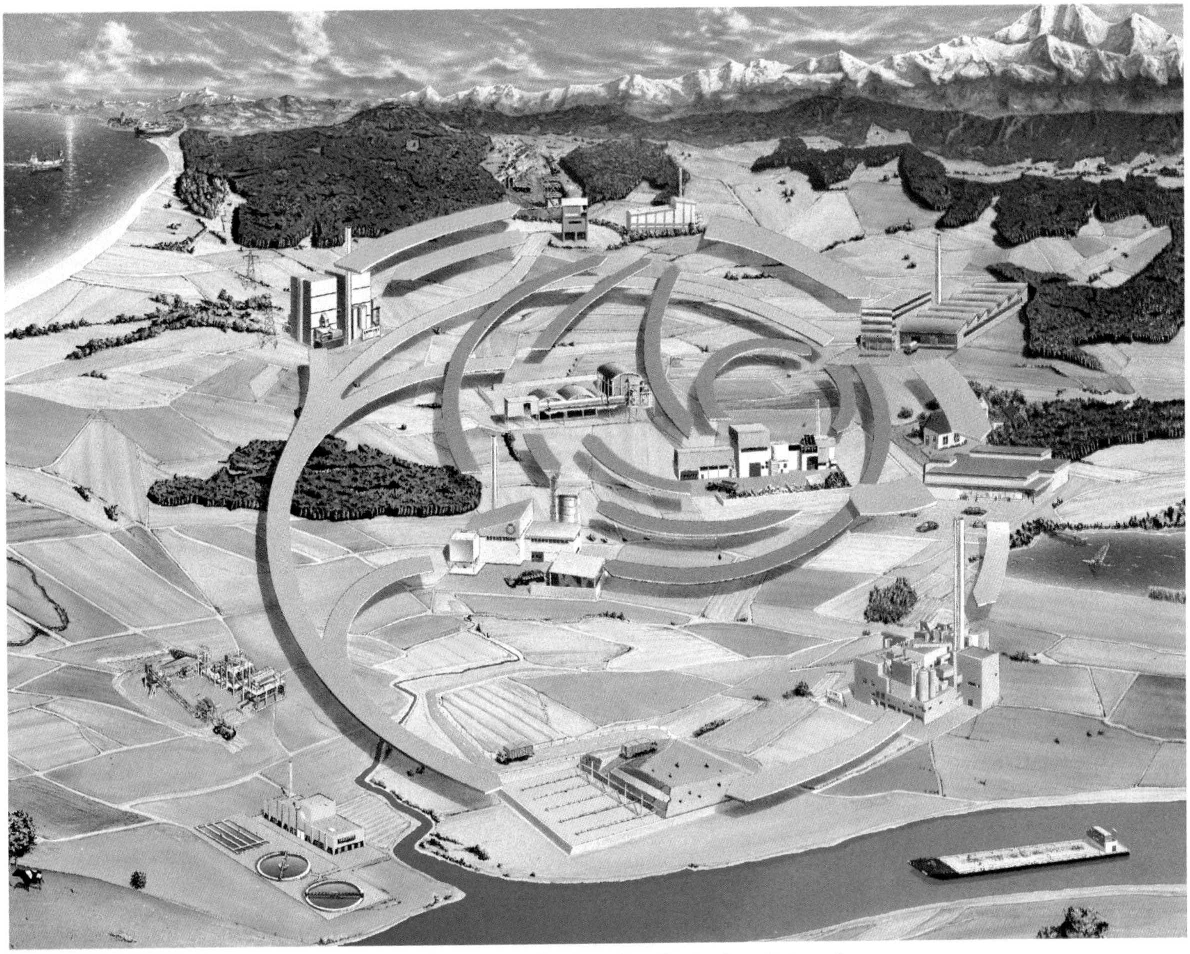

Comprehensive solutions for the industrial cycle.

"Advanced technologies in basic industries."

METALLGESELLSCHAFT AG
Reuterweg 14, P.O. Box 10 15 01, D-6000 Frankfurt am Main 1
Telephone: (69) 159-0, Telefax: (69) 159-2125, Telex: 41 225-0 mgfd
METALLGESELLSCHAFT CORP.
520 Madison Avenue, New York, NY 10022
Telephone: (212) 715 52 00, Telefax: (212) 715 52 91/92, Telex: 422 681
NIHON METALLGESELLSCHAFT KK
Hibiya Park Building 1-8-1, Yuraku-cho, Chiyoda-ku, Tokyo 100
Telephone: (81-3) 3281-7341, Telefax: (81-3) 3281-7379, Telex: 26 684 mgtok
Subsidiaries and affiliates in all major marketplaces of the world

Here's to a happy break-up in '93

Tom Peters

"Imperial Chemical Industries plc, Britain's largest industrial company, reported gloomy profits today," the *New York Times* revealed on July 31st 1992, "but its shares soared as it announced a plan to split itself in two." In 1991 the company almost fell victim to a hostile raider, Lord Hanson—who vowed to break it up. Now, the behemoth plans to do the job itself, splitting off ICI Bioscience, which would include a parcel of fast-growing businesses, from more traditional chemical operations.

That is a story that is going to be repeated time and again next year. Watch out too for the failure of yesteryear's big mergers to become increasingly obvious. For example, the 1980s were an era of bank mergers. Why? The pursuit was on for synergy, efficiency and, of course, increased profits. How is it working out? "The average bank merger in the 1980s didn't cut costs, didn't raise productivity, and actually made the combined bank slightly less profitable," *Business Week* reported this summer.

"Battleship IBM is trying to become a fleet of nimble destroyers." That's how the *New York Times* headline read, following the most dramatic decentralisation in corporate history.

Tom Peters: author of "Liberation Management: Necessary Disorganization for the '90s", published in 1992, and "Thriving on Chaos".

Despite the concurrent announcement of a $3 billion, one-time restructuring charge, the stockmarket instantly signalled its delight by boosting the firm's share price.

Break up and boost your worth: that is the message from Wall Street. The raiders, bred of easy financing, led the way in the 1980s. But their aim was to squeeze money from underused assets. This time the motivation will be to produce the most efficient management.

Which takes us back to IBM, the company that the United States Department of Justice dreamed of breaking up because of its seeming armlock on the computer industry. After a lawsuit that lingered for a decade, Ronald Reagan let IBM off the hook in 1980, but its 50,000 competitors (the number that IBM chairman John Akers claims) haven't been so kind.

"Breaking up IBM" blared the cover of *Fortune* on July 27th 1992. Inside, the reader was treated to the striking contrast between IBM and AT&T. IBM's stockmarket value was $34 billion in January 1982; by June 1992, it had increased 65% to $56 billion. In 1982, AT&T kowtowed to the Federal Reserve and agreed to break itself into eight pieces—AT&T and seven "Baby Bells". Over the next ten years the value of the combined entities jumped 275%, from $48 billion to $180 billion.

In "The New Industrial State", the Harvard economist John Kenneth Galbraith sung the praises of the handful of huge industrial enterprises (mostly American) that had achieved

"near perfection". They were leading the United States to an unprecedented domination of the planet's economy.

In May 1992, just 25 years after Galbraith's gushy tribute to gargantuans, a *Business Week* cover shouted, "Johnson & Johnson, a Big Company That Works!" (Yes, replete with exclamation mark.) We are now stunned when any giant outfit performs well! (And note that *Business Week* felt pressed to add, on the cover, that "J&J's secret is keeping its businesses divided into small pieces. Managers are given a free rein to take big risks... but they had better produce.") So much for Mr Galbraith's managerial technocrats ensconced in tall towers with masses of fellow bureaucrats.

Luck or nothing

Understandably, Herbert Kaufman's provocative "Time, Chance, and Organizations" isn't commonly found on coffee tables in the offices of Fortune 500 chieftains. In this tightly-argued book on organisation theory, he concludes: "The survival of some organisations for great lengths of time is largely a matter of luck."

Attempts to induce flexibility in response to changing circumstances, Mr Kaufman cautions, are doomed to failure. The "ravages of time" that beset large organisations are irreversible. "Organisations by and large are not capable of more than marginal changes", he adds, "while the environment is so volatile that marginal changes are frequently insufficient to assure survival."

For economies taken as a whole, the answer is unmistakable: welcome, rather than deplore, what Mr Kaufman labels "organisational replacement". Welcome the corporate raiders when they succeed and bust up a firm. Applaud the high business-failure rate in California's Silicon Valley and China's Guangdong Province.

The mess is the market's productive message. According to the late Nobel laureate in economics, F.A. Hayek: "Order generated without design can far outstrip plans man consciously contrived." In his last book, "The Fatal Conceit", he added that modern economies "resulted not from human design or intention but spontaneously... Evolution leads us ahead precisely in bringing about much that we could not intend or foresee."

Chance, Mr Kaufman and Hayek say, is the driving force of the universe. Why was IBM so successful from 1960 to 1980? Because the approach Thomas J.

Watson Sr, the founder, developed for a very different time (the 1920s and 1930s) happened to pay off in the computer industry a quarter of a century later. (IBM's longstanding devotion to service set it apart in an age of unreliable machines, while its technology-obsessed competitors focused on gee-whiz equipment.)

IBM employees worked hard, to be sure. (So did their competitors' staff.) But timing, chance—blind luck—was the real key. I am not alone in holding this view. Tom Watson Jr, who followed his father on to the throne, writing in *Computerworld* in June 1992, said he considered calling his autobiography "Blind Luck". He chose "Father and Son & Co" instead. Too bad.

ICI decides to split. IBM edges up to splitting. Siemens coughs and splutters, then shifts tens of thousands of troops closer to the front line. Philips lays off tens of thousands in the middle ranks, trying to force decision-making closer to the markets. AT&T breaks up—and the eight pieces surge (not without ditching hundreds of thousands of jobs).

Silicon Valley prospers, courtesy of an enormous business-failure rate—and chaotic energy. Germany spits out exports at a breathtaking rate, mostly thanks to its unsung medium-sized companies, the *Mittelstand*. (Many have no more than a few dozen employees, yet dominate some high-value micro-niche around the world.)

100 people is too many

Take the case of ABB, a worldwide electrical-engineering company. When its boss, Percy Barnevik, went on a buying binge in anticipation of a unified Europe, he set the example for any would-be raider. Mr Barnevik sacked approximately 95% of the staff who sat in headquarters. Furthermore, he has atomised his giant operation into some 5,000 surprisingly independent profit centres, each of which averages just about 50 people.

Or consider Chromalloy Compressor Technologies, part of the $2 billion Sequa Corporation. The company repairs very expensive aircraft-engine parts for the world's airlines. In 1989 it broke itself into 16 tiny bits. The bits run between 18 and 70 people. When an outfit gets to about 100 people, it automatically splits up—with the new,

independent company formed several miles away from its "parent".

This kind of 1993 company, like a German *Mittelstander*, is a maniac for focus; it just repairs one or two turbine blades, say, for 727 engines. Loaded with expertise, fanatical about state-of-the-art equipment and training, it is a tiny master of a tiny piece of the universe, doing its job fast, cheap and with exceptional quality.

And ponder Ben Lytle, chief executive of the $2 billion Associated Group, of Indianapolis, Indiana. He was as proud as a peacock of his effort to decentralise the financial-services company in 1982—that is, until he got into the elevator one day.

"I was really excited about having gone from a functional organisation into

"Applaud a high business failure rate . . . mess is the market's productive message"

five major business units," he said. "A claims processor was in the elevator too, and I asked her, 'How do you like working in the new structure?' And she said, 'Oh, real well.' And I asked, 'Where do you work?' I expected her to say something like, 'I work in the commercial division, we support small businesses.' However, she replied, 'The 14th floor'.

"That experience really made me look at how to change culture. You have to change what people see, where they live, how they're paid, everything." Change everything he then did, creating dozens of small, tightly focused companies (collectively called Acordia). Each one has a CEO, about 100 employees, its own facilities, total profit-and-loss responsibility, a local board of directors (including outsiders), even the right to make acquisitions. Acordia Business Benefits of Evansville, Indiana, for example, has a potential market of just 11 counties.

Thermo Electron, a high-tech

Massachusetts-based company ($800m in 1991 revenue), goes even further. The Company's founder and CEO, George Hatsopoulos, egged on the entrepreneurial spirit from the company's start in the late 1960s by granting stock options to divisional executives. But Mr Hatsopoulos discovered that with continuing growth such incentives were not enough to keep entrepreneurship flourishing. His answer: sell minority interests in subordinate units to the public. Thermo has done so with eight businesses, including its former central R&D operation.

Thermo's approach reverses conventional spin-off wisdom. "Before we arrived on the scene, 'spin-off' might have implied 'How do you get rid of a dog?' " said John Wood, CEO of Thermedics, the first spin-off. "We've used it in quite the opposite way: 'How do you take a jewel and raise money to finance its growth more rapidly than you could afford to if it remained part of a larger corporation?' "

The historic response to marketplace change, starting with Du Pont and General Motors in the 1920s, has been decentralisation.

But that's not enough. The problem is that decentralisation seldom takes hold. A still sizeable corporate headquarters and the pronounced culture that led the big companies to success in the first place continue to cast long shadows over subsidiary operations.

The only medicine that works is radical and painful:
• virtual decapitation, the effective removal of all headquarters staff (ABB's 95% central staff reduction—in Germany, Finland, Sweden, Switzerland and the United States);
• creation of modest-sized, market-focused units that must serve their micro-niches extremely well, or go out of business (ABB, Acordia, Chromalloy Compressor Technologies);
• selling parts of divisions off to the public to induce true accountability and independence (the Thermo Electron approach);
• or just plain breaking up (ICI, AT&T, IBM and many others by the end of next year).

The volatile marketplace is, in short, destroying the old forms of organisation. The process is messy. The pain is great, the alternative nil.

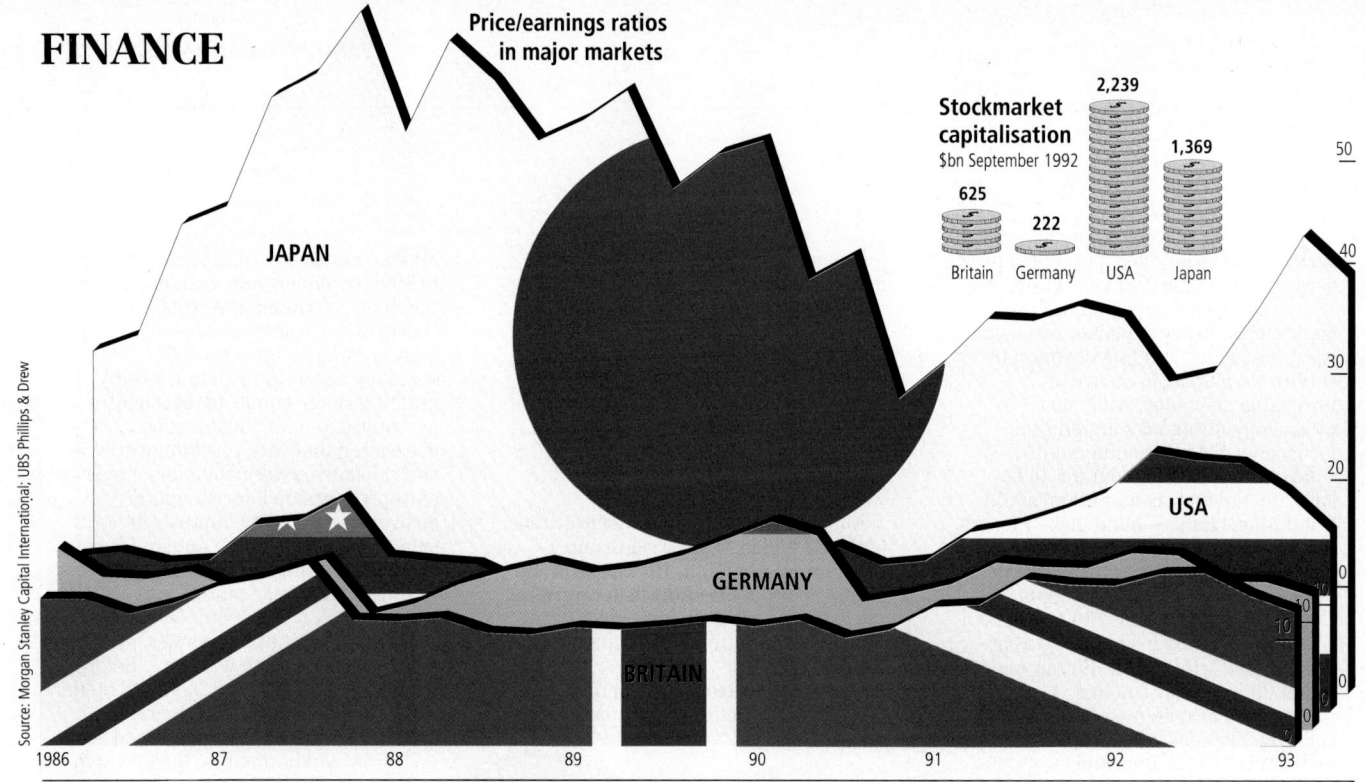

Price/earnings ratios in major markets

JAPAN

Stockmarket capitalisation
$bn September 1992

625 Britain
222 Germany
2,239 USA
1,369 Japan

USA

GERMANY

BRITAIN

Source: Morgan Stanley Capital International; UBS Phillips & Drew

1986 87 88 89 90 91 92 93

How not to lose money next year

Hamish McRae

Maybe the cult of the equity is over. 1993 will be a year when the wise global investors will go back to basics. It will be clear that the world economic recovery will be a slow one, and that the trend of inflation continues down. So investors in equities, bonds and currencies will be looking for security and value. They will be sceptical of the experts in every market, for the lesson of the early 1990s is that experts are frequently wrong—they failed to warn of the plunge of the dollar, the gyrations of the Japanese equity market, the delay in the British economic recovery, the minefields on the path to European currency union. Instead of listening to the experts investors will listen to their own sense of history.

In equity markets the common theme will be a search for value. This is likely to encourage a downgrading in the United States and a change in corporate behaviour in Japan. In bond markets there will be an awareness that low and falling inflation has radically changed the relationship between bonds and other financial investments. And in currencies, purchasing-power parities will start to pull harder in 1993.

All equity markets face tough questions, for any investors who moved into

Hamish McRae: associate editor, the *Independent*.

the major equity markets in the summer of 1987 would, by the summer of 1992, have done better had they stayed in cash. The detailed questions vary from market to market. The prime one for investors in the United States is whether it is reasonable for a market in a slow-growth economy to trade at more than 24 times earnings, when a typical historic P/E would have been 12-18. American share values in the autumn of 1992 were putting a lot of pressure on corporate performance: United States Inc is unlikely to be able to justify such an aggressive rating in 1993.

In Japan, confidence in equities has been shattered. The great adjustment of Japanese share prices, bringing them back towards (though not completely in line with) ratings in the rest of the industrial world, has taken place. The absurdity of ranking companies on P/ES of 70 times earnings, or a dividend yield of less than 0.5%, had been shown up. But the Japanese market, on those two measures at least, was in late 1992 still somewhat over-valued. (The P/ES of over 30 are to some extent supported by conservative accounting practice which understates corporate profits, but the yield of about 1% is low by any standards.)

While some justification for a demanding rating can be made on the basis of Japan's low inflation and good growth

record, the mismatch between return on equities and on bonds and cash cannot be sustained. The test for Japanese business in 1993 is whether it can turn its priorities from considerations such as market share and protected employment towards profits and dividends. Sony's chairman, Akio Morita, suggests it should, and he has been an important force in shaping Japanese corporate attitudes.

Valuations in the main EC markets are less extreme. In the autumn of 1992 the British market was trading on a P/E in the mid-teens, roughly its 1980s average. Germany was rated more towards the top end of its recent range, with France closer to the bottom. Although none of these ratings is particularly demanding, the question for investors in any EC equity market is whether tensions within the EC will damage business and hence undermine the recovery.

The case for bonds...

The question which needs to be resolved during the 1990s is whether the long bull market in equities which has, with a few exceptions, ruled since the end of the second world war, has run its course. Before that war the investment norm was for equities to yield more than bonds because of the greater risks involved. High inflation and rapid growth of company profits

GEFCo

Guaranteed Export Finance Corporation PLC

Barclays de Zoete Wedd was lead manager in the issue of £100,000,000 9 1/4 per cent guaranteed bonds due 2008. Guaranteed by the British Government acting by the Export Credits Guarantee Department.

JULY 1992

P&O

The Peninsular and Oriental Steam Navigation Company

Barclays de Zoete Wedd was lead manager in the issue of £125,000,000 11 1/2 per cent bonds due 2014.

MAY 1992

Abbey National Treasury Services plc

Barclays de Zoete Wedd was lead manager in the issue of £250,000,000 10 1/2 per cent guaranteed notes due 1997.

APRIL 1992

B·A·A

BAA plc

Barclays de Zoete Wedd was lead manager in the issue of £150,000,000 11 3/4 per cent bonds due 2016.

APRIL 1992

The expertise to make it happen.

changed this balance and the various markets switched from a yield gap in favour of equities to a reverse. (In Britain the cross-over came in 1959.) But now the 1990s appear much more like the 1890s than, say, the 1960s. The long-term trend of inflation is down; growth is expected to be slow. Yields will not cross back in 1993 (it would be astounding if they did), but already the financial markets have started to narrow the gap. That trend will continue in 1993 leading to relatively poor overall returns on equities but much better returns on bonds.

Typically government bonds in the industrial world give a real (ie, post-inflation) yield of 5-6%. This would be the top end of the range for such securities in the 19th century, suggesting that even if inflation fails to fall further, bonds are cheap. Were inflation to fall to 1-2% worldwide during the 1990s, bonds at their present levels would be even cheaper. On a five-year view: sell equities, buy bonds.

...and the dollar

But in which currency? How long can the undervaluation of the dollar continue, and how will the exchange-rate mechanism develop?

1993 should see the dollar fighting back. It was deeply out of fashion in 1992, hitting new lows against the D-mark, despite being between 25% and 40% undervalued on purchasing-power parities against both the ERM currencies and the yen. All past experience shows that currencies can diverge for many years from these parities—but that they win out in the end. By the end of 1992 the elastic had become very stretched: the dollar had overshot. Signs of any convergence between D-mark and dollar interest rates could cause the dollar to snap back, if not to its purchasing-power parity of around DM1.80, certainly to above DM1.60.

The ERM showed its flexibility and political staying power in 1992. Except for Britain, every major European country, even Maastricht-denying Denmark, even non-members like Austria, is committed to its success. Expect sterling to move somewhat shamefully back into it in the course of 1993. Expect a gradual fall in D-mark interest rates to gather pace in the spring of 1993, allowing other ERM interest rates to fall, and tensions to subside. Expect, too, evidence of the core ERM countries moving closer to monetary union, but with a question mark lingering over the French franc.

For the yen, there should be some revaluation overall, the most likely scenario being one where the yen rode up with a recovery of the dollar and then hardened a little further.

Are central bankers human?

Marjorie Deane

If anything is certain, it is that the role of monetary policy will not decline in the foreseeable future. It will continue to be the centrepiece of macroeconomic policy; fiscal policy is a mess almost everywhere and will stay so. Furthermore, monetary policy will remain dedicated to price stability.

But, literally, stability, a world of zero inflation? Yes, says Federal Reserve chairman, **Alan Greenspan**, an obsessive number-watcher. Yes, echoes the Bank of England's **Robin Leigh-Pemberton**. But here's an oddity: the German Bundesbank's president, **Helmut Schlesinger**, a draconian financial disciplinarian, is inclined to add ''or 2%'' when a zero-inflation target is mentioned.

This shows savvy. The Bundesbank knows that the success of its anti-inflation policy over the years, challenged only by the costs of German unification, has owed much to the support of the German public—business and individuals. An obsession with an academic goal—doesn't zero

Marjorie Deane: private consultant and journalist.

inflation smack of that?—endangers that support. Central bankers may do well to take lessons in public relations.

The climate has become much less friendly for them since the former Fed chairman, **Paul Volcker**, entitled an address to international bankers two years ago ''The Triumph of Central Banking?'' His question-mark seemed almost absurdly cautious at the time. No longer. In the interval, the commitment to stable money has paid off handsomely in terms of low inflation, but failed to bring the economic growth it is supposed to promote. A backlash against central banks seems inevitable.

Nor have they shown up particularly well in the foreign exchanges. Here their role is reduced to concerted intervention to try to moderate extreme movements in currencies. Technically, they are good at it. But they have no illusions that they can jack up a currency if a gap has opened up in international interest rates that tells the markets to sell it—as it did when the dollar hit new lows against the D-mark.

Struggling economies promise to

1993 INDICATORS

Gross public debt includes all the short- and long-term liabilities of central, state and local government. Net debt subtracts from this total governmnent assets like loans to the private sector, cash and foreign reserves. The Japanese gross debt will rise. It will all but vanish when assets are counted. Debt in Italy and Belgium will overshadow domestic politics and swallow up a fifth of public spending. Austerity in Belgium and reform in Italy will be lent new urgency by the commitments to thrift made at Maastricht. Spain will have plenty of reserves to help keep the peseta within its ERM range. Expect the sackfuls spent by central banks propping up overvalued currencies in September 1992 to start showing up in diminished reserve totals as 1993 gets going. Britain's politicians will be worried by the budget deficit but overall debt will put the least strain on spending of the major European countries.

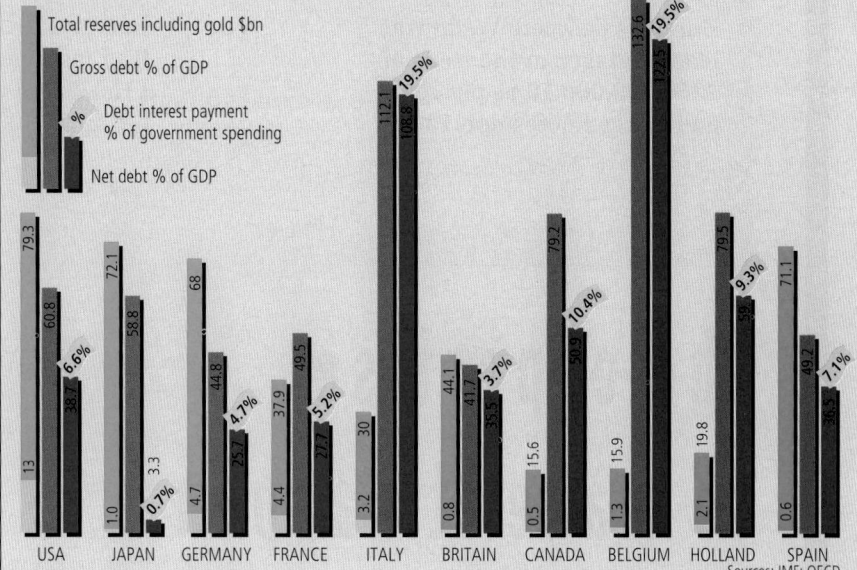

Sources: IMF; OECD

NFC plc

Barclays de Zoete Wedd was
lead manager in the issue of
£82,500,000 7 3/4% convertible
bonds due 2007.

OCTOBER 1992

WPP Group plc

WPP Group plc

Barclays de Zoete Wedd was
equity adviser to the co-ordinating
committee of the bank syndicate
for the financial restructuring
of the WPP Group.

AUGUST 1992

Hanson PLC

Barclays de Zoete Wedd was
lead manager in the issue of
£400,000,000 10 per cent
bonds due 2006.

JULY 1992

Telefonos de Mexico SA de CV

Barclays Structured Finance was
arranger for a project line of credit
for US$115,693,000 for the supply of
digital public telephone exchanges
by Bell-Alcatel N.V.

MAY 1992

The ability to innovate.

Bundesbank gets a new man

Marjorie Deane

Here's a name for 1993. **Hans Tietmeyer**, 61. Economist, political scientist. Boss of German money from next summer and master of all our European fate. He joined the Economics Ministry in Bonn in 1962 and stayed there 20 years, heading the directorate in charge of European Common Market Affairs before becoming responsible for economic policy. Then, in 1982, as State Secretary to the Finance Ministry, he became Chancellor Kohl's "sherpa", charged with preparations for world economic summits. A Bundesbank director since the beginning of 1990 (except in the spring of that year when advising Mr Kohl on unification) and vice-president since August 1991. A great believer in economic and monetary union (EMU)—on Germany's terms. A tough talker, strongly anti-inflation, but a pragmatist, preferring to think in terms of international co-operation rather than co-ordination. Highly regarded by foreign central bankers.

As the new president of the Hesse state central bank, with Frankfurt in its terrain, **Horst Schulmann**, 59, will also bring international expertise to Bundesbank council meetings. After working in the World Bank in the early 1970s, he was Chancellor Schmidt's

sherpa from 1978 to 1982, serving as state secretary in the Finance Ministry just before Mr Tietmeyer. From 1984 he headed the international bankers' think-tank, the Institute of International Finance in Washington. Less tough than Mr Tietmeyer—some say too nice for his own good—he will nevertheless want to play an active role.

Next year's gnome

called "derivatives"—a whole variety of financial futures, options, swaps, with cross-links perhaps to equities or commodities—has increased eightfold in the past five years. Yet more products are on the way, with still more complex twists. Banks are major players in these markets. But central banks, as usual trailing behind, are hardly near to even understanding these exotic instruments. There have been no disasters so far, but links with the cash markets mean that potential risk from derivatives is high.

It is on the broad shoulders of **Gerald Corrigan**, president of the New York Federal Reserve Bank, that problems of international financial risk come to rest. As chairman of the Basle Committee on Banking Supervision, he strives for co-operation between bank supervisors throughout the world to strengthen the payments system. A workaholic, he will have his work cut out in 1993. But there are broad issues coming up beyond his jurisdiction.

Bank or regulator?

Rather astonishingly, formal involvement of central banks in banking supervision ranges the whole gamut, from nil in the Bundesbank's case through a shared role for the Fed to total responsibility for the Bank of England. As the walls between financial markets tumbled, the conventional wisdom was that supervision of banking and securities business, maybe life assurance too, should come under one roof—that of the central bank. The tide is turning the other way, at least in Europe. Central banks want independence from political pressure above all else, and fear that responsibility for supervision may make them seem too powerful.

If EMU does come about according to the Maastricht treaty, all EC central banks will have to be given independence—the sort the Bundesbank already has. Some are pressing for it earlier. The Bank of Italy has already made progress towards it; the Bank of Spain hopes to do so in 1993. The Bank of England will be the laggard, but don't be surprised if the price of getting more independence is the relinquishment of its powers of supervision.

That step would alter the Old Lady's relationship with the City—the present governor and his predecessor think it would lose valuable influence. Yet it could still have the "strong voice" in regulatory matters that Mr Volcker favours. The Bundesbank manages to have one without dirtying its fingers in actual supervision; the separate supervisory agency in Berlin is forced by statute to consult the central bank. Pehaps not a bad arrangement, all said and done.

make 1993 an inward-looking year for central bankers. Who might lead them to greater things than navel-watching? Japan has a stronger governor in **Yasushi Mieno** than it has had for some time, but he has his hands full getting Japanese financial markets and banks robust again, after the beating they have taken. The man to watch out for is **Hans Tietmeyer**, now waiting in the Bundesbank's wings.

Europe offers central banks the best chance to shine in 1993. Oblivious of the brouhaha after the Danish referendum, EC central bankers, under the guidance of the Danish governor, **Eric Hoffmeyer**, continued to plan for economic and monetary union (EMU) as if it were due tomorrow. Groups of experts have beavered away at harmonising money-market techniques, laying the foundation for a single monetary policy, broadening the use of the ecu, even getting a headstart on procedures for issuing new notes representing a single currency (a process judged to take three years from start to finish).

Even if EMU never comes about, some of these developments will stick. Management of monetary policy will move closer

together in EC countries. And the ecu will be more attractive to use.

However, a new uncertainty looms. The Bundesbank gauges German interest rates—which set the pattern for other countries in the European exchange-rate mechanism (ERM), as they never cease to complain—by tracking a broad measure of money. That it can do what most other central banks have been forced to abandon does not reflect special aptitude, but rather the slowness of Germany to deregulate. It has resisted the innovations that have made flows in the Anglo-Saxon financial markets so much harder to capture.

Now Germany is catching up, having its own Big Bang. The advent of the single market, giving financial firms a single passport in the EC, will hasten this process. Add the uncertainties from unification, and the Bundesbank's money management could be up the creek. Watch for whether it does the smart thing and adjusts its techniques before it makes some awful mistake.

Risk and supervision seem old hat but will take on new dimensions in 1993. Activity in the new financial instruments

APV Finance Limited

Barclays de Zoete Wedd acted
as private placement agent for
US$100,000,000 senior notes
due 1999 and 2002.

AUGUST 1992

Blenheim Holdings Inc.

Barclays de Zoete Wedd acted
as private placement agent for
US$75,000,000 senior notes
due 1999.

AUGUST 1992

Pemex

(Petroleos Mexicanos)

Barclays de Zoete Wedd
acted as arranger for a
US$38,000,000 private
placement to re-finance
four offshore drilling
platforms due 1997.

APRIL 1992

Harrisons & Crosfield plc

Barclays de Zoete Wedd acted as
private placement agent for
US$120,000,000 of senior notes
due 2002 and 2004.

MARCH 1992

The power to place worldwide.

Das neue Kapital

Hans-Joerg Rudloff

After a decade of obsession with debt, equity capital will fuel the return to investment and growth of companies in both the West and rapidly developing countries. But where is this capital going to come from?

The "shortage of savings" in the world is a fashionable theme, to which even the managing director of the International Monetary Fund, Michel Camdessus, paid lip service in his address to the Rio conference on the environment. Seeing a shortage at a time of increased demand, pundits have made gloomy forecasts of a rise in the real cost of equity capital. This will not happen. New sources of capital will come on stream just as western economies rebound.

There are three main springs from which these savings will flow: changes in demography, financial liberalisation, and a return to traditional savings patterns in Latin America, Eastern Europe and, above all, Asia. The combination of people living longer and having fewer babies will lead to a rise in the dependency ratio—defined as the population aged 65 and over as a proportion of the population aged 15–64. In Europe, these old folk, who formed 22% of the population in 1980, will make up 40% in 2040. In Japan their increase will be even sharper: from 13.4% in 1980 to 37.5% in 2040. More old people will demand more pension payments and need more health care. Unless baby-boomers are prepared to accept a much lower standard of living in retirement than they have enjoyed in their salad days, personal-savings rates in the West are going to have to rise substantially, and soon.

These increased savings will mostly find their way into life-assurance companies and pension funds. Assets under institutional management in the EC could double by the end of the decade; indeed, if these institutions throughout the EC were to grow as large in relation to GDP as they currently are in Britain, assets under management would quadruple. That would mean some 6 trillion ecu ($8 trillion) at current prices.

These savings will grow rapidly larger just as restrictions on cross-border investment by institutions are relaxed or, even better, scrapped. This will lead to a tripling of such flows from the EC to over 1

Hans-Joerg Rudloff: chairman and chief executive of Credit Suisse First Boston.

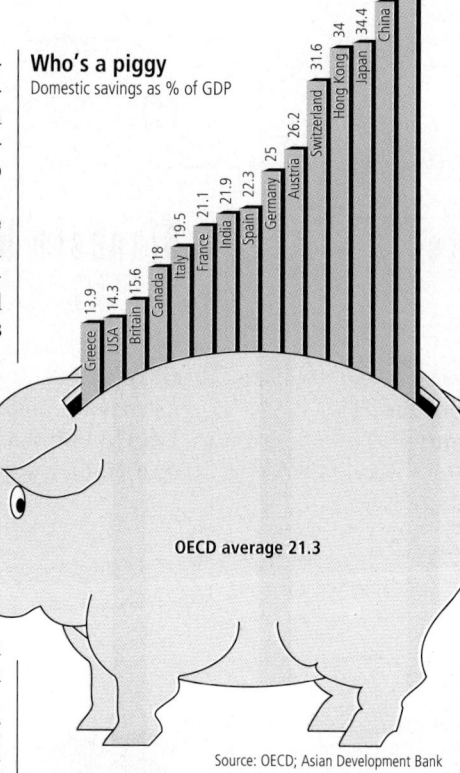

Who's a piggy
Domestic savings as % of GDP

Greece 13.9
USA 14.3
Britain 15.6
Canada 18
Italy 19.5
France 21.1
India 21.9
Spain 22.3
Germany 25
Austria 26.2
Switzerland 31.6
Hong Kong 34
Japan 34.4
China 37.4
Luxembourg 44.7

OECD average 21.3

Source: OECD; Asian Development Bank

trillion ecu by the end of the decade.

But capital-hungry Asia, Latin America and Eastern Europe will not want to pin their hopes for rapid development on the financial concerns of the Woodstock generation in middle age. Nor will they need to. They should be able to cater for their own investment needs. Personal-savings rates in these countries have historically been high. Since 1985 savings ratios have fluctuated between 28% and 38% in Taiwan and between 27% and 39% in Indonesia. Latin-American countries should also be able to finance much capital formation domestically.

Companies will not only benefit from fresh supplies of savings; old users of capital, notably the property market, will no longer be so greedy. In future, households will be more inclined to invest their savings in machines and managers rather than bricks and mortar.

For these reasons, the average cost of equity capital for companies around the world is unlikely to go up. But corporations in the West should not be complacent. An unchanged average can disguise radical shifts in particular costs. As once-trapped capital is free to move into the rapidly-growing markets of the developing world, western firms will have to show higher returns if they are to com-

pete for funds. The cost of capital will not rise for those western companies which swim with the tide of comparative advantage. The laggards, however, will be punished as the cushion of captive capital is withdrawn.

All this will keep investment banks on their toes. The process by which savings are transformed into productive capital will be very different in the 1990s. The role of the investment banks will be less obvious and less secure. In the 1980s investment banks prospered from an activity called "disintermediation". Traditionally, commercial banks had played the key intermediary role in the channelling of capital from savers to borrowers. In the 1980s investment banks helped companies bypass the commercial banks (and their margins) and gave them direct access to investors through the securities markets. For this service, investment banks earned generous fees.

In the 1990s institutional investors such as pension funds and life-assurance companies will turn the tables on the investment banks and deal directly with companies which seek their investment. The investment banks' past success was based on superior information and an ability to commit capital and assume risk. This competitive advantage is being eroded as quickly as a sandcastle by the incoming tide. Access to information about companies has become laughably cheap. And capital-seeking companies are finding that they can cosy up to leading institutional investors without paying for the match-making services of investment banks.

The scandals and excesses of the 1980s have led to tighter regulation of investment banks, which has diminished their appetite for risk. Pension funds and life-assurance companies, on the other hand, remain relatively loosely regulated and the current trend is for further deregulation of their investment policies.

The sidelining of investment banks in the flows of equity capital to companies will hurt their shareholders more than their employees. As fee incomes diminish, investment banks will shed staff. But investment bankers are nothing if not agile. Many of them will discover a new enthusiasm for the breeds they have traditionally despised but always depended on. Pension funds, life-assurance companies and the financial departments of large corporations will be the glamorous places to work in the 1990s. Since regulators seem incapable of closing the stable door before the horse bolts, they are also the places where the financial scandals of the decade will happen.

KfW

KfW International
Finance Inc.

Barclays de Zoete Wedd was
lead manager in the issue of
£100,000,000 9 7/16 per cent
notes due 2008 unconditionally
and irrevocably guaranteed by
Kreditanstalt für Wiederaufbau.

AUGUST 1992

European Coal and
Steel Community

Barclays de Zoete Wedd was
lead manager in the issue of
£52,700,000 floating rate
notes due 1997.

MAY 1992

ITT RAYONIER
FOREST PRODUCTS

ITT Rayonier Forest Products

Barclays de Zoete Wedd was
adviser for the acquisition of
timber cutting rights and related
assets from the New Zealand
Government for US$197,000,000.

MAY 1992

REMY·COINTREAU

Rémy Cointreau

Barclays de Zoete Wedd was
global co-ordinator in the
international offering of
2,086,301 shares and public
offering in France of 1,000,000
shares, together with warrants
to acquire shares.

MARCH 1992

The capability to
cross borders.

The Economist dollar index of commodities
Quarterly averages, $ terms
1985 average = 100
Metals
All industrial
Non–food agriculturals
All items
Food

Roll up for the roller coaster

David Blackwell

Common sense is the best distributed commodity in the world—for every man is convinced that he is well supplied with it, said Descartes. Common sense suggests that 1993 will see most commodities in abundant supply around the world, and consequently prices are likely to remain low. However, cynics may well ask: since when has common sense had anything to do with commodity markets?

The **gold** market has certainly seen its share of madness over the years, but now it appears to have lost its allure for investors—and their disinvestment has led to abundant supplies. In the first half of 1992 Europeans cut their gold-bullion holdings by nearly 9.6m troy ounces—equivalent to half the annual output from South Africa, the world's biggest producer. Even central banks have been getting out of gold—the Belgian National Bank sold 6.5m troy ounces, worth $2 billion last June. This unspeakable act will be repeated by others in 1993.

The Gold Institute, the international Washington-based trade association, is expecting annual production to rise by nearly 5.5% between 1991 and 1995, to 71m troy ounces, dashing any hopes that a fall in output will lift prices. The gold price averaged $362 an ounce in 1991, the lowest real level since the 1970s; it is expected to continue to decline.

Silver and **platinum** are now widely regarded as industrial metals, having lost

David Blackwell: commodities editor at the *Financial Times* since 1987.

almost all claims on investors' hearts. This leaves them more vulnerable to recession than gold. Silver, which spent a good part of 1992 above $4 an ounce, could go as low as $3.

Japan is the biggest consumer of platinum, and its economic troubles have hit world demand. Automotive exhaust catalysts account for nearly 40% of platinum consumption, but it is South Africa's political stability, not a revival in the fortunes of the motor industry, that will determine the metal's price in 1993.

The performance of the Russian and East European metal industries has spawned a whole lot of predictions, but no one knows the truth about their production and consumption—least of all the Russians themselves. Russia has had the most obvious effect on the markets for both **nickel** and—above all—**aluminium**, which it shipped out in massive quantities in 1991. Much of that metal must have come from stock, and, once again, no one knows how much is left.

Sales in 1992 have fallen back. According to Sumitomo of Japan, whose guess is as good as any, Russian aluminium exports were 720,000 tonnes in 1991 and 580,000 tonnes in 1992—a level they expect to be maintained in 1993 before a further fall to 400,000 tonnes in 1995.

The Russian exports have led to the accumulation of huge aluminium stocks on the London Metal Exchange. However, aside from aluminium, base-metal stocks

overall are relatively low at less than ten weeks of consumption. When recovery comes stocks will fall fairly rapidly, lifting prices.

The **copper** market, where supply and demand are more or less in balance, has also had to keep an eye eastwards. Although concentrates—an intermediate material which needs smelting—have been in good supply, smelters in Russia and Kazakhstan were called into service in 1991 to ease the severe shortage of western capacity. In addition, the Chinese have re-emerged as buyers. China's economy is booming (industrial production up an estimated 18% in the first half of last year) and the country, regarding a price of 105 cents a lb as bargain-basement level, has snapped up 200,000 tonnes.

For those interested in economic theory, an important shift in thinking is taking place: base metals are developing into a leading, rather than lagging, indicator of economic health. Price improvements towards the end of 1992 indicate that the metals cycle is on the turn and recovery is on the way in 1993. If western industrial output were to rise by 5% in 1993, as some analysts have forecast, base-metal prices should start to move ahead, perhaps attracting further buying from non-income generating capital growth funds disillusioned with gold. Copper could even hit the 150 cents a lb level, giving an astonishing return to mines like Chile's La Escondida, which has operating costs of only 45 cents a lb.

The past couple of years have brought only bad news to growers of **coffee** and **cocoa**: prices have been at the lowest levels for 20 years, in cash terms, and the lowest ever historically, in real terms. International agreements in both commodities have disintegrated.

With arabica coffee prices near 50 cents a lb and robustas near 30 cents, producers look increasingly likely to take their own measures to force prices up. This is likely to be successful only in the arabica sector, where producing countries are few in number and concentrated in Central and South America. The first task of any cartel would have to be the reduction of consumer stocks of around 18m bags (60kg each).

The same applies to cocoa, where supply has actually fallen below demand by about 100,000 tonnes in 1991-92, and an expected 195,000 tonnes in 1992-93. Despite the huge stocks still available after eight years of surplus production, some analysts are now predicting the start of a bull phase for cocoa, with prices hitting £1,000 a tonne in 1993—almost double the 1992 low. Enjoy that chocolate bar while you can.

In today's global markets you need
an investment bank that has
the power to execute as well as
the intellect to innovate.

That crosses borders as easily as
today's investor.

That can understand corporate issues
as well as it places capital issues.

That has power bases in
every major market as well as
a strong capital base.

And that has the integrity
to recommend not doing something
as well as the power to make
things happen.

Hurrah for the property bust

Richard Ingram

You only have to take a look at the property pages of the *New York Times* or *Le Monde*, the Toronto *Globe* or the London *Independent*, the *Asahi Shimbun* or the Brussels *Echo*. In property, it is the worst of times—the only proviso is that worse still may be on the way.

Throughout Western Europe (Germany is the only exception), right across North America and in Japan, property has crashed. In many cities the proportion of office space lying empty is now at a post-war high; residential property prices are static, or edging down, everywhere.

It is fashionable to blame recession. But that has not been the only problem. Over-supply and over-pricing are the two greater villains. And they are the reasons that property prices won't budge in 1993 or 1994 or 1995.

Revolutions create winners as well as losers. The revolution under way in the western world's property market will alter the next stage in the business cycle—and alter it much for the better. That stage of growth, quite unlike its post-war predecessors, will take place without the inherent destabiliser of property inflation. It will last longer and produce more real wealth as a result.

If your capital is tied up in commercial property development in London, Los Angeles or Osaka, you're a loser. Yet most businesses and people are not providers of property, but consumers. For them the outlook is different.

The cost of setting up an office in Tokyo or Manhattan is being slashed. For the entrepreneur beginning or expanding in business in any of these capitals, one of his biggest, deadweight costs will be both stable and low.

The biggest winner of all must be the economy at large. The boom-bust cycle that has afflicted both commercial and residential property in Europe and the United States has distorted investment and deepened recession. Britain, for example, has seen three booms and three busts in less than two decades, and almost every EC country has been up and down the cycle in the 1980s.

Now we are in for a decade of stability. On the housing market, the baby-boom bulge already has a roof over its head; Europe is starved of teenagers to be the next decade's first-time buyers. Changes in corporate structures will have

the same effect: gone are the days of the big company headquarters or the prestigious factory site. These are good reasons to believe that over the next decade property prices will be less volatile.

Property is an asset, but a peculiar one. As assets go it is highly inflexible and this inflexibility is a cause of much trouble. Unlike paper assets (equities or securities, say) it is not easily tradable at the best of times, and when values are falling it is often not tradable at all. Because property is partly land and land is limited, it is subject to much, often unpredictable,

Estate of unreality
Office rent, 1985=100

Source: Hillier Parker; The Economist estimates

regulation. And because property is partly development and development is rather slow, supply is often out of tune with the rest of the economy.

The greater this inflexibility, the more dramatic the boom-bust effect. While a house takes an average of just under two years from conception to completion, a long enough wait, that is nothing to the rigidity of large-scale commercial office development which can take eight or even ten years to complete. A project dreamed up at the height of the boom drops off the end of the conveyor belt a decade later, gleaming and unwanted.

The only capitalist economy that has escaped the cycle in the past couple of de-

cades is Japan, the entire landmass of which now has a theoretical value of more than all the United States, a country some 25 times larger than Japan.

But the key word here is "theoretical": Japan's land values are paper values, and they are paper thin. The country's long boom has taken it up to the edge of a vertiginous bust, and it will take great skill from the Ministry of Finance to bring prices down without precipitating a crash.

Officially, the commercial-property market in Tokyo is ticking over; unofficially it is frozen solid, with most reported transactions being notional intra-corporate deals. This is reflected in falling rents and rising vacancy rates: discounts of 20% or more on quoted rents are failing to melt the ice, and since existing projects will increase building stock in Tokyo by 32% between now and 1997, these discounts will only grow more favourable.

Like much of the rest of the EC, the property bust in Britain is being exacerbated by low inflation. However, Britain's economy is increasingly regional, and the north of England and Scotland remain exempt from the crash.

In London, however, the glut of commercial space is at last freeing up the capital's restrictive leasing practices, while residential property prices have only a little further to fall. A decline of 33% from the high of the late 1980s seems the likely floor.

Until recently, the United States was an object lesson in the need to treat property markets on a strictly regional basis. The boom towns of the south-west had their bust in the mid-1980s, while the north-east followed at the beginning of the 1990s, and California, as usual, followed nobody.

Now there is hardly a region that is not somewhere on the downward curve. Bel Air mansions can be had for half the price of two years ago, and if you are looking for office space, Los Angeles is the place for you. Vacancy rate: 25% plus. In Manhattan, there are landmark office towers in the financial district where office workers say a prayer before they get in the lift: they pray the lift won't stop on one of the many empty, stripped, darkened floors.

The combined effect of smaller employed labour forces and much lower corporate staff requirements will keep property prices (particularly commercial ones) moving at or below inflation. Across Europe and the United States, residential property is beginning to offer good value once more. This promise of stability is good news. It might be the beginning of the best of times.

Richard Ingram: freelance journalist.

PHILIPPINE AIRLINES PUTS ASIA,

AUSTRALIA, EUROPE, AND AMERICA

RIGHT IN THE PALM

OF YOUR HAND.

Across vast oceans and continents we fly to 35 cities all over the world. Touching each and every one with an exceptional warmth and hospitality found nowhere else. And bringing them all within your reach.

Philippine Airlines

SHINING THROUGH

A worldwide explosion of markets

Richard C. Breeden

The past few decades have been a truly remarkable era in world securities markets. Total market value has grown enormously, with world equity market capitalisation increasing from $741 billion to $9.5 trillion during the 1980s alone. Trading volume has increased even more rapidly: the average daily trading volume on the New York Stock Exchange in 1960, about 3m shares, now occurs on average in the first six minutes of trading.

In the United States, institutions own an ever-increasing share of the equity market. In 1975 institutions held about 30% of the total value of American equity securities. By 1992 that ownership stake had risen to about 54%. Institutions now represent 70-80% of total trading volume in American markets. Despite this steady and continuing growth in the proportion of institutional holdings, more than 50m individual investors also own over $2 trillion worth of equity securities. These are both historic highs.

One reflection of this growth in institutional money was the creation by the Securities and Exchange Commission (SEC) in April 1990 of an entirely deregulated offering and trading market for institutional investors. In slightly more than two years, more than 195 issuers (120 of which were foreign firms) have placed over $22 billion in securities using this new "Rule 144A" market.

Institutions have driven hard to lower the costs of their transactions. Average commissions per share on institutional trades have been driven sharply downward, squeezing the margins of block traders and creating pressure to divert trading from high-cost exchanges towards markets or trading systems with lower costs.

This is one reason that more than ten new electronic proprietary trading systems have been approved by the SEC over the past five years. Institutions have also followed a steady trend toward the indexation of their investments. Indeed, indexed assets of the 200 largest pension funds in the United States increased almost sixfold in the 1980s.

Recent decades have witnessed the

Richard C. Breeden: chairman of the United States' Securities and Exchange Commission.

creation of several major new types of financial products. Following on from standardised options in the 1970s, and stock index options and futures in the 1980s, a wide range of "OTC derivatives" of different types and terms are growing rapidly in the 1990s. Products such as interest-rate or currency options and swaps help firms manage currency risk and fundamental business planning. By turning market risk into credit risk, however, these products create new regulatory challenges.

Separately from derivative instruments that allow risk shifting but do not raise any capital, innovation has also given birth to new instruments for raising capital. In the United States, so-called "junk bonds" provided access to the capital markets for smaller and financially weaker companies in the 1980s.

These may prove increasingly

"The SEC will not abandon the protection it provides to 50m American investors simply to achieve a common world standard"

important in the 1990s as bank loans become unavailable as a result of the Basle capital accords; these push banks into becoming, in essence, government bond mutual funds. Indeed, junk bonds represent the quite logical and efficient extension of commercial paper into the medium and long end of the maturity spectrum.

Securitisation of financial receivables has helped to bring greater liquidity and efficiency to different types of financial instruments. Though the first mortgage-backed securities were not issued in the United States until the late 1960s, more than $1.2 trillion of such securities are outstanding today. Indeed, such securities finance almost half the single family home mortgages in America. At the SEC we are trying to encourage development of a secondary market for securities that pool interests in small business loans in a manner similar to

the secondary market for home mortgages.

Among the most important areas of growth, however, have been new markets for traditional products. Here, the growth of international investing has been spectacular. In 1982 foreign transactions in United States' equities aggregated about $80 billion. By 1991 that total had increased more than fivefold to $410 billion. Similarly, American investment in foreign equities has increased about 18 times from $15.7 billion in 1982 to $274.2 billion in 1991. More than 300 mutual funds in the United States now specialise exclusively in foreign stocks.

American markets have a rapidly growing number of foreign listed companies, with almost 150 new foreign companies entering the American market for the first time with public offerings in the past three years, and over 540 foreign companies trading in American markets. Today, large offerings are frequently structured as "global" transactions, tapping capital in major North American, European and Asian markets. This makes it more desirable for regulators to reduce differences in accounting and disclosure standards among markets if this can be done without sacrificing investor protection or transparency of corporate earnings. It also means we must guard against manipulation and gun-jumping in different international markets.

Internationalisation has certainly not been limited to the developed securities markets. Indeed, one of the key trends of the late 1980s was the renewed emphasis on equity securities markets in the developing world. In the 1970s many developing countries learned that economic development financed solely with bank loans was a disastrous course.

In country after country, discredited central planning and inadequate centralised banking systems have been invigorated by growing equity securities markets. In several dozen "emerging" markets like Mexico, Argentina, Chile, Thailand, Taiwan and even China, securities markets have been put to work to foster economic growth.

These fledgling stockmarkets have grown remarkably in size and financing capacity. Aggregate market values in Taiwan and Mexico, for example, are larger than those of Sweden and Spain. Throughout the emerging markets in 1991 more than 1,000 companies raised more than $18.2 billion in the domestic markets and another $6 billion in international markets.

These emerging markets present huge risks along with the potential for significant gain. Significant supply-and-demand imbalances are not uncommon in such markets, liquidity can be uncertain, and clearance and settlement systems are often fragile. Protections against market manipulation and other abuses are typically weaker than developed markets. Accounting systems in many emerging countries may also be less reliable, making financial statements difficult to evaluate.

Internationalisation will continue to create major regulatory challenges. At the outset one should avoid the assumption that, because the markets are more international, we need to have a single international securities code that of necessity would reflect the lowest common denominator. A system of diverse national rules—some good, some not so good—is better than a system that is uniform but inadequate.

For example, in the present international discussion of capital standards for banks and securities firms, several countries have argued for standards that would not have been adequate to prevent widespread failures among firms in the event of market declines of a magnitude we actually saw in 1987 and 1989.

Some proposals for an "international" minimum standard would set capital levels so low that they would be patently inadequate to protect either customers or market stability. The recently adopted capital-adequacy directive of the European Community seems to suffer from exactly this defect by permitting a 50:1 maximum leverage. The SEC will not abandon proven capital standards—and the protection they provide to 50m American investors against the failure of a securities firm—simply to achieve a common world capital standard, if that common standard is worse than no standard at all.

Lastly, any review of the 1980s and prediction for the 1990s has to note the problems of market stability. The market crash of October 1987 and the aftershock in October 1989 reminded us that equity markets can fall massively and suddenly. Japan's prolonged slide from 1990 to 1992 demonstrates that massive price deflation can also occur over a lengthy period rather than as a sudden and violent squall.

In times of market stress, attention turns to the clearance and settlement system. Despite its size and efficiency, the American settlement system for equities still functions on a five-day cycle and makes payment in next-day funds. High on the agenda of the American markets is the need to achieve three-day settlement with same-day funds. Three-day settlement alone would reduce the risk to the centralised American clearing agents by 58% in the event of the failure of an average large member in a normal market.

Systemic stability must remain one of

One global derivative too many

the pre-eminent concerns of regulators. Achieving that requires back-up market trading systems, redundancy in communications and data processing, and conservative capital levels coupled with careful oversight. Public confidence is critical. It is fundamental to the stability of every market.

It must be noted that in the United States, market financings of all types were about $700 billion in 1991, by far the highest level in American history. Public offerings are up another 55%, leading to the potential for more than $1 trillion in new financings for the full year of 1992. These growth rates reflect more than temporary market trends.

Bad Basle

By giving government securities a 0% capital weight and overlooking all interest-rate risk, the Basle capital accords have made the banking system in the United States more vulnerable than ever. In only three years the Basle standards have helped artificially to encourage a massive shift of more than $250 billion in bank assets into government securities.

These massive holdings of securities do not require any capital requirements under the Basle accord, and they are also reported under unrealistic cost accounting practices. The experience of the late 1970s and early 1980s demonstrates that banks can fail from spread problems just as easily as from problem loans. Financing billions of dollars of long-term, fixed-rate bonds with overnight deposits is a proven formula for enormous losses.

Ironically, the Basle standards encourage the creation of exactly this exposure. Thus, by driving banks out of loans and into bonds, the Basle rules have distorted capital flows, not reduced risk. In addition, these rules have played a major role in producing sluggish economic growth in the United States by depriving small businesses of vital bank financing.

Given these trends, securities markets in the 1990s should play an increasingly important role in financing economic growth around the world. Overall, world-capital needs are likely to sharply exceed world-capital availability in the next decade, making the investor more important than ever before. Markets that provide the highest quality information and protection will attract the most capital in 1993.

Shedding a few more veils

John Maddox

April next year will see the 40th anniversary of the discovery of the central role of DNA in regulating the processes that keep living things alive. Throughout 1993 there will be a mass of new understanding of how particular genes made of DNA determine the character of organisms, in both health and disease. The marvel is that so much has been accomplished in a mere four decades.

But 1993 will also bring another set of triumphs for the reductionist doctrine that the behaviour of complicated systems can be explained by the properties of the atoms and molecules of which they are made. Ever since the second world war, people have been seeking to design molecules that, when clumped together, would yield entirely novel properties. Now there is likely to be a flowering of this ambition.

There have already been great successes. For many purposes, nylon makes better fibres for the clothing industry than wool or cotton. Carbon fibres, made by the deliberate alteration of synthetic polymer molecules, are used to form materials stronger than steel but only a fraction of the weight. Chemists now routinely design molecules to function as catalysts for cracking oil or doing other jobs with all the confidence of an architect placing windows in a building to make the best use of sunlight. Designing drugs on the same principles has become one of the pharmaceutical industry's ambitions.

But that is only the beginning. 1993 will see the first fruits of plans to construct novel electronic materials by manipulating individual atoms and molecules—"nanotechnology" is the trendy name. It will soon be possible to construct electronic devices from patterns of atoms of different kinds, perhaps laid down on the surface of a piece of silicon. Until recently that would have been an impossible dream. But now it has turned out that the device called the scanning-tunnelling microscope (STM), originally developed, at IBM's Zurich laboratory, for studying the

John Maddox: editor of *Nature* magazine.

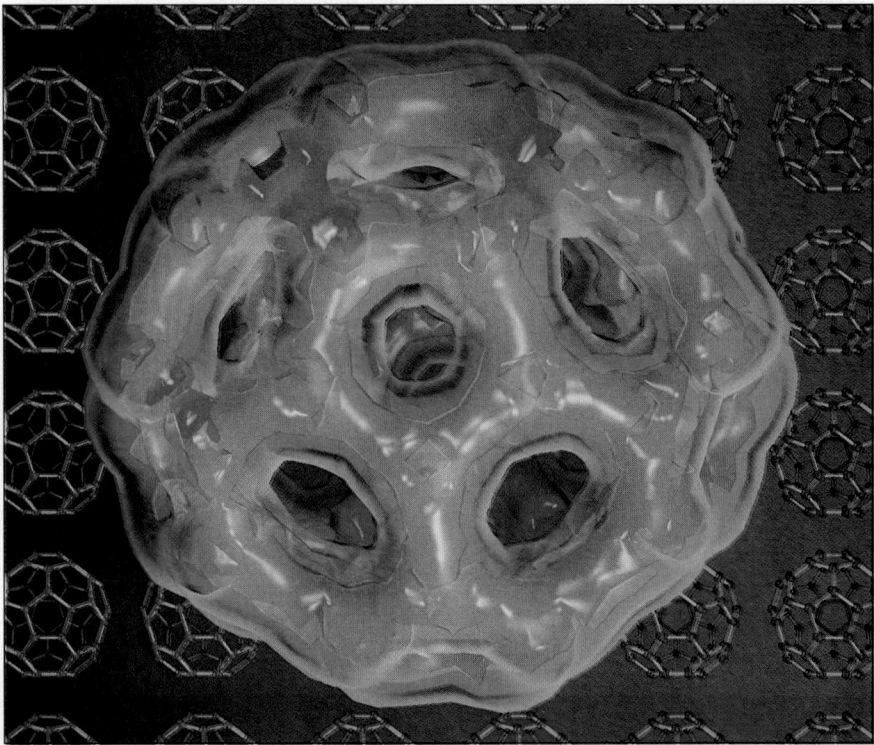

Buckminster Fuller would have been proud

arrangement of atoms on the surfaces of solids such as silicon, can also be used to move particular atoms to predetermined positions on the surface. A Japanese group at Tsukuba is already enthusiastically at work constructing "atomic wires" consisting of strings of rubidium atoms floating on a flat silicon surface. No doubt that group is only one of many.

Put together the economic incentive to make much smaller electronic devices with the new-found means of manipulating individual atoms physically—and you have nanotechnology.

The name nanotechnology is not inappropriate. "Nano" is the third in the sequence of prefixes, beginning with "milli" and "micro", denoting successive subdivisions of some unit by factors of 1,000. A micrometre is a millionth of a metre and is roughly the smallest dimension that can be seen in an optical micro-

scope. A nanometre is a thousandth of that and is roughly ten times the diameter of the smallest atom, hydrogen.

The thing that has made nanotechnology exciting, as well as logically necessary, is a quite unexpected development—the recognition in 1987 that pure carbon can exist in a previously unrecognised form known as C_{60}. To begin with, this discovery seemed an intellectual curiosity; but C_{60} was quickly shown to be a molecular form of pure carbon. It consisted of 60 carbon atoms held tightly together by chemical bonds to form a closed and nearly spherical ball with a hollow at the centre. Each ball is just under a nanometre in diameter.

In a few hectic years, several developments have pointed to the value of C_{60} as a building block for nanotechnologists. One of these is the discovery that if C_{60} molecules are allowed to form into crystals in the presence of potassium, potassium atoms are incorporated into the crystal at regular positions. The resulting crystals are super-conducting, that is, they will carry an electrical current but show no resistance to its passage.

Even more suggestive, the architectural principle on which C60 molecules are built is that of Buckminster Fuller's geodesic dome (at least one macroscopic example of which seems now to be erected at each world's fair). So some chemists call C60 "Buckminsterfullerene". What researchers have now shown is that the versatility of the geodesic architectural principle also holds at the molecular level.

So people are now constructing long closed tubes of carbon atoms, just one nanometre across, on the C60 principle, and wondering what will happen if they fill the tubes with other kinds of atoms, perhaps making electrically-conducting wires in the process. Hardly ever can a new technology have been as well blessed with such a stimulus to the imagination as C60 has give nanotechnology.

Brain work

The painstaking business of understanding how the brain works will have a profitable 1993. Now, after many previous occasions when people have been almost persuaded that they were within an ace of answering the question, there is a proper appreciation of the complexity of the problem. Simply to describe the brain in exhaustive detail will not explain it.

But the detail helps, especially that now being provided by molecular biology. The functioning of many psychotropic drugs, both "recreational" and therapeutic, is on the way to being understood. The outcome should be much more effective treatment of psychiatric illness by means of drugs. It is not surprising that many of the pharmaceutical companies are now switching their research programmes in that direction.

And while it may be disappointing that the neural network theory, which describes how large groups of nerve cells can act in concert so as to store images and other evidence of the senses, has not by itself explained what kind of computer the brain is, researchers are at last turning their attention to the prior philosophical questions. The question of what is consciousness cries out for an answer.

1993 should almost complete people's understanding of what is called the cell cycle, the rhythmic progression of newly-formed cells through several distinct stages until they reach the point at which they divide into two replicas of themselves. The criteria that must be satisfied to allow progression from one stage

to the next are only now being pieced together, largely as a result of intricate genetic analysis (in yeast) by Paul Nurse at the University of Oxford. The issue is evidently of the greatest importance for the understanding of life itself, and of senescence, not to mention aberrations such as cancer.

Next year offers the continuation of several tantalising conundrums. In fundamental physics, for example, it is a safe bet that the missing ingredient of nuclear matter, called the "top" quark, will not be found: no new particle accelerator dramatically more energetic than those now working in America and Geneva is due to come on stream. Nor, for that matter, will anybody find the "Higgs boson", required by theories of the interactions of particles like electrons. If the managers of the European High-Energy Physics Laboratory, CERN, in Geneva decide to go ahead with what they call the Large Hadron Collider, there may be something to show by 1997. But that long period will have sceptics chiselling away at theories that must fall if the particles they predict do not exist.

There is a curiously similar situation in cosmology, where it seems agreed that the mass of all the matter in the universe is greater than that represented by the

galaxies observed by the world's telescopes. Put crudely, the conclusion is that the universe would be expanding more quickly than it is if the visible mass were all there is to hold it together.

But what does this missing mass consist of? Stars too small to glow, perhaps? Or is it that some of the particles of matter called neutrinos, now supposed to be utterly devoid of mass, have enough of it that their gravitational attraction holds the universe together in its present form? Or is there something wrong with the standard picture of what the universe is like, its origin in the Big Bang and all that?

The experience of the past few years offers only more frustration. Several candidate constituents of the missing mass have been suggested, and have been ruled out in succession. The sole survivor, called the "17-keV neutrino", is unlikely to have a long lease on people's attention. There will simply be a hole at the heart of the standard cosmology. That prospect was not mentioned when, in 1992, the operators of the United States' COBE satellite hyped their first data about the thermal radiation filling the universe, saying that it proved the Big Bang to have been a reality. It would be good if 1993 put that tale in a cooler perspective.

The human genome project: biology's blockbuster

Leroy Hood

One of the most striking features about the three-year-old human genome project is the emerging paradigm changes that it is engendering in biology. The human genome project, biologists' most ambitious endeavour to date, seeks to decipher the human genome and, hence, human heredity.

This project proposes to map the 24 different human chromosomes (two sex chromosomes, X and Y, and 22 non-sexual chromosomes, 1-22) present in each cell. These chromosomes direct the development of every individual, starting from one cell, the fertilised egg, and ending with nearly a million trillion cells in the adult. Each chromosome is a single DNA molecule that may be visualised as two intertwined strings of pearls of four different colours or letters of the DNA language. There are 3 billion DNA letters in the human genome, encoding perhaps 100,000 units of information (genes) positioned

Leroy Hood: Gates professor; director, NSF Science & Technology Center; chairman, Department of Molecular Biotechnology, University of Washington.

across the chromosomes. Each gene makes a distinct protein, which once again may be visualised as a single string of pearls comprised of 20 different colours or letters of the protein alphabet. Each protein folds in three dimensions to constitute a molecular machine that catalyses the chemistry of life or helps to build the structural framework of our body.

Defective genes lead to genetic diseases such as cystic fibrosis or to the predisposition of particular diseases such as rheumatoid arthritis or Alzheimer's disease. This deciphering of the human genome promises to lead to fundamental insights into human genetic diseases.

To decipher the human genome, three types of maps are being determined. The genetic map orders the genes encoding particular traits (for example, eye colour or Huntington's disease) on their respective chromosomes by following the passage of these traits through human families. Once a detailed genetic map is available for all human chromosomes, uncharacterised disease genes can readily be mapped (located), as can the multiple genes encoding the major components of common human disorders such as cancer or heart disease. Once defective genes are identified, rational approaches can be used to design therapies to prevent disease consequences.

The physical map for each chromosome is comprised of a complete set of DNA fragments, each contained in a recombinant DNA vector and thus capable of infinite expansion. The physical map of each chromosome is essentially a linear jigsaw puzzle. These fragments are used specifically to identify the genes generally localised by the genetic map and they constitute the substrate for generating the sequence map.

The third map, the sequence map, of each chromosome specifies the order of

be developed that are 100-1,000 times more efficient (and less costly) than those currently available. The development of powerful new mapping tools and computer hardware and software for assembling, storing and analysing the map information has been an important aspect of the project. These technological developments are accelerating and powerful new mapping and computation tools will undoubtedly emerge over the next year.

Changing the way we are

The genome project is catalysing a series of emerging paradigm changes in biology and medicine as we move into the 21st century:

• The sequence of the human genome and its 100,000 genes will be in a computer, readily accessible to all biologists

learn to design new tools as well as apply these tools to leading-edge problems in biology and medicine. In many cases these tools will require the application of interdisciplinary approaches from applied mathematics, applied physics, chemistry, computer science and engineering. The challenge is how to bring together scientists from very different disciplines who speak and think in very different languages.

• Biologists and physicians will become totally dependent upon computers for storing information and for thinking about the complex systems and networks of biology. Indeed, the human genome programme will foster for the first time a vigorous and healthy theoretical biology devoted to the understanding of how genes and proteins work in the context of human development and disease. Computational tools will also revolutionise the education of scientists and physicians.

• With detailed genetic and sequence maps it will be possible to identify the multiple genes contributing significantly to many of the major diseases of mankind (for example, heart disease, cancer and auto-immune diseases). If in 25 years we have identified perhaps 100 or so genes that contribute significantly to major human diseases and have appropriate preventive therapies to circumvent their potential for causing disease, then medicine will become preventive rather than reactive (in other words, keeping well people well rather than making sick people well). The possibility for relatively inexpensive preventive medicine has important implications for rapidly escalating medical costs.

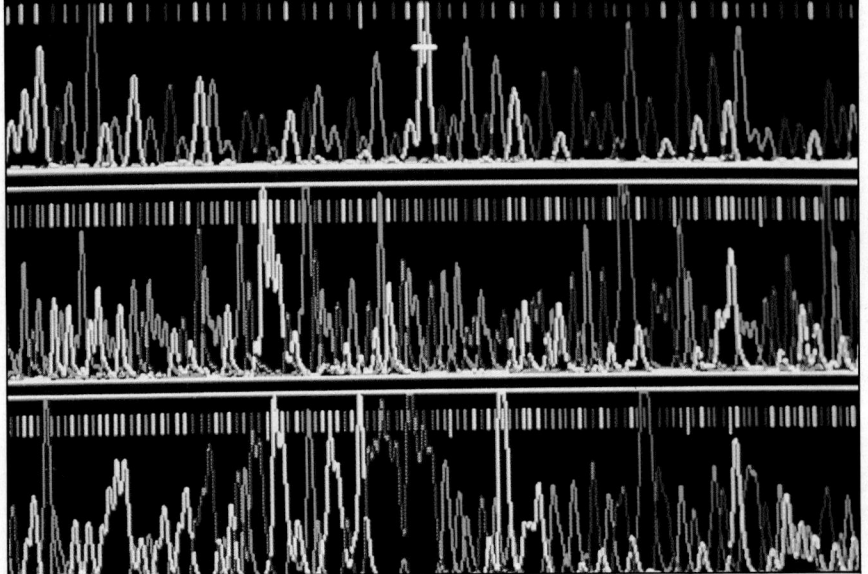

A map of your life

DNA letters in each DNA molecule. This map will eventually permit us to read, in sequence, all of the DNA letters comprising each of the 100,000 human genes and this will provide important insights into understanding the complex processes of human development and disease.

During next year, significant advances will be made in generating more detailed genetic maps. These have already led to the identification of particular disease genes (for example, cystic fibrosis and neurofibromatosis) and more will soon be identified. Perhaps the most striking result of the human genome programme to date has been the physical mapping of two chromosomes, Y and 21. In 1993 additional human chromosomes will be physically mapped.

The sequence map is progressing very slowly because sequencing tools need to

and physicians. Scientists will then be able to study how these genes function rather than spending most of their time, as is now the case, identifying and characterising them. Just as the road system of any country provides a critical component of the transport infrastructure, so will the genome sequence provide a unique and powerful infrastructure for practising biology and medicine.

• The genome project has aptly illustrated the importance of pushing the development of new technologies to drive advances in biology. Many of the future challenges in biology relate to the analysis of complex systems and networks (for example, the 100,000 human genes that constitute a developmental network). Powerful new tools must be developed to decipher these biological networks. The critical point is that some biologists must

• The human genome project has highlighted a variety of ethical, legal and social questions already posed by the previous advances of human genetics. Who has a right to the genetic information concerning disease predisposition (for example, employers, insurance companies, potential marriage partners)? How will this knowledge affect the practice of abortion or future applications of human genetic engineering? The human genome project is now spending about 5% of its resources on these issues, making it the first scientific programme to combine science with ethical, social and legal issues. The critical issue is how society can balance the enormous opportunities this technology presents against the concerns that it evokes. The critical issue here is the imperative to educate our citizens so that they have some basic understanding of science and its impact on society, and the need for scientists to interact effectively to educate society on these complex and thorny issues.

Science of the seas

John Woods

Five per cent of world GDP comes from the ocean. But whether wrung from commerce or defence, from fishing or science, it is a very uncertain 5%. Those who use the seas remain remarkably ignorant about them. In 1993 and beyond significant chunks of that ignorance will start to fall away.

Oceanography is entering a new era of robotic monitoring. A reliable flow of data describing the state of the world ocean—its flows and salinity, its inner storms and outer wrath—is just starting to be available. This is the kernel of really long-range climate forecasting: an accurate reading of the oceans could predict variations a decade ahead.

For example, it should be possible to predict fish stocks. They respond to ocean changes that science can monitor. A start is being made in the Pacific. Every few years Peru's fisheries are devastated by El Niño, a climatic disturbance which begins months earlier in the ocean 5,000 miles away off the Philippines. The 1992 El Niño was accurately predicted one year ahead, thanks to scientific observations that would have been unthinkable only a few years ago. Now 11 nations have agreed permanently to monitor the Pacific, thousands of miles away from the fisheries they seek to protect.

The ocean's secrets will be cracked only by such international research programmes. The most ambitious is the eight-year World Ocean Circulation Experiment, in which instruments will be lowered kilometres to the ocean floor at 24,000 different spots. Assimilating the data into mathematical models will yield the first comprehensive description of the state of the ocean.

New cost-effective methods are being developed to monitor large-scale change in the ocean. Remote sensing from space is showing the way. Two satellites launched in 1992 carry radars to measure ocean currents, waves, wind stress, and ice cover.

But instruments in space can only map the surface of the ocean: changes occurring deep inside are just as important. The ocean is warming on average at five

John Woods: director of Marine and Atmospheric Sciences at the National Environment Research Council; chairman of the committee planning the Global Ocean Observing System.

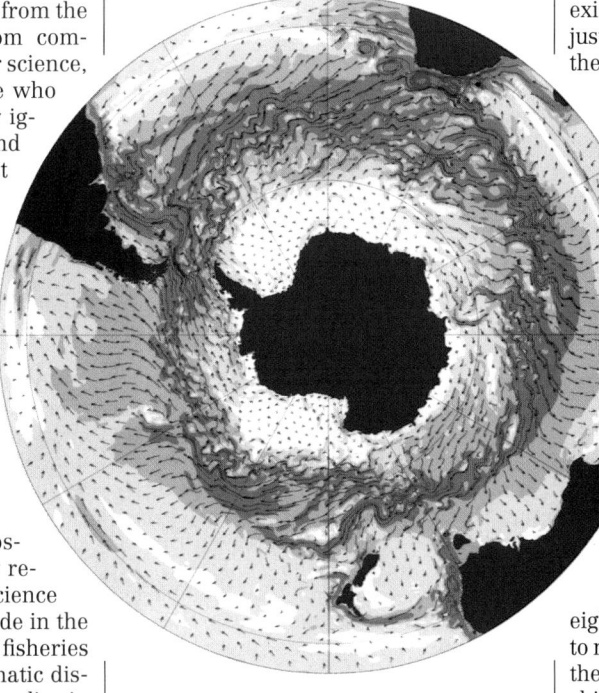

20,000 storms under the sea

millidegrees a year, but mathematical models developed in Klaus Hasselmann's laboratory at Hamburg predict considerable variations across the world, depending on depth and region.

In 1992 Walter Munk, at Scripps Institute of Oceanography, determined deep ocean temperatures to millidegrees of accuracy from the travel time of sound pulses radiating across the world from Heard Island, in the Indian Ocean. Local nets of sound can be used to monitor the transient weather systems inside the ocean.

Such acoustic tomography will be important in regions (for example, off southern Africa) where energetic storms inside the ocean control the larger-scale permanent currents carrying heat, water and chemicals around the world.

Also in 1992 a team led by David Webb, working at the Institute of Oceanographic Sciences' Deacon Laboratory, demonstrated that storms mapped by satellite altimeters could be simulated by computer models fed with widely-spaced observations collected decades earlier. This is a critical breakthrough, which will bear much fruit in the years ahead.

Variations in the salinity of the seas are all important. Although the concentration of salt averages 3.47%, regional differences are considerable, depending on evaporation, rainfall, river inflow and sea-ice change. The circulation of fresh water around the world by ocean currents has long been known to exist but its precise measurement is only just beginning. These currents depend on the gradients of density of the sea water, its temperature and its salinity.

It is impossible to monitor salinity to the required precision from space or acoustically, so salinometers must be deployed inside the ocean. In 1992 John Gould, from the Institute of Oceanographic Sciences, discovered that the north-east Atlantic has freshened substantially since a survey 15 years earlier.

Of course such snapshots do not reveal the spectrum of variation. That needs a costly series of annual, or even monthly, surveys. One way to speed things up is to tow a salinometer (known as a SeaSoar), to undulate behind a ship travelling at eight knots. In three months it is possible to map the salinity of the Atlantic between the Azores and Greenland; so a dedicated ship could survey this critical region, where most of the ocean's deep water is formed, with considerable accuracy. Raymond Pollard, head of the James Rennell Centre, led a successful trial in 1992 and plans to start permanent Vivaldi ("four seasons") monitoring in 1995.

The next step towards cost-effective monitoring of the ocean will be to use unmanned robots, programmed to range the oceans from top to bottom, continent to continent, mapping the changing distributions of temperature, salinity and currents. A start is being made with existing technology. A British firm, Marconi, has modified a naval torpedo to carry instruments in trials along the edge of the polar ice-cap during 1993. But the limited range, pay-load and depth of torpedoes make them unsuitable for global monitoring. Peter Hedgecock and Peter Collar, at the Deacon Laboratory, are developing unmanned submersibles suitable for global monitoring. The "autosub" project is scheduled to deliver in 1998 a fully-tested vehicle equipped to map the oceanic ecosystem as a contribution to the International Geosphere Biosphere Programme. Hundreds of these robots will be deployed to monitor the oceans of the world, at less than one-tenth the cost of doing it by ship.

Marine chemists, biologists and geologists are adapting their instruments to fit into the "autosub". Most exciting is the prospect of mapping the distributions of microscopic plankton which moderate the greenhouse effect in global climate change. The bewildering biodiversity of plankton poses a problem. Ocean biologists, working in England at Plymouth, are developing new methods to replace labour-intensive taxonomic analysis. Genetic or other molecular probes will automatically count and classify the plankton, by distinct functions that can be represented mathematically in models.

Together these advances will soon make it possible to design an operations system for monitoring the global ocean. It will take 20 years to plan, finance and establish such a system; starting now the Global Ocean Observing System could be working by 2015. The first step will be a ten-year trial beginning in 1995 under the auspices of the UN Inter-governmental Oceanographic Commission. The permanent system will cost about the same as weather forecasting: $2 billion a year. With serious scientific attention being paid to monitoring it, the ocean will every year become less of a mystery.

The green agenda, '93

John Hemming

The United Nations Conference on Environment and Development, or "Earth Summit", in Rio de Janeiro did not achieve all its objectives. However, it did assemble the greatest gathering of heads of government ever, and it did get some 150 countries—almost all humanity—to sign many powerful and binding environmental pledges. The task for environmentalists next year is to make sure that these pledges stick.

The most important documents signed at UNCED were conventions or treaties on climate change and on biodiversity. Despite erratic rainfall elsewhere, the catastrophic drought in southern Africa seems to confirm most scientists' conviction that mankind is causing the earth to warm unnaturally fast. The Convention on Climate Change obliged signatory nations to strive to stabilise their greenhouse-gas emissions. Each country has to report regularly what it is doing to curb energy consumption and switch to less-polluting means of transport, industry and energy generation.

All nations present at Rio de Janeiro also signed Agenda 21, a 500-page plan for environmentally-sustainable development into the 21st century. The problem during 1993 is to get nations to honour their pledges. The UN is establishing a Sustainable Development Commission; but, like other UN agencies, it will have no coercive powers.

Bill Reilly, head of the United States Environmental Protection Agency, likens the UNCED agreements to the east-west Helsinki accords of the 1970s. At the time, Helsinki seemed a public-relations exercise; now, it can be seen that it was an important step in ending the cold war. But Helsinki succeeded thanks to the gallant

efforts of Lech Walesa, Vaclav Havel and others who monitored their governments' non-compliance. The Earth Summit needs similarly tenacious non-government organisations (NGOs) to make every country enforce its undertakings. This is where the international conference of environmental NGOs called by John Major for mid-1993 will be important.

Another political objective is to get environmental concerns into both the current and future GATT rounds. International trade needs a level playing field, not

Acid eats its way through Europe

a levelled rain forest, in environmentally-sensitive produce. In other words, the GATT negotiators must not permit environmental vandals to compete unfairly with those who honour UNCED's pledges on sustainable development.

If major projects are to be financed by the World Bank and other aid agencies, they require increasingly tough environmental impact assessments, as well as genuine consultation with local communities. The bank's environmentalists continue to fight to get environmental damage and resulting losses properly costed on the debit side of future projects' balance sheets.

The other achievement of the gathering in Rio de Janeiro was to put the environment into all the world's media and most of its classrooms. The problem for 1993 is to maintain this publicity momentum. Editors may think that their audiences are weary of environmental Jeremiahs. But mankind's battering of its fragile planet will be controlled only if it is reported. Also, amid the gloom are good stories: of reductions in pollution caused by cleaner new technologies and of gains by environmentally-conscious managements encouraged by often-maligned green activists.

Many who drafted the Rio de Janeiro agreements wanted to introduce the principle that "the polluter pays". A few enlightened governments may introduce carbon taxes in 1993, particularly on vehicles. But some of the world's worst polluters are in the industrialising "second world" of China and the former Soviet block, too poor to pay such a levy.

However, governments in Eastern Europe and even China are conscious of pollution caused by their dirty coal, antiquated factories, profligate dumping of waste, hazardous nuclear plants and catastrophic development plans. They are seeking western help and new technology to lessen such damage. If such environmental cleansing is built into aid packages for those countries, it could be the most important advance of 1993.

One issue that was too sensitive to be mentioned at the Earth Summit was population growth. Mankind's numbers will continue to increase inexorably during 1993, despite pious hopes that greater prosperity will yield a spontaneous slowing-down in the rate of growth. In the long term, this demographic explosion combined with heightened consumption is the greatest environmental threat of all.

John Hemming: director and secretary of the Royal Geographical Society.